Women's Life-Writing

Women's Life-Writing:
Finding Voice/Building Community

Linda S. Coleman, editor

Bowling Green State University Popular Press
Bowling Green, OH 43403

The excerpts from Vera Brittain's *Testament of Youth, Testament of Experience, On Being an Author, England's Hour*, and *Selected Letters of Winifred Holtby and Vera Brittain*, and from Vera Brittain's letters and articles, are included with the permission of Paul Berry, her literary executor. Brittain's papers are housed in the Vera Brittain Archive, William Ready Division of Archives & Research Collections, McMaster University (Canada).

Copyright © 1997 Bowling Green State University Popular Press

Library of Congress Cataloging-in-Publication Data
Women's life-writing : finding voice/building community / Linda S. Coleman,
    editor.
        p.   cm.
    Includes bibliographical references.
    ISBN 0-87972-747-0 (clothbound). -- ISBN 0-87972-748-9 (paper)
    1. English prose literature--Women authors--History and criticism.
    2. American prose literature--Women authors--History and criticism.
    3. Women and literature--Great Britain.   4. Women and literature--United
    States. 5. Autobiography--Women authors. 6. Community in literature.
    I. Coleman, Linda S.
    PR756.W65W66   1997
    828'.08--dc21   97-12724
                                                                          CIP

Cover design by Dumm Art

To Casey, for her patience, her sharp and critical eye, her constant confidence in the project, and most important, for the safe place.

Contents

Introduction

"I hope I will be able to confide to you, as I have never been able to confide in anyone, and I hope you will be a great source of comfort and support" (2). So begins one of the most widely read of life-writings, *The Diary of a Young Girl* by Anne Frank. Shortly after undertaking her task, Frank reveals that it is her lack of "a friend" that prompts her turn to the diary, a friend with whom she can go beyond the "ordinary everyday things" (6). So she creates Kitty, to whom the diary is subsequently addressed. Three months later Frank marks her success: "So far you truly have been a great source of comfort to me, and so has Kitty, whom I now write to regularly. This way of keeping a diary is much nicer, and now I can hardly wait for those moments when I'm able to write in you. Oh I'm so glad I brought you along!" (2).

Like many girls and women before and after her, Anne Frank sought an understanding of herself in the world of life-writing. Yet in this explicitly self-directed act, this private search to find a meaningful voice, she turned outward as well, building first in the pages of the diary, and later in the friend she has created to be her reader, a community within which to feel understood, comforted, stimulated. It offered relief from her own alienating and narrowly defining real world, and within it she came to better and independently understand herself as a girl, a daughter, a lover, and a Jew.[1]

Modern western culture has attempted to order itself around a gendered division into private and public spheres, privileging the voices of the public male and, in turn, silencing, or at best limiting to the private, the female voice.[2] These collected essays on life-writing by women, both obscure and familiar, often marginalized, offer us a complex understanding of how individuals have responded on the most personal of levels to this imposed world order. Across the many subgenres, with their varied opportunities and limitations, we discover a fundamental and common strategy for coming to a meaningful understanding of the self and for establishing the needed authority and strength to negotiate or even to subvert external or internalized norms that might silence that self. This strategy is the construction of an empowering and sympathetic other, a community of readers. Its shape varies, from the explicit to the implicit, the conscious to the unconscious, the community of one—including the writer's own self, past, present and/or future—to people and places far

1

beyond the writer's immediate experience. Ironically, of course, the source for this turn to community is the very gendered socialization fostered by the public/private division. As recognized by feminist psychologists and sociologists, female socialization largely centers upon relationships. Though the intention of this socialization may be an erasure of the self in service of others, women across their differences of time, place, age, race, class, and sexual preference have subverted the dichotomy to instead employ their sense of connectedness to discover and even reconstruct a self/selves. In the pages of these life-writings we trace both the costs and the successes of their actions.[3]

In the last two decades, life-writing by women, with its immediate yet complex access to everyday life, has gained a wide readership, popular and academic, female and male.[4] Before this, the same gendered norms that marginalized female experience severely restricted our knowledge of people and cultures: women's private lives were silenced by an historical and critical bias against the apparently private genres they most often employed (diaries, daybooks, and journals), and their explicitly public voices (memoirs, confessions, autobiographies) too often were discouraged, silenced, or denied. In addition, narrow and dichotomous critical definitions of genre kept related forms, such as the letter or the advice book, forms employed by marginalized writers for ad hoc purposes, from even being considered. These restrictions have limited severely our critical assessments of women's life-writing. Now, however, having completed our first stages of discovering texts and of giving value and breadth of definition to these genres, readers can explore more fully and fairly this pivotal genre, challenging, like the life-writers themselves, the gendered and artificial barriers between private and public experience, the individual voice and its community.

Women's Life-Writing organizes our readings of seventeen British and American life-writers around their choice of genre and their place in the historical evolution of modern gender codes, from their emergence in the seventeenth century to the present. "Lives Considered and Reconsidered Day by Day" and "Retrospective Constructions and Negotiations" cluster writings according to the writers' relationship in time to the events, thoughts, and emotion in their works, and thus to their readers as well. In the first section, for example, May Sarton scrutinizes her daily struggle with depression, first for herself, as a map to future recovery, and later for her readers, as a guide to May Sarton's creative life. In the second section, by contrast, pioneer Anne Ellis's life is remembered whole in her old age, when the demands of the pioneer life, which we so eagerly share, no longer limit her creative time to the kitchen and her family. And we trace the "day by day" evolution of novelist Fanny

Burney's intellectual and emotional independence in her letters and diaries, noting the contrasting selves she must construct for personal satisfaction and public reputation, while Vera Brittain's "retrospective" and more broadly public outreach to the unsympathetic youth of post-war Britain is motivated by her holistic understanding of war reached only during its aftermath. Few of these works would fit into a simple private/ public generic division typical of earlier critical typologies of largely male autobiography. For example, in Mary White Rowlandson's subversion of an existing publicly focused form, the captivity narrative, she acts out a personal agenda and shapes what Parley Ann Boswell terms a "narrative of the mother" around her private need. The third section, "Crossing the Boundaries," allows us insight into less easily categorized works and the opportunity to observe both conscious and implicit appropriation of nontraditional life-writing forms for autobiographical purposes. Mary Wollstonecraft traverses both terrain and genre, intentionally redefining her culture's gendered aesthetic notions in the process. Lydia Maria Child, via her merger of the epistolary, the journalistic essay, and the travelogue, achieved personal solace as well as access to a wider audience for her abolitionist goals. Her role as traveling observer was an explicit violation of the norm that reserved the required freedom of movement and observation for men. Gathering together Virginia Woolf's diverse life-writing forms, both the immediate and the retrospective, the public fictional essay and the private autobiography, we weave an enlarged and complicated knowledge of how Woolf came to understand her personal experience of gender and masculine repression in relationship to fascism and patriarchy. That Woolf could only negotiate this understanding in separate spheres, in different genres, is part of what we must identify to understand fully her struggle to know herself.

This collection also is organized chronologically within each section, though not more narrowly limited by the traditional literary or historical periodization and its restrictive aesthetic and social parameters. By proceeding through time, we can observe the changing connotations for terms such as "diary," and thus we better understand the factors that encouraged or discouraged voicing, and that shaped the expected community of the diarist. Mary Rich, for example, openly kept her diary as part of a then-current practice. The freedom to keep such a diary, however, carried with it clear reader expectations that shaped and limited both its form and its content. A generation later, the diary had become dangerous territory for the young woman who risked public censure for private reflection, as Fanny Burney discovered when her father found her diary. The act of transgression, however, became for Burney a lesson in subversion.

The second wave of feminism, at least in part, has explored gender as a systematic, structural element in the shaping of who women are supposed to be and/or who we have been. For its authors, life-writing has been the site where the boundaries have been negotiated. For readers, it serves as well to connect our past with our present, ourselves with other women. Too often, however, even those of us engaged in feminist analysis have overgeneralized from limited or particular female experience and thus seriously limited our understanding of the social construction of gender as well as genre. That is, we too often create a rhetoric that universalizes the nature of female experience, without regard for differences in historical circumstance, race, age, class, sexual preference, and ethnicity among other things.[5]

Understanding of the limitations of essentialism motivates, in part, the diversity and organization of these essays, thus allowing, for example, the voice of the formerly enslaved Elizabeth Keckley to enter into tangential conversation with those of three Confederate women imprisoned for their commitment to the South. All respond to their common national crisis but each from the distinct position that gender, class, and race construct for her. Keckley feels she can only voice an American identity by erasing the traces of her gender and race experience; the three white women act on regional identity at the expense of the protection their class and gender once had offered them. In addition to attending to race and class differences, these essays offer insight into life-writing's place in the negotiation of sexual identity via two early modern women, the lesbian Anne Lister and mystical Quaker Mary Penington, for both of whom the diary is a site of safe exploration and experimentation before they act in a world ready to harshly penalize any explicit or public enactment of their desires. Within each section, too, the span of three centuries is reduced to the common denominator of gender as, for example, the seventeenth-century Mary Rich struggles against the imperative of female silence to legitimate her voice, and the twentieth century May Sarton struggles still with "discursive resistance" to gain control of her life. The differences, of course, are there as well, in Sarton's conscious and public control and her explicit knowledge of a sympathetic community of readers.

In addition to the insight gained through the three-part division of these essays, readers can interrogate these texts for their disclosure of the material conditions within which women voiced their lives and sought or constructed responsive communities. What barriers—real or perceived—have women overcome or subverted to achieve voice, and at what cost? Avra Kouffman, in writing about Mary Boyle Rich, looks to the links among religion, gender, and genre as a source of limitation, acknowledging the firmly entrenched acceptable codes for spiritual diarists of the seventeenth century, including the journal's role as self-monitor, yet she finds in Warwick both participation with, and resistance to, these codes. Anne Lister shares with Rich a problem of encoded expectations; however, according to Jennifer Frangos, the issue for Lister was a need to escape ill-suited secular sex-and-gender codes, and only in her diary, where she acted as writer, reader, and subject, did she find complete freedom.

And what, then, in any given historical and personal situation has enabled these life-writers to find their voices. For advice-manual writer Dorothy Leigh, it was her own impending death and, as with Mary Rowlandson, the culturally sanctioned authority of a mother. Her obligation to educate her children transcended the gendered silence of the Christian woman. For the African American Shaker Rebecca Jackson, personal strength had both worldly and spiritual dimensions and intentions, and from the intersection between them came what Sylvia Bryant calls "self-creation." Feminist Mary Wollstonecraft, too, suffered extreme personal circumstances and from them, and her own subversive philosophical strength, came not only a personal voice but a newly defined form of writing, violating the norms that in her lifetime, according to Angela Jones, separated public and private voices.

How explicitly conscious have women been of shaping these voices and of trying through them to build new communities? In the diaries and letters of novelist Fanny Burney, readers find a desire for a community more accepting of difference. Failure to identify a single coherent community necessitates her multivoiced life-writings. This is explicitly in contrast to the accommodating and sheltered woman to whom we are so often introduced by histories based on her public life. Mary Rowlandson's narrative, too, reveals in its language an explicit awareness of the need to manipulate the reader's encoded Puritan expectations, to shape and form her reader, in order for her "mother narrative" to reach the sympathetic community with whom she desired to communicate. By contrast, activist Lydia Maria Child discovered her confessional voice and role almost by chance, finding in her informal letters and the readers who responded to them a connection to a city and a life she had felt estrangement from in her more outwardly defined formal role as editor and writer. Jennifer Brantley identifies multiple communities within a single work: the people of Anne Ellis's past, of her present, and the sympathetic fictive community of readers she creates within her prose, people she sought in life but too seldom found. And while World War I's well-known *Testament of Youth* was, in part, Vera Brittain's quest for personal reconciliation, it was also her quest to radically transform her nation to one so schooled in the limitations of nationalism that the future might be spared such suffering as her own generation had experienced.

Interdisciplinary techniques and self-conscious readings characterize the essays included here, locating each text in its time and place and requiring modern readers to negotiate the similarities as well as the differences among writers and readers of widely diverse experience. Gathering readings that help us, as modern readers, to read "then" through the lens of "now"—and, in turn, to read "now" through "then"—has been a primary goal for this collection. Like Mary Field Belenky and her colleagues, I believe that a woman's voice is critically connected to her awareness of, and responses to, dominant definitions of femaleness, and that "when the woman's voice is included in the study of human development, women's lives and qualities are revealed and we can observe the unfolding of these qualities in the lives of men as well" (7). I would only change "woman's voice" to "women's voices."

Notes

1. The "Women's Lives and Letters" sessions organized by Marie Campbell at the annual Popular Culture Association convention have been a recurring site for the negotiation and exchange of ideas on the topic of women's life-writing. It was as a panelist and chair in these sessions that I began to form the thesis for this collection. I wish to thank as well Janet Eagleson Dunleavy, whose encouragement first nurtured my interest in life-writing by women.

2. See my discussion of Michael McKeon's critique of early modern culture in "Gender, Sect, and Circumstance" in this collection.

3. The work of Belenky et al. has been integral to the development of this collection and to my own work on women's life-writing. Their paradigm of women's ways of knowing is most explicitly used in my own essay, "Gender, Sect, and Circumstance," and in Linda Lang-Peralta's "'Clandestine Delight': Frances Burney's Life-writing."

4. See Estelle Jelinek's *Women and Autobiography* and *The Tradition of Autobiography*, groundbreaking texts in the rediscovery of women's autobiographical writings. For historical and theoretical considerations of the genre, see also Domna Stanton's *The Female Autograph*, Sidonie Smith's *A Poetics of Women's Autobiography*, Bella Brodzki and Celeste Schenck's *Life/Lines*, Shari Benstock's *The Private Self*, Bettina Aptheker's *Tapestries of Life*, Marlene Kadar's *Essays on Life Writing*, as well as the many valuable essays by Suzanne Juhasz, Mary Mason, Sara Heller Mendelson, and Mary Beth Rose.

5. See, for example, Elizabeth Spelman's *Inessential Woman: Problems in the Exclusion of Feminist Thought.*

Works Cited

Aptheker, Bettina. *Tapestries of Life*. Amherst: U of Massachusetts P, 1989.

Belenky, Mary Field, et al. *Women's Ways of Knowing: The Development of Self, Voice, and Mind*. New York: Basic, 1986.

Benstock, Shari. *The Private Self*. Chapel Hill: U of North Carolina P, 1988.

Brodzki, Bella, and Celeste Schenck. *Life/Lines: Theorizing Women's Autobiography*. Ithaca: Cornell UP, 1988.

Frank, Anne. *The Diary of a Young Girl*. Trans. Susan Massotty. Ed. Otto H. Frank and Mirjam Pressler. New York: Doubleday, 1995.

Jelinek, Estelle. *The Tradition of Autobiography*. Boston: Twayne, 1986.

——. *Women and Autobiography*. Bloomington: Indiana UP, 1980.

Kadar, Marlene. *Essays on Life Writing*. Toronto: U of Toronto P, 1992.

Smith, Sidonie. *A Poetics of Women's Autobiography*. Bloomington: Indiana UP, 1987.

Spelman, Elizabeth. *Inessential Woman: Problems in the Exclusion of Feminist Thought*. Boston: Hall, 1983.

Stanton, Domna C. *The Female Autograph*. Chicago: U of Chicago P, 1984.

Lives Considered
and Reconsidered Day by Day:
Diaries, Letters, and Journals

1

"Why feignest thou thyselfe to be another woman?": Constraints on the Construction of Subjectivity in Mary Rich's Diary

Avra Kouffman

In 1666, at age 40, Mary Boyle Rich, Countess of Warwick, began a spiritual diary which she was to keep for the twelve years until her death.[1] On first reading, the diary succeeds more as a representative cultural document than as a testament to an individual psyche or narrative persona. It is, in effect, a collaborative effort, inscribed by mid-century clerics whose manuals and guidebooks taught readers the received method of composing a Christian diary. Local religious advisors also advised Rich on the "best manner" of keeping a journal.[2] Even after her death, the vestiges of her self-presentation were manipulated by others: In the tradition of printed eulogies, her chaplain, Anthony Warwick, and later, the editor Thomas Woodroofe, selected and published only those passages of her diary that best displayed the countess's "saintly character" (Mendelson, "Diaries" 207). Nonetheless, the published versions of the diary reflect the tensions between Rich's desire to fashion and express a private subjectivity, and her compunction to adhere to the models of self-presentation set out for her. As a spiritual diarist, Rich's text is strongly marked by the expectations of genre, and her writing both adheres to and subverts the dictates of a well-established tradition.

Although diaries and journals are commonly regarded and represented as a safe, secret space where one's private thoughts may be recorded freely, diary practice was very much a topic of discussion and instruction by the mid-seventeenth century. The diary served an important function in terms of cultural subject production: It taught diarists to construct and monitor themselves as Christians with specific positions in the hierarchy of God, man, and wife. Protestants, particularly, were asked to keep a strict record of all of their sins, to account for their time as well or poorly spent, and to chronicle God's mercies in every area of their lives. In 1656, John Beadle calls the diary a "Register-Book for conscience to keep courts by" (9). Religious diary-keeping manuals like his explained which questions one should regularly ask oneself, and included precise directions as to how the faithful should behave, organize and render up every aspect of daily existence.

For several reasons, titled women like the countess were regarded by the religious establishment as an important contingent to influence. Aristocratic women were among the elite minority who were able to read and write. These women were frequently influential in their counties, and often accessible: In the case of country estates, the local cleric could develop a mentor relationship with the lady of the manor while her husband went off to war or to London. A friendship with one's patroness could enhance a cleric's success in the district; unsurprisingly, several Christian guidebooks were dedicated to wealthy gentlewomen.

The gentry and middling sort also participated in diary writing. After all, the Protestant clerics who kept spiritual diaries and helped to popularize the practice were rarely titled themselves. It is likely that the Reverend Beadle taught both the Countess of Warwick and Elizabeth Walker—the wife of Rich's chaplain—to keep journals. In these diaries, Rich and Walker gauge the probability of their salvation by the same means: They seek signs of God's favor in everyday occurrences. The women seem to believe some Christians to be among the "elect" and thus destined for Heaven, as opposed to the reprobate masses, who are doomed to Hell. Rich and Walker articulate a worldview that prizes a religious, rather than solely aristocratic, elite. The diary-keeping itself serves to reenforce the view that the individual life is important and worthy of record for all Christians.

In the late Stuart era, the diary would have been viewed as a particularly appropriate genre of religious instruction for women. No social stigma was attached to the writing of these private texts. Female diarists, unlike female playwrights or novelists, could not be accused of setting themselves up as authors and competing with men in a public marketplace or arena. Women could keep diaries and worship God without intruding into spaces that were culturally designated as male. Indeed, diary-writing was actively encouraged as a means by which women could fashion a pseudo-private, though publicly celebrated, subjectivity. The public aspect of keeping a daily record derives from both the diary manuals and from printed funeral sermons. These sermons often incorporated the deceased woman's diary excerpts, as a means of displaying and praising her virtue and Christian worth. Yet the diarists are consistently and adamantly depicted as writing for entirely private intents and purposes. In *Eureka, Eureka: The Virtuous Woman Found* (1678), Anthony Walker announces that Lady Rich had been "Great by her

Pen"—an allusion to her diary. He then rushes to declare that Rich meant her writing to be entirely private, and that any public perusal of it was "without her knowledge, or allowance, and wholly beside her expectation" (48). Whereas female Restoration playwrights and poets were expected to apologize for the audacity of writing as women, in the eulogies, women are actually encouraged to write, as long as they write only spiritual diaries, and as long as they have no ambitions to make the contents of these diaries public. The ostensibly private nature of woman's written subjectivity is, through the printed funeral sermons, publicly authorized and celebrated.

During the diarist's lifetime, the primary use of her journal was to function, metaphorically, as a form of seventeenth-century spiritual Panopticon.[3] The journals were a mechanism by which women learned to monitor their own actions and thoughts in the absence of external overseers. Mary Rich, for example, castigates herself for muttering angry "passionate words," although no one sees or hears her. She writes, "though no other did hear, yet, O Lord, thou didst" (224). Her journal becomes a space to record, examine, agonize over, and repent of her failings. Its very dailiness helps to explain its powerful ability to affect and shape the way she imagines and represents her subjectivity. Days, weeks, and years of repetition and adherence to standard diary form take their toll, and Rich writes her life as a series of religious duties and repentances. As a spiritual diarist, she articulates a subjectivity in the religious discourse available to her, until the textual Rich is shaped by the genre itself.

By virtue of its habitual nature, the diary was a powerful tool. Once a woman took charge of monitoring her own subjection, she could be trusted to absorb and promote the spread of Puritan ideology throughout her household and family. Mary Rich preached religious discipline to her husband, friends, and servants. She also tithed a large portion of her substantial income to the church.[4] Her inner resolve had public, outward effects.

Sidonie Smith, in her work on personal narrative, writes of the subject who "actively negotiates cultural discourses as an agent of resistance" (393). Can this categorization apply, at all, to Rich? Or is her self-depiction entirely beholden to the instructional literature she read? Certainly, she consciously attempted to copy the models that were laid out for her. She borrows in both content and expression from at least three Christian guidebooks: Isaac Ambrose's *Media* (1654), John Featley's *A Fountaine of Teares* (1646), and John Beadle's *A Journal or Diary of a Thankful Christian* (1656) (Murray). Ambrose, in *Media*, suggests that diarists review their entries to search for "mercies of God" and instances of sin, and Rich follows this procedure (73). Featley exhorts his female readers to be "weeping daughters of Jerusalem" and to cry often and copiously (5-6), and Rich's diary is filled with pointed references to the "abundance" (72) and "great plenty" of tears that she sheds almost daily (140). Beadle suggests in his book that diarists monitor the state of the nation and thank God for both deliverances and afflictions. Rich, accordingly, prays for "the crying sins of the kingdom" (86) and praises God for having preserved her from broken bones (252), fire (115), the plague (148), and the likelihood of eternal damnation. Heeding John Beadle's injunction to "Blesse God for every twig of his rod" (197), she writes that "all the crosses and afflictions God had been pleased to exercise me with, had proved advantageous for the good of my soul" (196). The sense that she deserves whatever burdens she must bear is present throughout much of Rich's diary, as she displays the subservient posture characteristic of the Puritan faithful. In one self-abasing passage, Rich employs the language of masochism to record her desire to humble herself before God:

[I did] beg supporting grace from God to enable me patiently to bear what afflictions he was pleased to lay upon me, that when he did strike me with his rod, his staff might support me, that I might not faint when I was corrected of him, but might make a sanctified improvement of his fatherly chastisements, which I was enabled from my heart to confess I did deserve. (170)

As a repentant sinner, Rich has been schooled to abandon hopes of earthly happiness, and cling to "thoughts of future glory" and the faith that heaven will make "amends for all the troubles" she has suffered in the world (171). Accordingly, she places the needs of others before her own. This quality of selflessness, which was widely viewed as an appropriate characteristic in a woman, delighted Anthony Walker, who claimed in his *Memoir* of Rich that she was "mistress and promotress, not to say the foundress and inventress, of a new science—the art of obliging" (21).

And yet, occasionally Rich uses her diary as a forum for a critique—if not of the subservient posture expected of her, then of her husband and his failure to adhere to Christianity's dictates. Lord Rich was less interested in godliness than was his wife, and they quarreled over her religiosity. One entry states: "was hindered by my Lord's commands from going to church, for which I was much troubled, seeing him so passionate about it" (128-29). Rich often records that she prayed for her husband, and she seems to take pleasure in her ability to intercede for him. She writes that she "did earnestly wrestle" for Lord Rich's soul "with great abundance of tears," and hopes that God will heed her request as "a person of so many prayers and tears" (100-01). Rich seems to feel a sincere responsibility to effect her spouse's salvation: "[I] did with abundance of tears beg that God would convert him, and make him that swears to fear an oath, and to wash him as clean from the guilt of all his sins as the blood of a God could make him" (97). At the same time, she clearly relishes her position as the morally and spiritually righteous partner. She makes the occasional ironic remark about her husband's shortcomings. As she writes of his propensity for swearing: "I did exceedingly adore and admire [God's] mercy, that did yet keep the plague out of my house, when that curse was so usually in my husband's mouth" (115). Lord Rich just happens to come to mind when she is pondering the "black abyss of eternity": "Whilst I was thinking what a sad thing it would be to be eternally miserable, God was pleased to stir up my heart to pray that my poor husband might be delivered from the wrath to come" (159-60). Rich even uses her power as God's agent to talk back to her husband at the dining table, telling him that he ought to "study gratitude" for the food which God provides (184).

Christianity becomes a means by which Rich can derive leverage and power in her personal relationships. She is emboldened by the thought that she is campaigning for piety and the triumph of the Christian way. Apart from begging her husband to change, she also importunes her servants, acquaintances, and friends to consider their future state. She writes, "I spent the whole afternoon in examining and exhorting my servants to prepare themselves to receive the sacrament. I was enabled to speak with much seriousness and affection to them, and I did much endeavour to bring them to a seriousness in the matter of their souls" (173). Several entries record her religious discussions with dying townsfolk; Rich always counsels them to keep faith in God and to hope for a better afterlife. One feels, reading her diary, that death is always hovering over the shoulder of the Stuart woman, as those around her fall prey to the very high infant mortality rate, incurable disease, fires, and wars. That she should feel a sense of urgency regarding one's future condition is not surprising; thus Rich cautions some "young ladies" to consider how things stand between them and God, and "to be more strict than ever in their lives and conversations" (195-96). Her husband's illness prompts even more vigilance in her spiritual care of him: "I did in a very serious and awakened frame tell him of his danger, and was very home with him about his everlasting state" (217). Rich allows herself a freedom and outspokenness in religious matters that she might not permit herself on other topics. She derives an unmistakable sense of power and authority from her adherence to societally acceptable doctrines, and she uses her position as a respectable Christian to authorize her advice towards others, and to oversee their conduct and behavior.

Central to Rich's text are related schisms: Her spiritual pride vies with her desire to be a humble Christian, and her attempt to suppress her fury in marital arguments is thwarted by her strong conviction that she is "ever so much in the right" (238). Rich's partial failure to suppress her secular ego affects her adherence to the commands given by John Featley in his 1646 guidebook, *A Fountaine of Teares*. In over 600 pages, Featley lays out the proper occasions and reasons for Christian women to cry. His table of contents include chapter headings for "Teares in the Night," "Teares in the Day," "A Virgin's Teares," "Teares of a Married Woman," "Teares of an Aged Woman," "Teares of a Barren Woman," "Teares of a Wife for the Sicknesse of her husband," "Teares of a woman lamenting the death of her beloved husband," and "Teares in a woman in the State of Widdowhood," among other topics. Featley lists 38 questions to ask oneself before bed, such as "What ould offence has been new sinned over?" and "What teares have I shed for it?" (90-91). Rich takes this edict to heart, and she tends to stress the amount of tears shed as a proof of spiritual vigor. She prays with "many tears, groans and sighs" (79) and cries "buckets" in the hopes that a sudden fire will not harm potential victims (80). Yet she rebukes herself that her tears are not entirely unselfish. In two separate instances, Rich cries over her husband's cruelty, and then professes guilt for resenting any one's shortcomings but her own:

I was so much troubled with his unkindness to me that I was weary of my life. . . . but afterwards I went to prayer, and therein did beg God's pardon for my shedding so many tears for anything but my sins, and for not being content with what his providence was pleased to order for me. (136)

[M]y lord, without any just cause given by me, spoke very bitterly and provokingly to me. . . . I found myself so much overcome with the unkindness of it that I wept exceedingly. . . . Afterwards, I was much troubled that I had shed any tears for anything but my sins, and begged God's pardon. (215-16)

Rich records her husband's unkindness and its effect on her, and reproaches herself for exhibiting enough ego to weep over his behavior. In this way, she at once critiques the ideology that encourages her to accept her husband as lord on earth, and simultaneously accedes to it.

In the abbreviated, published edition of her diary, Mary Rich's voice often seems lost or suppressed. Her entries chronicle routine religious activities: she prays, reads devotional literature, hears sermons, and weeps. Her word choice is familiar and repetitive, as she endlessly transcribes phrases from the devotional literature of the time. Although, in a tradition made popular by John Bunyan,[5] she attempts to document the vacillations of her soul, she does not delineate her spiritual trials and successes with Bunyan's precision and nuances. She usually ascribes to herself one of two primary emotional states: Either Rich's heart is "dull and untoward" during prayer (93), or she achieves a "sweet, refreshing" communion with God (115). This lack of literary originality may partly be attributed to the constraints of a genre in which Rich's uniqueness was *meant* to be subverted to a detailed recital of God's attentions and mercies. Accordingly, her secular autobiography, written in the 1670s, displays more originality and a better literary style.

However, it is probable that Rich's manuscript diary is more exciting than the bland 1847 edition published by the Religious Tract Society (the only substantive edition in print). Nineteenth-century efforts to standardize and regularize the diary's form and content appear to have altered significantly the substance and even the look of Rich's original text. The Tract Society entry for July 25, 1666, for example, contrasts significantly with an unedited version of the same entry, published in Charlotte Fell Smith's 1901 biography. The unedited entry suggests a text that is fuller and more vibrant than what has been published thus far. Smith's transcription features signs and symbols absent from the Tract Society edition:

Why dost thou faine thyself to be realidgious and yet art not one that delightest thy selfe more in God? Why dos thy heart goe out after anything but him in whom thou shouldest sett all thy heartes dealight? This thought [God was] pleased to melte my heart by, to give abundance of teares to mourn for my not dealighting more in him. I came into my closett and [cypher—? prayed], then went to private prayer, ♥ L[my heart was] cared out for preservation in those times of siknes from the noysome pestilence, and for the comfort of friendes when bettar then I had themselves shut upe from them. u L pleased to give abundance of teares at the consideration of His unmerited goodnes to me in the preservation of my selfe and famely. Then I went to famely prayer the ♥ went out towardes u in desires and breathings after him. After diner came the news of hearing the gunes and that our flete was ingaged. The ♥ was much afrited at the consideration of the protestante blood that would be spilte, and of soe many Souls that would presently lanech into eternity, my heart was cared out exseadingly to compashenate them and to pray u to spare the sheding of the blood of those for whom + shed his pretious blood. I got Mr. Cla[rk] to pray priuately in the clossett for them. u gave [tears] of compassion for them. Then in the

evening went lone into the parke and begde for mersy again, and to give me
ashewrance of my one euerlasting condition, that what every becom of my body
my S may be safe. Then went to famely prayer, the ♥ breathed after u. After
supar comited my S to u.[6]

Rich, in this entry, personalizes Reverend Beadle's instructions to
record and interpret current events for their religious significance.
Rather than dwell on the battle between the English and the Dutch as a
manifestation of God's wrath, she describes herself as "much afrited"
by the event, and claims to feel extreme compassion for its victims. Her
partisan emotional concern is displayed in her wish that "protestante
blood" not be spilt, and in the entry's final wish that her own soul will
be safe, come what may. The attention to her own spiritual welfare in
the midst of a national catastrophe occurs again, when Warwick house
is in danger of burning in a fire. She notes: "I thank God I found my
heart more affected for the common calamity and sufferings of others
than for that" (79). This comment encapsulates the paradox of the religious worldview that Rich embraces. As a humble sinner, Rich should
put all others before herself. Yet the state of her own soul and psyche is
important enough that it must be constantly monitored and assessed, by
both herself and her creator. Thus Rich can thank God for her spiritual
progress in forgetting herself in a time of crisis, even as she mentally
marks, and later records, her triumph in being so self-effacing. This
simultaneous rejection of, and implicit valuing of, oneself forms the
central schism expressed in the majority of Stuart women's diaries.

Ultimately, what fascinates most about Rich's diary is its length.
Perhaps the force of Rich's personality resides in the very weight, dedication, and discipline of those 9,000 manuscript pages. Anthony Walker
tells us that Rich altered her daily schedule and rose early in order to sal-
vage quiet moments in which to write (*Memoir* 28). She must have cher-
ished what she perceived as time spent alone with her journal and her
God. The intimate relationship of the believer to the Almighty is likely
to have been an appealing aspect of doctrine to women who found themselves, despite their wealth or position, disappointed by their lives. Rich
herself experienced the death of her children and marriage to a difficult
man. She was receptive to an ideology which assured her that Christ, her
true bridegroom, awaited her in a better life-to-come. The passages
where she writes of her desire for Christ are the most vibrant and erotic
in the journal: Rich hopes to have "sweet communion with him"; she
records many "spiritual breathings and yearnings after him" (128) and
she desires to "blow my languid spark of love into a more ardent fire,
which I would fain to have blazed with more than seraphic heat" (75-

76). Although these phrases are borrowed from religious discourse, they also symbolize Rich's intense and heated desire for a balm for her earthly existence.

Mary Rich begins her first diary entry with a worried query. She asks, "What if God showld say to me as the Prophet Ahijah to Jeroboas wife: why feignest thou thyselfe to be another woman? Why dost thou faine thyselfe to be religious and yet art not one that delightest thy selfe more in God?" Rich does not explore further the implications of her own question—nor does she answer it. She merely writes that she cried an "abundance of tears to mourn for my not dealighting more in him" (qtd. in Fell Smith 169). Although it is impossible to answer for her with any certainty, I would hazard the suggestion that Rich had a need to pretend to delight more because that is what she was enculturated to do. The "other" that she feigned to be was the woman modeled in the manuals of the time; the woman who submitted quietly to the cruelty of fate and those around her, who always put herself last and committed her happiness entirely and passively to God and his agents on earth. In her final published diary entry, Rich writes, "God was pleased to give me a very humbling sight of myself, and to enable me to offer up the sacrifice of a broken and contrite heart; and, with great loathing of myself, to judge and condemn myself" (266). With more than 300 years of distance and theory at our disposal, it is easy enough to suggest that it was not "God," but rather the discourse of an insidious and pervasive ideology that encouraged Rich "with great loathing . . . to judge and condemn" herself. That the genre of spiritual diary played such a transformative role in the process, seems to me to make it worthy of more attention, discussion and extended study.

Notes

1. Following seventeenth-century practice and the example set by John Beadle's *A Journal or Diary of a Thankful Christian* (1656), I use the term "diary" and "journal" interchangeably.

2. Anthony Walker comments on Mary Rich's diary practice in his printed funeral sermon, "Eureka, Eureka: The Virtuous Woman Found" (1678). This sermon is excerpted, reprinted, and expanded in Anthony Walker, Memoir of *Lady Warwick: Also Her Diary from the Years 1666 A.D. to 1672 A.D.* (London: Religious Society, 1847). My citations refer to the Religious Tract Society edition of Rich's diary, except for the reproductions of Rich's July 25, 1666, entry, copied from the transcription in Charlotte Fell Smith's 1901 biography, *Mary Rich, Countess of Warwick (1625-1678): Her Family and Friends*. Rich's original manuscripts are lodged in the British Library: BL Add. MSS 27351-6.

3. For Michel Foucault's discussion of the Panopticon, see his *Discipline and Punish: The Birth of a Prison* (New York: Pantheon, 1977).

4. Walker explains in his *Memoir* that when he suggested that Rich "consecrate to God" a seventh of her estate earnings, she replied that she "would never give less than the third part" (52-53).

5. Bunyan's *Pilgrim's Progress* is considered a Puritan classic. Different sources have classed Rich variously as a Puritan, a Presbyterian and an Anglican. She appears to have embraced several dissenting influences, judging from her eclectic group of religious advisors. Diary-writing itself was practiced by both Anglicans and dissenters, but popularized, from the 1640s on, by by the latter group, whose influence appears in Rich's attempts to chart her mental-emotional state in writing.

6. I transcribed this entry from pages 169-70 of Charlotte Fell Smith's *Mary Rich, Countess of Warwick (1625-1678): Her Family and Friends* (London: Longmans, Green, and Co., 1901). Smith assures her readers that "the first day's entry in the Diary is reprinted below verbatim et literatim, signs and all. Punctuation is slightly amended" (169). Words or phrases in brackets signify Smith's interpretation of Rich's symbols.

Works Cited

Ambrose, Isaac. *Media, the Middle Things in Reference to the First and Last Things* . . . 2nd ed. London: Printed by T. R. and E. M. for Nathanael Webb and William Grantham, 1652.

Featley, John. *A Fountaine of Tears* . . . Amsterdam: Printed for John Crosse, 1646.

Fell Smith, Charlotte. *Mary Rich, Countess of Warwick (1625-1678): Her Family and Friends.* London: Longmans, 1901.

Foucault, Michel. *Discipline and Punish: The Birth of a Prison.* New York: Pantheon, 1977.

Mendelson, Sara Heller. "Mary Rich, Countess of Warwick." *The Mental World of Stuart Women: Three Studies.* Brighton, Sussex: Harvester, 1987. 62-115, n. 203-07.

——."Stuart Women's Diaries and Occasional Memoirs." Ed. Mary Prior. *Women in English Society, 1500-1800.* London: Methuen, 1985.

Murray, Germaine Fry. *An Annotated Edition of John Beadle's* A Journal or Diary of a Thankful Christian. Diss. St. Louis University, 1991.

Smith, Sidonie. "Who's Talking/Who's Talking Back? The Subject of Personal Narrative" *Signs: Journal of Women in Culture and Society* 18.2 (1993): 392-409.

Walker, Anthony. *Eureka, Eureka. The Virtuous Woman Found, Her Loss Bewailed, and Character Exemplified in a Sermon Preached at Felsted in Essex, April 30, 1678 . . . To Which Are Annexed Some of Her Ladyship's Pious and Useful Meditations.* London: Printed for Nathaniel Ranew, 1678.

——, and Mary Rich, Countess of Warwick. *Memoir of Lady Warwick: Also Her Diary from the Years 1666 A.D. to 1672 A.D. . . . To Which Are Added, Extracts from Her Other Writings.* London: Religious Tract Society, 1847.

Warwick, Mary Rich, Countess of. *Autobiography of Mary, Countess of Warwick.* Ed. T. C. Croker. London: Printed for the Percy Society by Richards, 1848.

2

"Clandestine Delight": Frances Burney's Life-Writing

Linda Lang-Peralta

Frances Burney (1752-1840) set ablaze all of her manuscripts, including a novel, on her fifteenth birthday. This destructive act reveals the anxiety that writing caused her as she created an identity within her community of family and friends. Despite her several attempts, she could not quash her desire to write. Referring to writing as her "clandestine delight," she indulged in that secret joy knowing that what she produced might threaten precious relationships, such as that with her father. Eventually she discovered, however, that writing not only strengthened the bond with her father but also helped to forge relationships with other writers in her family's social circle. This circle included members of the London literati such as Edmund Burke, David Garrick, Hester Lynch Thrale, Joshua Reynolds, Richard Brinsley Sheridan, and Samuel Johnson. During Burney's long life she produced several novels, poems, plays, a political tract, and copious journals and letters.[1]

Frances Burney was a writer when that label was not affixed to one of her sex without raising eyebrows. Writing was not only her delight but also her duty as amanuensis to her father, Dr. Charles Burney, who had gained his own measure of literary fame with his book on the history of music.[2] Writing down her father's ideas was expected, as was penning entertaining letters to friends and family. Whenever one of them traveled, witty letters would be shuffled back and forth across the distance. Frances wrote often to her sister Susanna Elizabeth Burney, for example, when they were not together, in order to share news, gossip, and affection. Writing was a way of life in the Burney household, but for a young girl to write novels for the public was another matter.

The anonymous publication of *Evelina* (1778) first brought fame to Frances Burney while she was in her twenties. The attention the novel received encouraged her to reveal her identity to her father and the world. Thereafter, the social community of writers, including the Blue Stocking Circle, welcomed her into their ranks. Her second novel,

23

Cecilia (1782), increased her literary fame, much to her father's delight. She was offered an appointment at the royal court as second keeper of the robes to Queen Charlotte but later resigned because of the oppressive demands of the position. She married the French General d'Arblay in 1793, with whom she had a child. The couple built "Camilla Cottage" with the proceeds from her 1796 novel, *Camilla,* and her pension from the years of court service, 100 pounds per year, helped to support her family. When interned by Napoleon, the d'Arblays resided in France for ten years. *The Wanderer,* her last novel, was published in 1814. She spent her later years editing the journals and letters, bound together in recent editions, which would provide readers after her death with an invaluable record of the growth of a woman writer in the late eighteenth century.

Selected journals and letters are the focus of this study. The various voices that emerge in her life-writing[3] document her constant struggle to practice her art and negotiate its place in her life. Although always aware that writing could jeopardize a woman's carefully constructed reputation, Burney felt that her journals opened up a private space where she could write to "Nobody," where she could offend "Nobody," where she could reveal herself to "Nobody." As she stated in 1769,

How truly does this Journal contain my real & undisguised thoughts—I always write in it according to the humour I am in, & if any stranger was to think it worth reading, how capricious—insolent & whimsical I must appear!—one moment flighty & half mad,—the next sad & melancholy. No matter! it's truth & simplicity are it's sole recommendations." (*Early Journals* 61)[4]

However, even in this supposedly private composition, Burney exhibited an awareness of a possible audience and provided an evaluation of her product. When her family and friends learned of her pastime, they also imagined with trepidation that her private thoughts might fall into the wrong hands. Burney's community constantly reminded her of the risks of writing.

A writer's community provides rich fodder for the imagination and a testing ground for the self. Comparing James Boswell's (1740-1795) journals with Burney's reveals the limitations of her experience in the brilliant but restricted society to which she had access. Boswell recorded in his letters and journals conversations with others from all levels of society, including prostitutes. Boswell's journals record, in Robert Folkenflik's analysis, the "trying out of the self upon others" because "he needs the sense of something palpably outside himself which can give him back the sense of being what he thinks he is because his own fragmented sense of self finds no interior stability" (1293). While Boswell tested his self on a variety of others, Burney recorded repeated instances of cutting herself off from those whose reputations might damage hers. She constantly limited her community according to the strict social codes as interpreted by her father. At fifteen, Burney wrote, "To be sure I am not frequently from Home, on the contrary, I seldom quit it, considering my Age & opportunities; but why should I, when I am so happy in it?" (*Early Journals* 60). While Burney was fortunate enough to interact in her own home with some of the most respected minds of her time, her social experience was limited to the upper levels of society. She had few relations with anyone of questionable repute, in other words, anyone (especially women) who had broken through the constraints by which she was so firmly bound for most of her life. This restrictive process limited the experience from which she could draw in her writing. In addition, rejecting people caused her much anguish and remorse, revealing that she did not accept this social code unquestioningly. Such constraints hindered her literary production while also providing the tension that made her art provocative. She learned to develop her voices as a woman and a writer.

Throughout this study of Burney's voices, I use the nomenclature developed by Mary Field Belenky and her colleagues in *Women's Ways of Knowing*. They used data collected from interviews with hundreds of diverse women to identify five voices that reveal women's epistemology. Using William Perry's *Forms of Intellectual and Ethical Development in the College Years*, Belenky and her colleagues discovered that these categories differed for women, a difference partly explained by Carol Gilligan's theories. Both the Perry and the Belenky studies schematized various ways of knowing as stages through which one progresses. While Burney's journals reveal this general development, some entries as well as selected letters also exhibit a curious mixture of voices that indicates her problematic relationship with her writing and her community. Burney's private writing not only provided a space for her to develop her writer's voice,[5] but also it reveals how carefully she manipulated her different voices to avoid censure. Burney often censored her writing so that it would not offend others or damage her own reputation. Using her ability to represent in print the voices that she heard in daily life, she carefully controlled her own voices in order to strategically negotiate treacherous waters. Her multiple voices also indicate her fragile sense of self in a society that allowed women only limited expression in writing as in life. The voices in these journals and letters expose resistance to the constraints that hindered a woman's life and writing in the late eighteenth century.

This study traces Burney's literary voice from the witty juvenilia of the quiet fifteen-year-old, to the letters of a mature woman negotiating relationships, to the "Windsoriana" of the renowned writer visiting the royal court. In these selected passages from her formative years, I demonstrate that while Burney's voices change dramatically depending on her audience, they also reveal major transformations in her ways of knowing. By controlling her voices, Burney succeeded in protecting her reputation while growing as a woman and a writer. Part of this process consisted in adopting the voice that Belenky calls "received knowl-edge,"[6] especially with her father. Reliance on authorities' views marks this voice, along with "either/or" thinking: things are right or wrong, good or bad, moral or immoral (35-52). Critics have often thought of Burney as a prude because she acted in accordance with received knowl-edge: judgments handed down from her father, from Mr. ("Daddy") Crisp, from social gossips. She even calls her friend William Locke her *"Oracle"* in 1791. A late eighteenth-century woman was expected to listen unquestioningly to authorities, whether fathers, husbands, or kings. If she had acted according to her own subjective reasoning, she quickly could have become one of the outcasts with whom she was forbidden to socialize. Most notably this voice emerged when there was a threat to her reputation. However, her journals and letters reveal ways of knowing far beyond this level of development.

The Juvenilia

The earliest extant journals reveal a public voice that was com-pletely subject to the power of others, but they also reveal the construc-tion of a private self in writing. Although Burney's public persona sug-gested a young woman with little or no perception of her own intellec-tual abilities, a voice Belenky and her colleagues call "silence," her jour-nals belie this image. At fifteen, when the journals begin, five years after her mother's death, Burney appeared as "the silent observant Miss Fanny" to a visitor (qtd. in Troide, Introduction xvi). The young Burney was not one to reveal herself or her private writing to others. Mr. Young, when a house guest, knocked at her bedroom door, supposedly desiring to see her journal. The journal describes her action: "I ran into a closet, & lock'd myself up—however, he did not pollute *my* chamber with his unhallow'd feet" (*Early Journals* 5). The assertive tone curiously con-trasts the timid action of running and hiding: Burney described the act of fleeing with an imperious air, as if a monarch were refusing admittance to an unworthy visitor. She guarded her right to privacy, her right to con-trol her own space, just as she protected her right to create a private world in writing. The journal allowed her the freedom to construct a self in writing that was at odds with her silent public persona.

Conscious from the beginning of the restrictions that an audience might place upon her written voice, Burney initially addressed her journal to "Nobody," an imagined friend and confidante. When her writing found its way into the wrong hands, she was terrified. Her father discovered some writing that she inadvertently had left out on the piano forte. It took her a day and a half even to ask her father about the purloined pages: "O Dear! I was in a sad distress—I could not for the Life of me ask for it—& so *dawdled* & fretted the time away till Tuesday Evening" (*Early Journals* 19). Evidently she feared punishment or embarrassment, and, therefore, could not bring herself to raise the issue with her father. When she did ask for her papers, he asked why she left them out. This question was enough to silence her again: "I could not say another word." Even though her father threatened to "stick [her journals] up in the market place" if he found them again, Frances was surprised by his benign response: "And then he kiss'd me *so* kindly—Never was parent so *properly*, so *well-Judged* affectionate." She considered giving up the project but admitted that she must write. She had no choice: "Well, to be sure, thought I, these same dear Journals are most shocking plaguing things—I've a good mind to resolve never to write a word more. . . . I was so frightened that I have not had the Heart to write since, till now, I should not but that — in short, but that I cannot help it!" (*Early Journals* 19). Possibly because of her lack of a voice in relations with authority figures such as her father, she needed to express herself in writing to "Nobody."

The silent persona that addressed her father transforms a short time later into an assertive one in Burney's account of a conversation with Miss Young (1721-1805). This adult friend advised her to give up writing in case it should fall into the wrong hands, possibly the hands of an admirer. Burney defended her practice, insisted that it was innocent, and argued for the right to record her thoughts:

I have been having a long conversation with Miss Young on journals. She has very seriously and earnestly advised me to give mine up—heigho-ho! Do you think I can bring myself to oblige her? What she says has great weight with me; but, indeed, I should be very loath to *quite* give my poor friend up. She says that it is the most dangerous employment young persons can have—it makes them often record things which ought *not* to be recorded, but instantly forgot. I told her, that as *my* Journal was *solely* for my own perusal, nobody could in justice, or even in sense, be angry or displeased at my writing anything. (*Early Journals* 21)

Again Burney expressed her inability to stop writing. Rather than a lack of control, which her previous "I cannot help it" implies, in this instance her "heigho-ho" suggests that it would seem ridiculous not to write. She relied on her journal as a "friend" with whom she could explore her growing sense of self in relation to others. She reasoned that she had the right to record anything that she desired. The "nobody" who could justly censure her (echoing the audience that she constructs for the journal), a few lines later, becomes her father: "Why dear ma'am, papa never prohibited my writing, and he knows that I *do* write, and *what* I do write" (*Early Journals* 21). This change in voices, from silence and deference in her interaction with her father to confident assertiveness with this friend of the family, could have various causes. Burney may have felt more confidence addressing Miss Young, who had no direct authority over her, than she did when addressing her father. On the other hand, perhaps Burney had become more comfortable with her writing in the short time since the incident with her father, described above, which had helped her to voice her rights. He did not forbid her to write, although he warned her to keep her writing private. She apparently interpreted this reaction as his approval of her avocation. Her voice in relation to her father usually was deferential and reverent, as in "received knowledge" in the Belenky schema. His word was her truth, and she rarely acted against his directive, and yet in relation to Miss Young we see an emerging sense of self.

Adding to the complexity of interpretation is the fact that this entry was added later to the journal when it was published, which could account for the change in voice (*Early Journals* 20). The issue of the public and private divide in writing seemed to haunt Burney into old age, when she spent her last years editing, excising, and rearranging her letters and journals so that they would not endanger anyone's reputation, as Miss Young warned her that they could. Of course, this revision process makes more complicated the task of tracing the writer's voices throughout her lifetime.

One must reflect not only on the silencing in which Burney and her editors engaged when they blackened lines, cut out sections, and rearranged sequences but also on the self-censoring that might have kept Burney from initially recording thoughts and events. This silence is what Ingrid Tieken-Boon Van Ostade calls "the inner layer" of Burney's journals, which, unlike the layers of ink that several editors have erased, "is not to be physically removed. Its existence is brought to light only by references in the journal itself to facts, events and circumstances which were not recorded because of their over-delicate nature" (159). This is not the silence, however, of one with no sense of self, as described by

Belenky; it is the self-protective voice of one who is aware of the risks of exposing a vulnerable self.

Reading gave Burney a way to test her self against others and question authority to some extent. In her earliest journals Burney recorded her reactions to reading authors such as Plutarch, Sterne, Goldsmith, and Dr. Johnson. When reading Homer, for example, she questioned the way that he depicted women as being, above all, vain:

I cannot help taking notice of one thing in the 3d Book—which has provoked me for the honour of the sex: Venus tempts Hellen [*sic*] [with every] delusion in favour of her Darling,—in vain—Riches—power—honour—Love—all in vain—the enraged Deity threatens to deprive her of her own beauty, & render her to the level with the most common of her sex—blushing & trembling—Hellen immediately yields her Hand. (*Early Journals* 37)

This passage disturbed her because she considered vanity a weakness. She further reflected on the veracity of this depiction of women: "Thus has Homer proved his opinion of our poor sex—that the Love of Beauty is our most prevailing passion. It really grieves me to think that there certainly must be reason for the insignificant opinion the greatest men have of Women—At least I *fear* there must.—But I don't in fact *believe* it—thank God!" (*Early Journals* 37). The distinction between learning knowledge from an authority and questioning that knowledge clearly emerges in this last statement. Burney read the masters to gain an education, but she resisted their depiction of women. This fifteen-year-old writer in 1768 demonstrated a clear sense of literature's role in shaping perception, and she articulated her knowledge that opposed Homer's male view. Her concluding "thank God!" seems to celebrate her ability to question authorities who misrepresent women.

In these early journals, Burney sounds much like a "subjectivist" in Belenky's terms, a woman who has begun to question authority, who arrives at knowledge individually but who rarely expresses herself publicly or tries to persuade others that she is right. A journal often provides such women with a place to express themselves freely, without the constraints that authorities might impose (35-87). Burney's voice to the "Nobody" that is her journal audience is full of wit and confidence, daring tentatively to question authorities, such as Homer. Her assertive stance with Miss Young was rare; more characteristic was a silent acceptance of other views while developing her own. The juvenilia reveal an adolescent writer with a growing sense of self, a savvy sense of audience, and a survivalist sense of a young woman's place in her society.

Adult Letters

Burney had learned to act according to her subjective knowledge by the time she was an adult. In several journal entries and letters of 1791, a stronger subjectivist voice defines itself in opposition to others, defending choices based on individual needs. Belenky and her colleagues often heard this subjectivist voice in women who had recently separated from spouses or divorced, women who were seeking an escape.

Burney certainly sought such escape from her oppressive role at the court of King George III and Queen Charlotte as second keeper of the robes. In her journal of 1791, she recorded a conversation in which she succinctly stated her case for leaving the court: "My conduct . . . all consisted in not pretending, when I found myself sinking, to be swimming" (*Journals* 1: 101). Rather than acting as if court life agreed with her, she had honestly admitted that her position was making her ill and requested to leave. Some time after she had gained her freedom, she visited her ex-supervisor at court, Mrs. Schwellenberg, who was the primary reason Burney was so miserable. Burney recounted, "I easily read that she still has not forgiven my resignation, and still thinks I failed in loyalty of duty, by not staying, though to die, rather than retire, though to live" (*Journals* 1: 88). These lines reveal her sense that others expected her to maintain what they saw as her privileged position. Burney is clearly adamant about her decision, and her many references to illness and exhaustion bear testament to the wisdom of resignation. Her father's disappointment must have been difficult for her to bear, because the social-climbing Dr. Burney "thought that going to court was like going to heaven," according to Thomas Babington Macaulay (qtd. in Doody 18). Nevertheless, Burney had learned to oppose authority when she felt herself abused.

Writing of "the tyranny of Mrs. Schwel." over one of her friends, she passionately exclaims, "Tis dreadful that Power thus often leads to every abuse!—I grow Democrate at once upon these occasions! Indeed, I feel always democrate where I think Power abused,—whether by the Great or the Little" (*Journals* 1: 89). The Burney who had rarely questioned authority in her youth, and adored her king and queen, sounds somewhat rebellious in this passage. As they had in her adolescence, her journals and letters to trusted readers provided a private forum in which she could express heretical ideas and record the struggles of conforming to public expectations.

The subjectivist voice gives way to a less defensive voice, marked more clearly by the use of reason in later letters. Belenky calls this position "procedural knowledge," and divides it into "separate knowing" and "connected knowing." Those in the position of "separate knowing" exercise doubt rigorously and strictly follow a rational method of discovering truth. They develop a public, adversarial voice or different voices, which they learn from authorities. Their lack of an integrated self can make them feel like "frauds" (Belenky 124). On the other hand, connected knowers learn by understanding how others think. They easily believe others and are open to their points of view, valuing their experience. A "capacity for empathy" allows them to understand other perspectives (113). Burney's letters of 1793, a very important year in her life, suggest "connected knowing" to a greater extent than "separate knowing." Suddenly entering a new social circle caused her to confront new perspectives, evaluate her methods of judging others, and dare to risk her carefully wrought reputation.

Burney's friendship with the French émigré Madame de Staël certainly posed, according to some, a serious threat to Burney's reputation on both political and moral grounds. The politics of the French Revolution united these two women writers; the politics of English society separated them. In 1793, Staël rented Juniper Hall in Surrey, England, and joined there a group of her French friends, who had escaped the Revolution. The émigrés became friendly with their neighbors William and Frederica Locke, close friends of the Burney family, and Mrs. Phillips (formerly Susanna Elizabeth Burney), Frances Burney's sister, who had a cottage at nearby Westhumble. Mrs. Phillips wrote detailed letters to Burney filled with conversations of the group, which included Maurice de Talleyrand, envoy to England; Louis de Narbonne, former minister of war; and Mathieu de Montmorency. Those letters were filled with excitement about becoming acquainted with these illustrious foreigners, which heightened Burney's anticipation of meeting them on a forthcoming visit. On this fateful visit Burney met both the man she would marry, the chevalier Alexandre-Jean-Baptiste Piochard d'Arblay, and Madame de Staël, author of "Letters on Rousseau" (1788), with whom she was to have a strange and ambivalent relationship.

Burney's first letters to her sister regarding the French residents of Juniper Hall indicate some fear that any relations with them would pose a threat to her reputation: "Mrs. L[ocke] talks of your & their Colony with continued praise & esteem. I think I shall offer to take poor Mr. Clark's place with them, & teach them English, for I am sure, else, I shall never speak with them, *French*, & in *this House*, being contrary to my Vows" (*Journals* 2: 7). Replacing the English tutor, Mr. Clark, was Burney's playful suggestion for avoiding a social situation that might jeopardize her relations with the court, of which she was painfully aware. Nevertheless, her reservations did not keep her from socializing with the émigrés and sharing their horror over the execution of Louis

XVI. As she related their pain to Dr. Burney in a letter dated 28 January 1793, she imagined, "What must be the feelings at the Q[ueen's] H[ouse]—how acute, & how indignant!" (*Journals* 2: 9). Her fear of breaking her vows, in other words, her fear of the court's authority, changed immediately to a genuine concern about the English royal family's response to the French executions. Moreover, a sincere affection for her new French friends had briefly superseded her concern for propriety and introduced her to new political and intellectual experiences. In particular, she expressed admiration for Staël: "She is one of the first women I have ever met with for abilities & extraordinary intellects." Her high regard for M. d'Arblay also is clearly evident in her description of him as "one of the most delightful Characters I have ever met, for openness, probity, intellectual knowledge, & unhackneyed manners" (*Journals* 2: 11). In this new situation she relied on her own powers of observation and judgment, using her society's time-honored criteria. As support she had her sister's and friends' positive accounts of these new friends as well as their social standings in their own country. Thus, she took advantage of the procedures for knowing that authorities had taught her.

Writing was the focus of Burney's nascent relationship with Staël. Burney reported to her father that Staël "has suffered us to hear some of her works in MSS. which are truly wonderful for powers both of thinking & expression" (*Journals* 2: 17). Comparing Staël with Mrs. Hester Lynch Thrale[7] in matters of style, Burney added that "she has infinitely more depth, & seems an even *profound* politician & metaphysician." Staël, in turn, expressed admiration for Burney's creative abilities. Burney wrote to her father with some pride that Staël "is enthusiastic in the highest degree about your FB & for a reason extremely amiable." When political events had devastated M. Necker,[8] Staël's father, only Burney's novel *Cecilia* could raise his spirits: "[I]t caught him . . . & 'soothed & regaled him, she said when nothing else could touch or interest or amuse him.—' I own I was not *very* much displeased at this circumstance" (*Journals* 2: 17-18). These two women who not only spoke different languages but wrote in different styles and lived in different ways eagerly began to form a bond. This bond was soon broken, but not forgotten.

The exciting friendship expired quickly because of Dr. Burney's warning about how the English perceived Staël's political activities and her relationship with Narbonne[9]: "[S]he has not escaped censure. Her house was the centre of Revolutionists previous to the 10th of Aug after her Father's departure, & she has been accused of partiality to M. de Narbonne—But perhaps all may be Jacobinical malignity. However, unfavourable stories of her have been brought hither" (*Journals* 2: 20). His letter concludes with a warning for Burney not to stay with Staël as planned, but to visit her nearby sister instead.

Although Burney cut off the friendship when advised to do so, which suggests the level of "received knowledge," her reaction to this letter reveals "procedural knowledge." As upset as she was—"I am both hurt & astonished at the acrimony of malice"—she employed reason to arrive at conclusions. Her letter skillfully blends logical rhetoric, using her own observations as support for her defense, with an intimate knowledge of her audience. Arguing to any extent against her father's assessment reveals a transition from "received knowledge." She did take his advice, but not without voicing her point of view and expressing confidence in her knowledge of the situation: "[I]ndeed I believe all this party to merit nothing but honour, compassion, & praise" (*Journals* 2: 21). She had come to her own conclusions based on an understanding of these friends' experiences, as different as they were from her own.

Burney's assertions such as this last are juxtaposed in the letter with deference to patriarchal authority, which she skillfully used to unite herself and Staël. The letter opens on a positive note: "What a kind Letter is my dearest Father's—& how kindly speedy." Immediately, however, she lodged her defense of Staël, presenting her friend as an adoring daughter:

Me de Stal, the Daughter of M. Necker, the *idolising* Daughter, *of course*, & even from the best principles, those of filial reverence, entered into the opening of the Revolution just as her Father entered into it: but as to her House having become the centre of Revolutionists before the 10th of August, it was so only for the *constitutionalists*, who, at that period, were not only members of the then established Government, but the decided Friends of the King. (*Journals* 2: 21-22)

Burney's respect for her father deftly shifts to Staël's respect for her father and then to respect for the French king. Burney tempers her defense of Staël with rhetoric that supports the external authority systems in which her father believes and by which she has learned to live her life. By presenting Staël as a dutiful daughter following her father, Burney depicted accurately that strong relationship that mirrored her own with Dr. Burney and appealed to his sense of patriarchal values. Thus, she used her father's language in order to persuade him that her own knowledge was valid.

As the letter to her father proceeds, the fervor increases as Burney defends Staël against charges of adultery: "The intimation concerning M. de Narbonne was . . . wholly new to me—& I do firmly believe it a gross calumny. . . . her whole coterie live together as Brethren. . . . their commerce is that of pure, but exalted & most elegant, Friendship" (*Journals* 2: 22-23). The hyperbolic language and sincere tone suggest Burney's "connected knowing," her "capacity for empathy." She easily believed others and was open to their points of view, valuing their experience (Belenky 113). This tendency to believe in her new friend's innocence may have blinded her to the passionate affair between Staël and Narbonne, which resulted in two children and is documented in extant letters between the two lovers. Apparently not knowing that her assessment of this situation was faulty, Burney felt confident enough to express her judgment before agreeing to Dr. Burney's strong suggestion. Unlike the fifteen-year-old who was afraid to ask her father for her journal pages, the more mature daughter had developed a voice, or actually, several voices with which she could both defer and argue. The "procedural knower" can adopt the voices of authorities when necessary to build a case. This ability came naturally to the writer of novels.

After Burney's bold and persuasive refutation of her father's report in this letter to him, she resumes her deferential tone: "I would, nevertheless, give the world to avoid being a *GUEST* under their Roof, now I have heard even the shadow of such a rumour,—& I *will*, if it be be *possible* without hurting or offending them" (*Journals* 2: 23). Indeed, she politely refused future invitations from Staël, although they continued to socialize at the Locke's home. Thus, the 41-year-old Burney continued to follow the social strictures that the 27-year-old Staël seemed to break without compunction. Puzzled over Burney's submission to her father, Staël remarked to Mrs. Phillips, "Mais est-ce qu'une femme est en tutelle pour la vie dans ce pays? . . . Il me paroîtque [Burney] est comme une demoiselle de quartorze ans." ("Is a woman under guardianship for life in this country? It seems that [Burney] is like a young girl of fourteen years.") Mrs. Phillips explained to Burney, "I did not oppose this idea, but enlarged rather on the constraint laid upon females, to me very unnecessarily, in England" (Forsberg 21). Burney's sister suggests with these words that English society expected women to remain as children. "Constraints" are the rules and strictures that women are expected to know well and follow without question. These women are supposed to develop a sense of self in their identification with roles as defined by others. Pleasing others by following their directives should bring them pleasure. Burney has moved far beyond the level of "silence" or of "received knowledge" at this point, even though her actions might suggest otherwise.

Burney felt anything but pleasure when forced to abandon her friendship with Staël and give up the community that had been so valuable. Her ambivalence and anger become apparent when one compares the letter to her father in which she capitulated to his wishes with the letter to Frederika Locke in which she expressed her resentment:

I have regretted excessively the finishing so miserably an acquaintance begun with so much spirit & pleasure, & the *dépit* I'm sure Made de St[aël] must have experienced. I wish The World would take more care of itself, and less of its neighbors. I should have been *very safe*, I trust, without such flights, & distances, & breaches!—But there seemed an absolute resolution formed to crush this acquaintance, & compel me to appear its willful renouncer. . . . I am vexed, however,—very much vexed at the whole business. . . . I fear [my connection] will pass for only a fashionable one. (*Journals* 2: 123)

The emotive language in this letter—"regretted," "miserably," "crush," "vexed"—reveals the Burneyan anger that Julia Epstein has made the focus of her literary study. Epstein argues that for Burney "[s]urface propriety was purchased at the price of internal rage; that the cauldron was covered only made it boil with greater heat" (5). Burney apparently felt that in trying to save her public reputation according to her father's wishes she had damaged her character as perceived by Staël, whose opinion she valued. She was now embarrassed by her initial attraction to Staël because she so quickly rejected the controversial woman. Burney realized that her behavior must have suggested to Staël that she was fickle or superficial. In following her father's advice and appearing to act according to "received knowledge," she was painfully aware of the sacrifice she had made to her own sense of self and her reputation among people who cared for her. In writing these lines to the liberal Mrs. Locke, Burney revealed her "procedural knowledge," which can make a woman feel a "fraud," because she is acting according to criteria established by authorities, rather than listening to her own inner voice. This angry tone never surfaces in letters to her father about the matter.

The persistent Staël made several more overtures to Burney; however, the two never met again, even when they both lived in Paris. When Staël returned to England in 1814 as a celebrated writer and enemy of Napoleon, Burney wrote to a friend, "I perpetually long to write to her, but imperious obstacles are in the way" (qtd. in Forsberg 45). The "obstacles" presumably are societal constraints that caused their initial rift.

Although the friendship died, Burney and Staël's appreciation of each other as writers did not. Evidence exists that they continued to read each other's works with admiration. Burney was delighted to hear that Staël had liked the first part of her last novel, *The Wanderer*: "The first Volume . . . was received by the reigning Critical Judges, with almost unbounded applause . . . Me. de Stael, Sir S. Romily, Lord Byron, Mr. Godwin,—& others whose names I do not recollect, sung its panegyric" (qtd. in Doody 371). Likewise, Burney described her passionate reaction to reading Staël's *On Germany*. She wrote of

the pleasure, the transport rather, with which I read nearly every phrase. Such acuteness of thought, such vivacity of ideas, and such brilliancy of expression, I know not where I have met with before. . . . I have rarely in the course of my whole life, read anything with so glowing a fullness of applause. (qtd. in Forsberg 45)

Regardless of social impediments and distance, Burney and Staël could read each other's works because they dared to add their creative voices to the growing chorus of women writers. Nevertheless, unlike Boswell, who could socialize with anyone and travel anywhere, Burney had to sacrifice this inspiring friendship in order to protect her tenuous position as a female in her society. Her ability to know through others, as in "connected knowing," was limited by the others whom her community allowed her to know. This process of restricting her social circle repeats itself over and over in Burney's letters and journals, just as her voices continually change depending on her audience.

The silencing effect of a particular audience is evident in Burney's letter to Dr. Burney even after she had married d'Arblay. Expressing fear that her letter would be unworthy, Burney addressed her father: "I have been longing to write my dearest Father ever since I last left Chelsea— but I have wanted something for an opening that he might not think a mere intrusion upon his time" (*Journals* 3: 1). To bore her father appeared, in her view, to be a worse offense than not writing at all. Although at this point she enjoyed a reputation as a celebrated novelist, the discriminating Dr. Burney still intimidated her to the point of silencing her. In "procedural knowledge" one consciously learns a "new language" in order to gain acceptance into the community. Awareness of the necessity of a certain form and procedure can inhibit women's expression: "[V]oice diminishes in volume; it lacks authority. . . . The inner voice turns critical. . . . Often they do not speak at all" (Belenky 88). Burney's letter to Dr. Burney exhibits signs of this type of voice: hesitant, lacking self-confidence, anxiety-ridden.

She concluded this letter as follows: "Adieu, Dearest sir,—will you forgive such a rustic Letter?—& indulge me, when you have a moment to spare, with the sight of the least little line of your beloved Hand?" (*Journals* 3: 4). This reverential tone reinforces her submissiveness to parental authority in what seems an exaggerated manner, perhaps *because* of her recent marriage and her celebrated novels. Burney's marriage to a Frenchman during the French Revolution was a daring act, about which her father initially had reservations. The daughter might also have wanted to protect her father's self-image by reassuring him that in spite of her fame, in which he appeared to delight, he was more talented than she. Conversely, acting as her father's amanuensis early in her life may have fixed in her mind that he was the writer in the family. In any case, this letter reveals a Burney who is curiously insecure in her use of language with this audience.

Windsoriana

Burney's tone changes dramatically in "Windsoriana," an account of her visit to court in 1796, which the celebrated writer sent to her father. After having been second keeper of the robes for Queen Charlotte for several years, she was welcomed back to the court as a visitor on several occasions. After completing *Camilla*, which she had begun during her employment there, she presented the royal couple with the first copies of the new book, which she had dedicated to the queen. Her journal recounts a conversation with King George III about writing *Camilla* that reveals her sense of self. When he asked her who else had seen the novel, she assured him that no one, not even her father or her good friend Mr. Locke, had seen it. When the king had "laughingly said 'So you kept it quite snug?—'" she explained, "Not intentionally, sir, but from my situation & my haste; I should else have been very happy to have consulted my Father & Mr. Locke; but I had so much, to the last moment, to *write*, that I literally had not a moment to hear what could be *said*!" (*Journals* 3: 177). The voice that emerges here reveals a passion for writing that had not diminished since the earliest journals and a confidence that required no bolstering from others. As much as she respected her father, Burney did not rely on him to edit her novels, which the king found amusing. When she told the king that only she had corrected her proofs, he replied,

Why some Authors have told me . . . that they are the last to do that work for themselves. They know so well by heart what *ought* to be, that they run on, without seeing what *is*. They have told me, besides, that a mere *plodding head* is best & surest for that work,—& that the livlier the imagination, the less it should be trusted to it. (*Journals* 3: 177)

Her confidence in taking full responsibility for her own work surprised him. By this time Burney, now in her forties, had written three novels (four, including the one that she burned), and she knew what she wanted to write and how she wanted to write it. She reveled in the act of writing as she always had, but now her fear of her audience had decreased: "And sure I am, happen what may to the Book from the Critics,—it can never cause me pain in any proportion with the pleasure & happiness I owe to it!" she tells the king. By this time in her life she not only had developed a strong authorial voice, but she also described herself as projecting a confident self to others, even royalty.

In this account, she described to her father chatting with a queen who seemed eager for her visits and catching up on new events in the princesses' lives. The princesses "made a thousand enquiries about my Book, & when & where it was written, &c, & how I stood as to *fright & fidget*." Her answer reveals a woman who was not nervous about publishing her work but rather one who had integrated her personal and professional life to an amazing extent in the eighteenth century:

I answered all with openness, & frankly related my motives for the publicatio[n.] Every thing, of house keeping, I told them, was nearly doubled in price at the end of the first year & half of our marriage, & we found it impossible to continue so near our friends, & the Capital, with our limitted income. . . .—I then, therefore, determined upon adopting a plan I had formerly rejected, of publishing by subscription. . . . My Garden, our way of life, our House,—our Bambino,—all were enquired after, & related. (*Journals* 3: 186)

Burney, the writer, the new mother, had turned herself into a breadwinner when that was necessary to keep her household near her friends and family. She not only published her third novel, but she published it in the most lucrative way possible: by subscription. She had turned her writing into a business that provided for those she loved. Her matter-of-fact tone in this passage suggests a woman who had reflected on her situation and adopted the most efficient means of ensuring her happiness and the well being of her family. She had juggled internal needs with external circumstances and been successful. The warm response of the royal family celebrated her achievement.

She proudly recounted the king's introduction to her husband: the king "most graciously bowed to him, & entered into a little conversation; demanding how long he had been in England, how long in the country, &c &c, & with a sweetness, an air of *wishing us* well, that will never, never be erased from our Hearts" (*Journals* 3: 191). For the English royal family to welcome her French husband exceeded Burney's hopes. When she departed, she promised to send copies of the novel, with the queen's approval, to all the princesses and vowed to visit annually, sure that her visits would be welcome.

As much as Burney followed the rules for a woman in her society and often acted according to "received knowledge," she did a remarkable job of eventually synthesizing external knowledge and subjective knowledge in order to build her life according to "constructed knowledge." According to Belenky, women in this position accept ambiguity and recognize the importance of a situation's context. At this stage women develop a voice with which they communicate their ideas to others. While a strong sense of self balances caring for others, self-awareness produces a voice that can help others (137). Burney certainly struggled between relying on her own inner voice and accepting the strictures of external authority.

"Windsoriana" reveals that the novels she dared to write, the Frenchman she dared to marry, and the life she dared to live had been accepted by the authorities in her life: her father, her king, and her queen. The journals from this period of her life celebrate an integrated public and personal self. Although the complete journals and letters span many more years, this study concludes with these writings because they show evidence that Burney attained the highest level in Belenky's schema, "constructed knowing."

In order to achieve this integrated voice Burney had to surmount many obstacles. On the personal level, her father presented the most intimidating presence in the journals and letters, but he also provided a lively intellectual atmosphere that was conducive to a writer's formation. Fortunately, her family's position in society allowed her ample opportunity for "connected knowing." Her education came largely through her associations with friends of the family and her extensive reading. Classical literature and the works of her contemporaries helped her to develop a literary voice in relation to others.

She also faced many social obstacles: to writing, to marrying a foreigner, and to living in a foreign country. The royal court became an obstacle to her well-being, while it also provided her family with the livelihood that allowed her to write. During her years of employment at court, her journals bear witness to the oppression and exhaustion that she suffered. However, once she extricated herself from that situation, her pension allowed financial independence, which she supplemented by publishing. *Camilla* made Camilla Cottage, her room of her own, possible.

By carefully using her voices to gain access to a world customarily reserved for men, she alienated a few but opened doors for many women. In a society that expected women to act according to "received knowledge" in Belenky's terminology, Burney shows that she could adopt this voice when necessary. As her letters and journals reveal, however, different voices reflect a growing sense of self. Voices emerge in Burney's writings that still characterize women today, suggesting that women's relationship to power has not changed in fundamental ways over the last two hundred years. By struggling to develop her voices as both a writer and a woman, Burney demonstrated that women in the late eighteenth century could be respected writers.[10]

Notes

1. See Joyce Hemlow's biography and Margaret Anne Doody's literary biography of Frances Burney.

2. Dr. Charles Burney was a writer, an organist, and a composer.

3. I use "life-writing" to refer to both journals and letters since the distinction between the two genres in Burney's case is blurred. Many of the earlier writings are private journals, while in later years Burney would send packets of journal entries to her sister or her father as in the case of "Windsoriana." Doody calls these entries "journal-letters" (26). In other cases, Burney addressed letters to a particular person for a particular purpose, as in the case of her letter to Dr. Burney concerning Germaine de Staël.

4. I quote from two recent editions of Frances Burney's journals and letters. Lars E. Troide has edited the most complete version of *The Early Journals and Letters of Fanny Burney*, which covers the years 1768 to the middle of 1791 (cited as *"Early Journals"*). Joyce Hemlow and others have edited *The Journals and Letters of Fanny Burney (Madame d'Arblay), 1791-1840* (cited as *"Journals"*).

5. Judy Simons has compared the writing in Burney's journals and novels in "The Fear of Discovery: The Journals of Fanny Burney."

6. I use "Belenky" to refer to all the authors of this study: Mary Field Belenky, Blythe McVicker Clinchy, Nancy Rule Goldberger, and Jill Mattuck Tarule.

7. Mrs. Hester Lynch Thrale, a writer, was a friend of the Burney family.

8. Necker had held powerful positions in charge of France's finances. He had fallen in and out of favor with Louis XVI and became a focus of the people's attention immediately before the storming of the Bastille.

9. Staël married Eric-Magnus de Staël-Holstein, ambassador to Paris of Gustave III, king of Sweden, in an arranged marriage. Shared political ideals formed part of the basis of Staël's relationship with Narbonne. They were excited by the prospect of a successful constitutional monarchy. Staël used her powerful connections to make Narbonne minister of war. She later saved his life, making sure that he was not killed while guarding the king on August 10.

She concealed him and others until she could arrange safe passage to England (Posgate 53).

10. For generous help with this project, I thank Herman Asarnow, Linda Coleman, Robert Folkenflik, Jane Hafen, Richard Lyon, Beth Rosenberg, Tracey Schwarz, Susan Taylor, and Susan L. Wood.

Works Cited

Belenky, Mary Field, et al. *Women's Ways of Knowing: The Development of Self, Voice and Mind.* New York: Basic Books, 1986.

Burney, Frances. *Camilla.* Ed. Edward A. Bloom and Lillian D. Bloom. New York: Oxford UP, 1972.

——. *Cecilia.* Ed. Peter Sabor and Margaret Anne Doody. New York: Oxford UP, 1988.

——. *The Early Journals and Letters of Fanny Burney.* Ed. Lars E. Troide. Vol 1. Oxford: Oxford UP, 1988.

——. *Evelina.* Ed. Edward A. Bloom and Lillian Bloom. New York: Oxford UP, 1968.

——. *The Journals and Letters of Fanny Burney (Madame d'Arblay), 1791-1840.* Ed. Joyce Hemlow et al. 12 vols. Oxford: Oxford UP, 1972-84.

——. *The Wanderer.* Ed. Margaret Drabble. London: Pandora, 1988.

Doody, Margaret Anne. *Frances Burney: The Life in the Works.* New Brunswick: Rutgers UP, 1988.

Epstein, Julia. Introduction. *The Iron Pen: Frances Burney and the Politics of Women's Writing.* Madison: U of Wisconsin P, 1989. 3-12.

Folkenflik, Robert. "Genre and the Boswellian Imagination." *Studies on Voltaire and the Eighteenth Century: Transactions of the Fifth International Congress on the Enlightenment* 192 (1980): 1287-95.

Forsberg, Roberta J. *Madame de Staël and the English.* New York: Astra, 1967.

Hemlow, Joyce. *The History of Fanny Burney.* Oxford: Clarendon, 1958.

Ostade, Ingrid Tieken-Boon van. "Stripping the Layers: Language and Content of Fanny Burney's Early Journals." *English Studies* 72 (1991): 146-60.

Perry, W. G. *Forms of Intellectual and Ethical Development in the College Years.* New York: Holt, 1970.

Posgate, Helen B. *Madame de Staël.* Twayne's World Authors Ser. 69. New York: Twayne, 1968.

Simons, Judy. *Diaries and Journals of Literary Women from Fanny Burney to Virginia Woolf.* Iowa City: U of Iowa P, 1990.

Troide, Lars E. Introduction. *The Early Journals and Letters of Fanny Burney.* By Frances Burney. Vol. 1. Oxford: Oxford UP, 1988.

3

"I love and only love the fairer sex": The Writing of a Lesbian Identity in the Diaries of Anne Lister (1791-1840)

Jennifer Frangos

Anne Lister was born in 1791 in Halifax, Yorkshire, to a prominent but declining family of that area. She kept voluminous diaries throughout her life, selections of which are available in two volumes: *I Know My Own Heart: The Diaries of Anne Lister 1791-1840*,[1] which covers entries from the years 1817-1824, and *No Priest But Love: The Journals of Anne Lister from 1824-1826*.[2] Lister's editor, Helena Whitbread, relates that Lister had always been a troublesome child, but that it was not until she was fourteen and at the Manor School in York that "her reputation as a 'tomboy' began to be viewed in a more serious light. . . . Lister's flirtations with her female contemporaries quickly acquired sexual overtones which she rapidly converted into sexual activity whenever the opportunity presented itself" (2).[3] In addition to beginning to engage in sexual activity while at boarding school, Lister also developed a class consciousness and social aspirations which brought her to view her family's decline in fortune with disdain. These two factors, her erotic attraction to other women and her preoccupation with bettering herself socially, are the overriding influences on her sense of self, the two axes by which she measures most other things in her life.

Upon the death of her only surviving brother in 1813, Lister became heir to the family estate, Shibden Hall, occupied by her bachelor uncle James and his unmarried sister (Anne's aunt) Anne. The promise of financial independence, and the accompanying freedom from certain family and social pressures (marriage, for instance), was at the foundations of the younger Anne's conception of herself.[4] In 1815, two years before her published diaries begin, she moved into Shibden Hall to begin preparation for her position as, as it were, "lord of the manor." It was not until 1826 that James Lister died and she was able to assume the responsibilities and freedoms of landowning, but those eleven years were characterized by her sharply focused anticipation of and planning for that event.

The two volumes of selections from her diaries show in particular Lister's process of self-definition, the struggle to present that self to the outside world, and the diary's important, even indispensable, role as primary tool of that process. Though she is remarkable for far more than her erotic life, I will focus on Anne Lister's deliberate construction of herself as a lesbian, as expressed in her journals, and on the frameworks she envisions and creates for validating, nurturing, and expressing that "queer" (or in her words, "odd") identity, inside and outside of the pages of her diary.[5] In any historical inquiry, what we gain is perhaps not so much a clear knowledge of what life was "really like," as an opportunity to examine (and even build) our own paradigms, categories, and definitions. As an especially lucrative source of information—particularly for the projects of lesbian history and queer theory—the diaries of Anne Lister have as much to teach us about the late twentieth century as about the years in which they were written. It is in this spirit which I propose the following essay.

Before turning to the lesbian diary in the title of this essay, I will briefly discuss the diary as a literary genre and what issues are at stake in considering it a consciously queer one. Felicity Nussbaum, writing on self-biography in the eighteenth century, which she defines, according to that period's conception of the term, as "deriv[ing] from a narrator and author who were the same, who existed in history, and who expressed an interior reality," thus including memoirs, journals, and diaries (2),[6] notes that "works of self-biography are less quests toward self-discovery in which the narrator reveals herself or himself than repetitive serial representations of particular moments held together by the narrative 'I'" (18). In a formulation very similar to Judith Butler's performative notion of identity,[7] we—the readers, *including the diarist*—see the narrative "I" coming into being through the relation of a series of acts (as opposed to seeing it as something that already exists and is revealed bit by bit). This narrative "I," or identity, creates the illusion of the continuity of a single writer, but is different from that writer, as the creator is from the created. Furthermore, the writer, in separating from the narrative "I," is able to recognize the diary's usefulness as a reflexive part of a deliberate self-definition; the diarist is able to interact with and manipulate (and later, become) the narrative "I" through activities such as resolutions for future conduct and selective recording of those events which will come to comprise the narrative "I" over time. The diarist, Nussbaum writes, "pretends to simply transcribe the details of experience, but clearly some events are more important to the narrative 'I' than others, and the minute particulars of an interiority increasingly become the diarist's focus" (28). Thus, the diarist is not writing to "find herself," but rather to construct the very identity she wishes to assume.

Nussbaum further states that "the diary produces a sincere yet changeable narrator and reader, whether self or other, who delights in smoothing over the contradictory strands in the text" (28). This "changeable narrator and reader" could take any number of forms, from the narrator who becomes the reader, to people invited to read the diary, to uninvited readers either during or after the diarist's lifetime. But as Nussbaum also observes, the reader (whoever she may be) takes the diary as a whole, unified by a single author and therefore expressive of that author. The reader succumbs to the illusion of the diary as actual experience, reflecting or portraying an identity or narrative "I" that is equivalent to the diarist.

Writing on the status of "experience," especially of a lesbian or gay subject, Joan W. Scott identifies the conflation of the narrative "I" and the author (in the terms used here) as a major failing in the historical evaluation of such subjects. Those scholars performing historical "rescue operations" that attempt to illuminate or retrieve the lesbian or queer experience often assume they know what a lesbian or a gay man is and project that assumption onto the texts in question, decontextualizing both agency and resistance as well as the subject herself. She proposes a constructed—indeed, performative—view of identity/subjectivity, coupled with an awareness of the linguistic context in which the identity is constructed, as the way to avoid decontextualizing historical subjects:

It is not individuals who have experience, but subjects who are constituted through experience. Experience in this definition then becomes not the origin or our explanation, not the authoritative (because seen or felt) evidence that grounds what is known, but rather that which we seek to explain, that about which knowledge is produced. To think about experience in this way is to historicize it as well as to historicize the identities it produces. (401)[8]

This type of contextualizing lends itself particularly well to an evaluation of a diary as mechanism in the performative process of identity-construction.

In examining a diary as a tool in the formation of a performative identity, especially a diary unpublished in the author's lifetime, the "truth" of what is recorded—whether what is written there actually happened or represents what the writer wants to believe happened, or what she wants to remember as having happened—is less important than what she does with what she records, how she works it into her series of performances in a way that both confirms the identity she perceives herself to have and supports the identity she wants to have. In the specific case of Anne Lister's diaries, I recognize that I have only Lister's version of certain events in her life, and that she often has a very clear agenda behind her relation of them, but it is the function of the diary and the uses to which she puts both diary and events which interests me. In what follows, I will examine Lister's use of her diary as something like a reflection of her overall identity (insofar as she defines herself in and through her activities and actions), as a "green room" for trying out aspects of her identity which she feels she can change, as a forum for processing experiences or interactions with other people, and as the site in which and from which she comes to understand herself.

Anne Lister's diary contains more than the day-to-day minutiae of events and musings typical of nineteenth-century women's diaries. Alongside the events of each day, daydreams, romantic encounters, frustrations, and future goals, she also records monthly expenses for both the household and herself, personal savings, dealings with domestic servants, travel agendas and expenses, strenuous education plans of her own devising, and financial planning for her future income. This conflation of various types of recordkeeping—those of master of the house, overseer of domestic affairs, accountant, tutor/pupil, travel writer, Casanova, and "diarist" in the usual sense of the term—which, if not done by separate people, might easily be done in separate ledgers or notebooks, suggests that Lister envisions herself in all of these roles all at once and seeks to unify rather than separate these aspects into her identity by expressing them all in the same forum. Performatively, Lister claims all of these identities as her own, creating her identity out of their compilation while simultaneously justifying their juxtaposition as elements of that overarching identity.

This composite identity actively informs her later actions. She evidently referred to past entries on a regular basis, making the journal an interactive tool in her process of self-definition. Her journals are organized by volume and everything is scrupulously indexed:

18 June 1824: From 2 to 6, looking over volumes 2, 3, 4, & 5 as far as p. 111 of my journal. Volume three, that part containing the account of my intrigue with Anne Belcombe, I read over attentively, exclaiming to myself, 'Oh women, women!' The account, too, as merely noted in the index, of Miss Browne, amuses me. I am always taken up with some girl or other. (*IK* 346)[9]

Rereading her journal entries, indexing them for ease in future reference, even reading just the indices, provides Lister with an identity, a definition of herself based on past actions. Repeated readings serve to solidify that identity. Even recording her reactions to reading about her own past activity feeds into that identity, for by doing so Lister attempts to preserve the sense of herself that she holds at the time of writing, so that when she refers back there is the illusion of continuity and consistency, of Lister the narrator/author expressing "an inner reality" (Nussbaum's term). The sense of self Lister acquires is simultaneously enabled and produced by the interaction of several factors: the performative process of diary writing, reference to what she has written in the past, and the promise of self-definition (if limited) inherent in financial independence and her class status.

Another use Lister makes of her diary is more conventional: the journal gives her a private, safe space to record what Whitbread calls "her intimate life." Adding another level of secrecy to an already private journal, Lister writes certain passages in a secret code or "crypt hand," as she calls it, devised for use in letters to her married lover Marianna Belcombe Lawton (referred to as "M–" in the first volume, "Marianna" in the second).[10] By making parts of her journals accessible only to those who can read the code, Lister establishes a space out of reach of most people with whom she came in contact. This secrecy could be taken to indicate shame or a sense of wrongdoing on Lister's part, but an equally viable explanation (more so, perhaps, given the relative lack of misgiving or impropriety concerning her sexuality elsewhere in the diaries) is the idea that Lister is manipulating her situation to her advantage. Assuming most of the coded entries to be concerned with sex or with Lister's attraction to other women, we might surmise that Lister, in coding or concealing her sexual or erotic experiences, is both bowing to and subverting a prohibition against same-sex desire, finding alternate modes of expression which serve the dominant social forces by concealing such activity, yet allow it to exist, even flourish, nonetheless. Her "crypt hand" (a type of "closet" really) serves her twin interests of lesbian practice and social status.[11]

Lister seems to believe that general knowledge of her lesbianism would mean ostracism from society; she forestalls this event by never making her "oddity" (her term) explicit in any social context, though she hints around it (especially to women with whom she pursues relationships). Whitbread notes that around Halifax Lister's nickname was "Gentleman Jack," which suggests that at some level most of the community knew or guessed at Lister's proclivities anyway. In dress and manner, she cultivates the image of village eccentric, another identity allowed by her impending inheritance—perhaps in the hopes that some time in the future when she is master of Shibden Hall and finally brings Marianna home to live with her, it will be just another quirky action on the part of a slightly batty spinster wealthy enough to have her own way in things. The attention to appearance begins soon after she moves into Shibden Hall. In 1817 she writes, "As soon as I was dressed, went to drink tea with the Miss Walkers of Cliff-hill. Went in black silk, the 1st time to an evening visit. I have entered upon my plan of always wearing black" (*IK* 14). The resolution to wear black is one that she adheres to for the rest of her life.[12]

The pattern of resolving in writing to act differently in the future establishes Lister's diary as a mediary or buffer between her inner imaginings and the "outside" world and exposes Lister's sense of control over her own identity. She feels free to manipulate elements of her identity, such as her appearance, and she uses her diary as a place to try those manipulations out. Writing them down, and thus making them "real" in the diary-world, lets Lister examine the impact they might have, as well as the various configurations they might take. For example, in looking forward to her eventual stewardship of the estate, she decides upon a reasonable annual income and mulls the means to secure that sum:

Having been talking about farming & rents, turned to my paper of memoranda. Added some fresh ones. Adding up & calculating till near twelve. My uncle must have now a clear income of nine hundred & above eighty pounds a year. By the time all centres in me, supposing my aunt to have fifty pounds a year Navigation stock, I can make thirteen hundred a year. It has just struck me, I will make the Cunnery cottages & barn into a farmstead & let off with it fifty out of the hundred & ten days work my uncle has in hands. This will give me another hundred per annum & I will fudge out one more, some way or another, so as to make an income of fifteen hundreds a year. (*IK* 318)

Much of her early writing is occupied with planning for the future, when she will come into her inheritance and will be free to live as she pleases. Within her journal, she works out a clear notion of what she wants in life, what she needs to attain that, and how to go about achieving it. When her uncle dies in January of 1826, her primary reaction is relief that the estate is finally hers. Lister easily assumes her new position as head of the family, calling her father and sister to Shibden Hall, locating and reading the will, arranging for obituary notices and mourning clothing, and attending to the funeral arrangements. The years of preparation, indeed, allow her to reject her father's self-serving offer to run the estate for her. She steps into her uncle's shoes and puts the estate into order, so that by June of that year she is in a position to travel again and to begin to put into action all the plans she has been devising over the last eleven years.

In operating as a buffer zone between Lister's interiority and the "real world," the diary also allows her to reconsider social situations and interactions with different people, especially those where she feels herself at a disadvantage, and save face by turning them to her favor. She maintains the illusion of objectivity by writing down even those events that might be painful to remember, thus allowing her future self to learn from those situations and perhaps be reminded that the diary is not the world in which she must live. In many ways, too, rewriting events as she puts them down in the diary—changing what happens (however slightly) or otherwise imposing the interpretation she wants to prioritize onto the scenes or people she describes—makes it seem that Lister has the same kind of control over the outside world that she has over her diary-world.

Such control through rewriting seems especially important when she considers the seduction of a woman and in the recording of harassment she suffers at the hands of anonymous men on the streets of Halifax. In an entry that shows Lister implicitly acknowledging yet attempting to deny the disparity between imagining and acting, she writes: "went to Anne [Belcombe, Marianna's sister], a little before twelve & staid two hours. At first rather lover-like, reminding her of former days. I believe I could have her again in spite of all she says, if I chose to take the trouble" (*IK* 139). Writing down this experience, Lister assumes the role of definer, the one who decides what this interaction means; she determines the interpretation of these events and, as access to these interpretations is limited (by virtue of being contained in a secret code in a journal), Lister is (almost) the only person able to reinterpret them or call those definitions into question. Nonetheless, Lister feels the need to qualify her statement—"if I chose to take the trouble"—for there's nothing easier to disprove than a direct statement. In this way, Lister reserves for herself a back door, a convenient way out of a situation where she might fail to get what she wants.

Another assertion of control over events within the diary-world is seen in Lister's dealing with a series of harassments from men she encounters in town. Typical of these entries is that of 5 January 1820:

[A] man in a greatcoat made like a soldier's followed me down our lane and asked if I wanted a sweetheart. He was a few yards behind & I said, "If you do not go about your business, sir, I'll send one that will help you." I heard him say, "I should like to kiss you." It annoyed me only for a moment, for I felt, upon coming upstairs, as if I could have knocked him down. (*IK* 113)

Lister asserts interpretational control over this demeaning situation by writing it down with emphasis on her own masterful behavior. In the recording of this interaction for her own future reference, what is preserved is Lister's successful handling of the event, her wresting control of the event from the man in the greatcoat. In the safe space of her diary, she is even confident enough to claim that she could have overpowered him had he tried to do more than talk to her; such an assertion is possible because there is no chance that it will have to be backed up with action. The man is gone and Lister is comfortable in believing that she could have defended herself if necessary.

Lister also engages in a certain amount of rationalization in her attitude toward Marianna, contriving to perceive events the way she wants them to be. In an optimistic moment, she conveys in a letter the kind of relationship she hopes to someday realize with Marianna:

Wrote the following crypt, "I can live upon hope, forget that we grow older, & love you as warmly as ever. Yes, Mary, you cannot doubt the love of one who has waited for you so long & patiently. You can give me all of happiness I care for &, prest to the heart which I believe my own, caressed & treasured there, I will indeed be constant & never, from that moment, feel a wish or thought for any other than my wife. You shall have every smile and breath of tenderness. 'One shall our union & our interests be' & every wish that love inspires & every kiss & every dear feeling of delight shall only make me more securely & entirely yours." (*IK* 145)

When her insecurities get the better of her, however, she records her doubts about Marianna's feelings:

I have doubted her love. I have doubted her sincerity. How often, with a bursting heart, have I laid aside my papers & my musings because I dared not pursue inconsistencies I could not unravel. I could not deem the dial true, I would not deem it false. The time, the manner of her marriage. . . . Oh, how it broke the magic of my faith forever. (*IK* 282)

The results of her attempts to reconcile her wish to find Marianna's love to be true with her sense of Marianna's betrayal are heartbreakingly tenuous. She tries over and over to create Marianna as a faithful, devoted lover, but again and again she is thwarted in the attempt.

In the confines of her diary, written in "crypt hand," kept for no one's use but her own, she can exert full authorial and interpretative control over the people and scenarios she writes about; once off the page, however, Lister loses some of her control to the other "selves" she shares space and time with. Outside of the journal's arena, Marianna becomes the untrustworthy, two-timing lover of Lister's worst fears, swearing fidelity without meaning it, ashamed to be seen on the street with Lister, and demanding secrecy about the nature of their relationship by saying, "I have a feeling on the subject which no earthly power can remove &, great as the misery which it would entail upon myself must be, I would endure it all rather than the nature of our connection should be known to any human being" (*IK* 266). When confronted with the "reality" outside of her safe journal space, the fictiveness of Lister's diary is exposed.

At this point, it may serve to turn from how Lister constructs a queer identity for herself and look more closely at precisely what this queer identity *is*. An important aspect of the eigheenth-century diary, as articulated by Nussbaum, is at play in Lister's sense of her own queer identity: "the eighteenth-century diary produces and reflects an individual who believes she or he is the source and center of meaning" (28). As the diarist comes to see herself as the source of meaning in her life (through writing), and as the diary comes to reflect that belief (in writing), an awareness of the diary as record of a series of acts and of the diarist's agency through the control of those acts is enabled. The performatively constituted identity is projected back onto the series of events which supposedly constitute it; this informs future performances and permits an individual's creative uses of the cultural tools available to her for the variation and subversion of normative identities, which, it could be said, is a goal of any queer individual negotiating the social reality in which she lives. In conceiving of herself as the center and source of all meaning in her life, Lister is thrown upon her own resources for self-knowledge, which reinforces her use of the diary in the process of self-definition.

Lister embraces this role as originator of her own identity, and takes it one step further. At the height of a crisis concerning Marianna's feelings toward her, she quotes Rousseau's autobiographical *Confessions*: "*Je sens mon coeur et je connais les hommes. Je ne suis fait comme aucun de ceux j'ai vus; j'ose croire n'être fait comme aucun de ceux qui existent.*" ("I know my own heart and understand my fellow man. But I am made unlike anyone I have ever met. I dare say that I am like no one in the whole world.")[13] Her (self-imposed) self-sufficiency easily leads to the conviction that she is the only one of her kind: when Lister identifies with Rousseau's isolation, she may be expressing not a wish of meeting someone like herself, but rather the desire to be the only one of her kind in existence. Searching for affection outside the bounds of a heterosexual norm, Lister seeks female companionship. Not similar women, for she feels unlike anyone she has ever met, but a potential lover and a relationship which seems to be modeled after a heterosexual couple—for example, she and Marianna call each other "husband" and "wife," as in the following passage of a letter from Marianna to Lister which Lister transcribed into her diary: "I shall not lose you, my husband, shall I? Oh no, no. You will not, cannot, forget I am your constant, faithful, your affectionate wife" (*IK* 129). In an illustration of what Sedgwick, in her discussion of "tropes of gender," calls the trope of inversion, Lister explains her lesbian desire by imagining herself in a traditionally "masculine" role, which suggests that she believes to some extent in "an essential *heterosexuality* within desire itself, through a particular reading of the homosexuality of persons," in this case, herself (*Epistemology* 87).

As Lister assigns herself the masculine role, the makeup (or economy) of this desire seems to necessitate that her attraction be for more traditionally feminine women. She further conceptualizes her erotic relationships with other women in terms of pursuer and pursued, where there is no relationship without Lister's initiation of a certain type of contact. Perhaps it is her own need to be "the first" with every woman, the desire to be the keeper of the knowledge and the one who indoctrinates novices. When Lister initiates a relationship, she sets the tone and defines the terms, assuring that it proceeds according to her plans. With a sexually inexperienced partner, she is also not subject to comparison with others or criticism in terms of practice or performance and so retains control of the definition and interpretation of both herself and of the relationship.

It has been theorized that lesbians' adoption of a male persona or a "masculine" role is often an assertion of active sexuality in a society where "male" and "female" are diametrically opposed, and constructed as "aggressive" and "passive" respectively.[14] Such an assertion is a bid for visibility, an act which defiantly confirms the existence of an active/aggressive female sexuality even while it seems to accept the terms of the dualistic equation, male (masculine) = aggressive/female (feminine) = passive. Lister's eccentric, decidedly masculine persona, while possibly serving to obscure the nature of her relationships (by signifying her strangeness in general), is also a defiant marker of her sexual activity, a subversion of gender and sex roles, a redeployment of her own sexuality against larger frameworks of heteronormativity.

Lister's economy of desire, based both on asymmetry of knowledge and on a masculine/feminine dichotomy, serves to support the conviction that she is the sole source of meaning in her life and the only one of her kind in the world; as such it is important in the formulation of her sense of self. Testimony to its importance is her reaction to a woman she meets in 1823. To the outside reader, Miss Pickford appears to be a person like Lister, a lesbian of the upper classes, well educated and concerned with making a place for herself in the world; in short, someone with whom she would have much in common. But issues of "closetedness," silence, and control reach a new level when Lister meets Miss Pickford:

She [Miss Pickford] is a regular oddity with, apparently, a good heart. . . . She is better informed than some ladies & a godsend of a companion in my present scarcity, but I am not an admirer of learned ladies. They are not the sweet, interesting creatures I should love. I take hold of her arm & give her the outside & suit her honor. (*IK* 237)

Lister finds herself in a dynamic with Miss Pickford which she does not like: she cannot allow herself to admire Miss Pickford because her education and knowledge (sexually and otherwise) rivals Lister's own. Also, Lister is used to being the arm-offerer; clearly she is uncomfortable in the reverse situation.

Indeed, perhaps Lister identifies a little too much with Miss Pickford for her own comfort. As they get to know one another, Lister devotes long passages of her diary to settling her feelings toward Miss Pickford, as in this passage:

Our conversation all in the confidential style, but it begins to strike me that were there not such a dearth of companions here I should not care much for the society of Miss Pickford. I would rather have a pretty girl to flirt with. She is clever for a lady, but her style of manner & character do not naturally suit me. She is not lovable. Flattery, well-managed, will go down with her as well as others & she is open to it on the score of mentalities. My attentions have pleased her & she is taken with me. . . . I do not greatly admire Miss Pickford, nor have I ever behaved to her as if I did . . . She has not divinity enough for me. (*IK* 240-41)

She wishes to locate herself erotically in relation to Miss Pickford, but is unable to because of "Pic's" "masculinity" (much too like her own): "she is too masculine & if she runs after me too much, I shall tire. Her manners are singular. Sometimes she seems a little swing-about" (*IK* 256). Lister's economy of desire will not allow her to find Miss Pickford attractive, yet Lister's primary mode of relating to women involves sexual interest and so the issue keeps sneaking into Lister's dealings with her. Perhaps the "swing-about" comment is a tentative way of resolving Lister's need for the upper hand in a romantic encounter: by supposing that Miss Pickford will switch roles (will act or appear masculine or feminine in order to complement the femininity or masculinity of the partner she is with), Lister allows for the possibility of the relationship proceeding on her terms. This fantasy recurs in Lister's final interaction with Miss Pickford. The tension between Lister's need to perceive desire on Miss Pickford's part and her wish to hold "Pic" in the familiar position of the woman whose favor needs to be won is underscored by the large amounts of space Lister devotes to writing about and trying to create/define the sexual dynamics between them.

Concerning Miss Pickford's relationship with one Miss Threlfall, Lister presses for details to satisfy her own curiosity while remaining silent about her own comparable relationship with Marianna, even to the point of lying to keep the position of power she finds herself in as Miss Pickford's confessor:

At 8.40, set off to walk with her . . . Got on the subject of Miss Threlfall. Went on & on. Talked of the classics, the scope of her reading, etc. & what I suspected, apologizing & wrapping up my surmise very neatly till at last she owned the fact, adding, "You may change your mind if you please," meaning give up her acquaintance or change my opinion of her if I felt inclined to do so after the acknowledgment she had made. "Ah," said [I], "That is very unlike me. I am too philosophical. We were sent on this world to be happy. I do not see why we should not make ourselves as much so as we can in our own way." Perhaps I am more liberal or lax than she expected & she merely replied "My way cannot be that of many other people's." Soon after this we parted. I mused on the result of our walk, wondering she should let me go so far, & still more that she should confide the secret to me so readily. I told her it would not be safe to own it to anyone else, or suffer anyone to talk to her as I had done. I think she suspects me but I fought off, perhaps successfully, declaring I was, on some subjects, quite cold-blooded, quite a frog. She denied this but I persisted in that sort of way that perhaps she believed it. I shall always pursue this plan. (*IK* 269-70)

In order to not put herself in a vulnerable position in relation to Miss Pickford, in order to maintain an asymmetry of knowledge and thus the possibility of sexual attraction, Lister disavows the very identity she has so carefully constructed for herself in her diary. She continues her charade, eliciting further confessions from Miss Pickford while elaborating her own cover-up as concerned and "liberal" but disinterested friend:

"Now," said I, "the difference between you & me is, mine is theory, yours practice. I am taught by books, you by nature. I am very warm in friendship, perhaps few or none more so. My manners might mislead you but I don't, in reality, go beyond the utmost verge of friendship. Here my feelings stop. . . . Now do you believe me?" "Yes," said she, "I do." Alas, thought I to myself, you are at last deceived completely. My conscience almost smote me but I thought of M–. It is for her sake that I first thought of being, & that I am, so deceitful to poor Pic, who trusts me so implicitly . . . We parted mutually satisfied, I, musing on what had passed. I am now let into her secret & she forever barred from mine. (*IK* 273)

To apply a concept articulated by Sedgwick, Lister masquerades as "the interlocutor who has or pretends to have the *less* broadly knowledgeable understanding of interpretive practice who will define the terms of exchange" (4)[15] and attempts to retain control of the discourse yet again. Lister has too much invested in maintaining her "secret"[16] (her lesbian sexuality) to give herself away, even to another lesbian; the closet Lister has built herself is too important to her sense of who she is: she has struggled too hard to establish herself as the sole source and center of meaning in her life and as the only one of her kind to acknowledge on any level that she identifies with anyone else.

Even once Lister has settled the matter of sexual attraction to her own satisfaction—she has decided that it exists purely on Miss Pickford's part—she presumes a greater (superior) knowledge of sex and sexual practices than Miss Pickford:

[Miss Pickford] said, very oddly, when I talked of a marriage of souls & hinted at bodies too, mentioning connections of *les esprits âmes et corps*, that it was all *esprit* on her side, insinuating that it was *les corps* on Miss Threlfall's part only. I looked surprised. "Then," said I, "there is only one alternative. Do you know it? No, of course you did not say." In my mind thought of her using a phallus to her friend. (*IK* 291)

This is an assertion of power over Miss Pickford's sexuality in the only way (superior knowledge) available to Lister, given that Miss Pickford's sexuality already exists and exists independently of Lister. It is this pre-existing sexuality that makes Miss Pickford an unsuitable object of Lister's desire and rules out the possibility that Miss Pickford could provide the kind of relationship Lister has been seeking.

Despite Lister's apparent disavowal and rejection of her, it is ultimately Miss Pickford who gives Lister perhaps the most profound insights into her own character. Miss Pickford's presence, her existence, causes Lister to ponder on 5 August 1823, "Are there more Miss Pickfords in the world than I have ever before thought of?" (*IK* 273). Though she never directly admits to identifying with Miss Pickford, this statement contains a rebuttal of the importance of Rousseau's singularity in Lister's world view. Admitting the possibility of more Miss Pickfords means acknowledging that she herself may not be unique, which means reformulating her own sense of identity that she has worked so hard to forge alone.

Lister never directly tells Miss Pickford of her deceit, though she does give her enough information to figure it out:

Asked her if she knew what lady-sick was. Said I could tell her something for which she would box my ears. She wanted me sadly to say it. I declined for the present (I meant I might sometime pretend I had gulled her, all I had said was a joke). "Is this," said she, "your philosophy? Does your conscience never smite you?", perhaps alluding to my having before so strongly denied the thing. (*IK* 290)

Despite Lister's spin on this event, Miss Pickford's genuine disillusionment is apparent. It would seem that Miss Pickford is looking for the company of equals, other lesbians with whom she could share her experiences and from whom she could learn. Lister's continued hoping to pass the whole matter off as a joke underscores her failure to grasp the importance of a lesbian (or queer) group identity, and demonstrates the problematic practice and solitary nature of her concept of lesbian love. On learning of Lister's deception, of her absolute unwillingness to participate in the kind of community Miss Pickford seeks, of her refusal to acknowledge the open secret they both share, Miss Pickford gradually begins her exit from Lister's life.

Miss Pickford's ultimate rejection of Lister throws Lister back into the problem of defining the sexual element of their relationship. For if, as Lister has decided, Miss Pickford is erotically interested in Lister and that is why she seeks Lister's company (which mirrors Lister's actions toward a woman she is attracted to), it does not make sense for Miss Pickford to walk away having received no satisfaction (something Lister does not do, or does not do easily). Thus, their whole dynamic must be reconsidered. In the last entry in which Miss Pickford appears, Lister records their final conversation:

"When," said I, "Shall I see you again?" "Perhaps never," she quickly answered. Altogether the last half hour did not please me & I parted from her sensible of her abruptness, her want of gentleness or tenderness of feeling & acknowledging to myself that I wished I had not staid so long with her. Yet I stood in the old bank watching the last of her as she turned up Horton Street.

Watching, I scarce knew why, as if I had not felt towards her as if I thought her so gentlemanlike as I had said. I stood watching her so long the people might stare at me. It has before struck me she likes me more than I might expect. It is very odd, but if I tried, would it be possible to make her melt at all? (*IK* 291-92)

As Miss Pickford finally wrests away Lister's control over the terms of their relationship by leaving her in the dust, Lister's response is twofold: desire, the first (and last) expression of a definite sexual attraction for Miss Pickford, and what could be construed as a longing for the company of a like person. The desire, however, is reached by forcing Miss Pickford into Lister's preferred sexual dynamic—"flipping the butch," in the terms of the twentieth-century American lesbian community—for it is Miss Pickford who must melt and succumb to Lister's advances in this fantasy. As it turns out, Miss Pickford disappears from Lister's life and thoughts, never to return even as a memory or a wistful recollection in the buffer zone of the diary.

After Miss Pickford's departure, Lister continues in her search for a wife, having affairs with two young widows in Paris, finally losing interest in Marianna, and ultimately settling on a woman named Ann Walker, whose fortune, as Whitbread suggests, may have been the primary appeal. The relationship was apparently not a good one, and in many ways Lister was as alone as she had been before the two of them set up house. Anne Lister died at the foot of the Caucasus Mountains in 1840, at the age of 49, while traveling with the reluctant Ann Walker. Knowing that she never realized her lifelong wish for a blissful married life forms a sobering undercurrent to the reading of these journals: after all of her longing for the day when she would be able to make her own decisions and live her life as she chose, after all the careful consideration of what it was that she wanted from life and the planning that went into being able to get it, it is discouraging to learn that when that day came she did not realize her dreams.

Nonetheless, Anne Lister's life and diaries have much to give us: not only do the diaries make for very entertaining reading, but they also provide a rich source of many different kinds of information, of particular interest to any number of scholars. The reading(s) I have presented might figure in the growing body of queer theory by considering Lister as a successful manifestation of queer subjectivity in a historical climate commonly regarded as hostile to such things and as one individual's deliberate interrogation of social constructs around issues of gender roles and attributes, eroticism, individual identity, and self-determination. Both objectives can be served, I believe, by using Anne Lister's diaries to suggest a way of thinking about identity construction within specific historical-cultural contexts.

These remarkable diaries are Lister's primary tool for self-imagining and self-definition, the arena where she formulates her identity based on examination of her past actions and projections of the future, where she tries out and reconfigures the plans she resolves upon, and where she self-consciously records the events which will form the foundation of the identity she continues to construct dialectically. And it is an invaluable tool, considering that the identity she formulates there is a queer one. In terms of ways of being queer, one of the most important elements is a "safe space" at least some of the time. In the late twentieth century, this often takes the form of a community of similar individuals; for Anne Lister, it is her journal.

Notes

A version of this paper was presented at the National Women's Studies Association annual conference in June, 1996 at Saratoga Springs, New York. I am deeply indebted to Deidre Lynch at SUNY Buffalo and to Karen Robertson at Vassar College (whose influence and assistance I have been remiss in acknowledging). This essay also could not have been written without the patience and support of Bess A. Rose.

1. Quotations from this volume will appear in the text as *IK*.

2. All biographical information is taken from the prologue and epilogue to this volume. Whitbread is reportedly at work on a full-scale biography of Lister.

3. Whitbread's attitudes toward her subject matter and her audience are thoroughly condescending and homophobic, though couched in a benevolently liberal heterosexual tolerance. Although I must rely on her presentation of Lister for biographical information, her formulation of Lister's psyche and lifestyle is, I feel, skewed in a way which does not lend itself to queer theory.

4. On the influence of financial independence in relation to lesbian and gay identity, see John D'Emilio, "Capitalism and Gay Identity."

5. I use these terms, especially "lesbian," extremely warily in this context, aware that some may take issue with what might be called an ahistorical application of a twentieth-century concept. I do not mean to imply a transhistorical lesbian-ness that is exactly the same in the early nineteenth century as it is in our current parlance, nor to deny that the historicity of a term such as "lesbian" is to be taken into consideration. Rather, faced with the absence of a better word for talking about a woman whose primary emotional and sexual relationships were with other women, I hope to suggest how "lesbian" can be productively

divested from its late-twentieth century political connotations without diminishing either the importance of those politics in some contexts or the usefulness of the term.

6. Subsequent references will appear in the text.

7. See Judith Butler, *Gender Trouble: Feminism and the Subversion of Identity* and *Bodies that Matter: On the Discursive Limits of "Sex."*

8. References are from *The Lesbian and Gay Studies Reader* and will appear in the text.

9. Whitbread's editing in the published version of these diaries elides information which could prove revealing about Lister and her concept of herself: the nature of Lister's organization scheme (where do volumes begin and end—chronologically or based on important events? what do the indices look like; how do the entries read? how does Lister make use of past volumes of her journal—does she return to look for specific topics or thoughts, or just leaf through, or a combination of both?) could speak volumes, so to speak.

However, the original diaries are in the Halifax archives in Yorkshire and my geographical reality has to date made access to them impossible. Furthermore, the only extant translated version of the diaries is apparently the one Whitbread made for her own work. For the moment, then, I must make do with the text as it is.

10. Whitbread's editing does not make it clear, however, where coded passages begin and end. She merely alludes to Lister's "intimate life" as the subject of these passages, implying that they all have to do with sex. It seems to me, however, that besides sexual activity there are any number of things Lister may have wished to shroud in extra levels of secrecy, details she might not want other members of the household to be aware of or have access to—her disdain for some of the residents of Halifax, hopeful anticipation of her uncle's death, changes in the management of the estate, disgust for her father and sister, to name just a few. (My suspicions are borne out in another section of the volume: see note 12.) Knowing which passages were coded would be immensely useful in analysis of Lister's concept of her own identity, as well as issues of propriety and privacy.

11. The tension between the privacy of a diary and the reader implied, even necessitated, by any kind of writing is compounded by the silences imposed on certain aspects of queer lives, namely those silences commonly grouped together under the denomination, "the closet." Eve Kosofsky Sedgwick writes: "'Closetedness' itself is a performance initiated as such by the speech act of a silence—not a particular silence, but a silence that accrues particularity by fits and starts, in relation to the discourse that surrounds and differentially constitutes it" (*Epistemology of the Closet* 3). Here, I read Lister's coded entries as a type of silence, although clearly it is not as simple as that. "Coding," like silence (the very act of *not speaking*), is itself a speech act, one that is influ-

enced by and simultaneously influences the other structures of interaction within a given group of people and which takes on a status of its own.

Speech acts themselves, Sedgwick argues, are indicative of and informed by the contentious dichotomy of hetero- versus homosexuality; the pressure of this antagonistic duality, she argues, is felt especially by those perceived (by themselves and/or others) as *different* from the norm. Not only is a lesbian's identity informed by her difference (her lesbianism), but also her difference informs her discourse (her patterns of coding, confiding, and withholding, which are in actuality different expressions of the same forces). Such dynamics will certainly inform what gets put down in a queer diary, as a pattern of silences is established and incorporated into the writer's performative identity.

12. In a footnote, Whitbread comments that Lister had never felt comfortable about her dress, and that she was "constantly the subject of criticism from her friends for her shabby and unfashionable wardrobe" (*IK* 14); she also divulges that when referring to her clothing and appearance, Lister wrote in the secret code, so the coded passages apparently aren't all about sex (see note 10).

13. *IK* 283; Whitbread's translation as quoted in Introduction xxiv.

14. See, for example, Elizabeth Lapovsky Kennedy and Madeline Davis, "'They Was No One To Mess With': The Construction of the Butch Role in the Lesbian Community of the 1940s and 1950s," as well as their *Boots of Leather, Slippers of Gold: The History of a Lesbian Community*, esp. chapter 6. See also Esther Newton, "The Mythic Mannish Lesbian: Radclyffe Hall and the New Woman."

15. *Epistemology of the Closet* 4. Sedgwick paraphrases Sally McConnell-Ginet's "The Sexual (Re)Production of Meaning: A Discourse-Based Theory," a manuscript quoted in Cheris Kramerae and Paula A. Treichler, *A Feminist Dictionary* 264.

16. I put "secret" in quotation marks here, for as her nickname "Gentleman Jack" and the tone of some of the conversation around Halifax suggests, Lister's "secret" is a secret only in that it is not explicitly acknowledged or spoken of in Lister's presence. It was probably the open nature of this secret that allowed Miss Pickford to find Lister in the first place.

Works Cited

Abelove, Henry, Michele Aina Barale, and David M. Halperin, eds. *The Lesbian and Gay Studies Reader.* New York: Routledge, 1993.

Butler, Judith. *Bodies That Matter: On the Discursive Limits of "Sex."* New York: Routledge, 1993.

——. *Gender Trouble: Feminism and the Subversion of Identity.* New York: Routledge, 1990.

D'Emilio, John. "Capitalism and Gay Identity." *Powers of Desire: The Politics of Sexuality.* Ed. Ann Snitow, Christine Stansell, and Sharon Thompson. New York: Monthly Review Press, 1983. Rpt. in *The Lesbian and Gay Studies Reader.* 467-76.

Kennedy, Elizabeth Lapovsky, and Madeline Davis. *Boots of Leather, Slippers of Gold: The History of a Lesbian Community.* New York: Routledge, 1993.

——. " 'They Was No One to Mess With': The Construction of the Butch Role in the Lesbian Community of the 1940s and 1950s." *The Persistent Desire: A Femme-Butch Reader.* Ed. Joan Nestle. Boston: Alyson, 1992. 62-80.

Lister, Anne. *I Know My Own Heart: The Diaries of Anne Lister 1791-1840.* Ed. Helena Whitbread. New York: New York UP, 1992.

——. *No Priest But Love: The Journals of Anne Lister from 1824-1826.* Ed. Helena Whitbread. New York: New York UP, 1992.

Newton, Esther. "The Mythic Mannish Lesbian: Radclyffe Hall and the New Woman." *Signs* 9.4 (1984): 557-75.

Nussbaum, Felicity A. *The Autobiographical Subject: Gender and Ideology in Eighteenth-Century Britain.* Baltimore: Johns Hopkins UP, 1989.

Scott, Joan W. "The Evidence of Experience." *Critical Inquiry* 17 (Summer 1991). Rpt. in *The Lesbian and Gay Studies Reader.* 397-415.

Sedgwick, Eve Kosofsky. *Epistemology of the Closet.* Berkeley: U of California P, 1990.

4

Speaking into Being:
The Gifts of Rebecca Jackson,
"Black Visionary, Shaker Eldress"

Sylvia Bryant

[I]f thou can climb to the heaven and take hold of the clouds, which are above thy reach, and have power over them, then thou can have power over thy light and trifling nature, and over thy own body also. Thy make must be unmade and remade, and thou must be made a new creature.

—Rebecca Jackson
Gifts of Power (1831)

The simple act of telling a woman's story from a woman's point of view is a revolutionary act.

—Carol Christ
Diving Deep and Surfacing (1980)

Women came to writing, I believe, simultaneously with self-creation.
—Carolyn G. Heilbrun
Writing a Woman's Life (1988)

The autobiographical writings of Rebecca Jackson (1795-1871), collected and published in 1981 by Jean McMahon Humez,[1] document one woman's "awakening" and response to the spiritual gifts bequeathed unsolicited to her in 1830, at age 35, during a spectacular thunder and lightning storm.

In the year of 1830, July, I was wakened by thunder and lightning at the break of day and the bed which had been my resting place in time of thunder for five years was now taking [*sic*] away. About five years ago I was affected by thunder and always after in time of thunder and lightning I would have to go to bed because it made me so sick. Now my only place of rest is taking away and I rose up and walked the floor back and forth wringing my hands and crying under great fear. I heard it said to me, "This day thy soul is required of thee," and all my sins from my childhood rushed into my mind like an over swelling tide, and I expected every clap of thunder to launch my soul at the bar of God with all my sins that I had ever done. I have no language to describe my feeling. (*Gifts* 71)

So begins this conventional record of an unconventional life—that of Rebecca Cox Jackson, a free black woman living in antebellum Philadelphia, for whom this initiatory moment of spiritual (re)birth as a new creature marked the truer beginning of her life as a spiritual being. What follows in *Gifts of Power*, a highly detailed, deliberately recorded collection of journal writings,[2] is the narrative of Jackson's spiritual life: beginning with her nascent sanctification as a child of God in 1830, leading to her embrace of Shakerism by 1836, and culminating in her establishment of a separatist women's Shaker community outside of Philadelphia in the 1860s.

Part religious tract, part doctrinal treatise, part intimate diary, *Gifts* presents a remarkable montage of exactly what Jackson experienced as a consequence of that stormy divine visitation, including miracles she received (the gift of literacy, of spiritual and physical healing) and miracles she performed (from healing the sick and restoring sight to the blind to altering the weather and communing with the dead.)[3] Equally remarkable in *Gifts* is the parallel record of everyday life, which maps Jackson's evolution from illiterate, hard-working domestic to tutored, eloquent itinerant preacher; from obedient sister and aunt and family caregiver to outspoken agent of her time and her days; from dutiful wife to fierce celibate; from committed African Methodist Episcopalian to prophetic visionary and Shaker eldress. Of the time prior to her 1830 conversion, Jackson provides, as Humez notes in her introduction to the volume, only "sketchy biographical information" (10). She never knew her father and was raised primarily by her grandmother, who died when Rebecca was seven; her mother, who worked to support her children until her death, entrusted to Rebecca the care of two younger siblings, thereby preventing any opportunities for formal education. At thirteen, upon her mother's death, Rebecca was taken into her brother's household, where she provided care and housekeeping for his several children; she eventually married but apparently had no children of her own. What we know of the time after 1830, however—the particulars of her days in the home of her preacher brother, Joseph; her life with and subsequent separation from her husband, Samuel; her livelihood in Philadelphia as a seamstress and domestic; her struggles against the ruling powers first within the A.M.E. church and later among the Shakers—not only situates our understandings of spiritual experience but also may serve as exemplar for human existence. More particularly, *Gifts of Power* also witnesses how interior experience may serve exterior living and how the particulars of one woman's life may speak to the intricacies of many others. In the traditions of women's life-writing, *Gifts* constitutes both an act of self-creation and a conduit for community, reflecting desires for autonomy and connection in the here and now, as much as in the hereafter. Sharing her "greatly enlightened" understanding concerning "how things visible are representations of things spiritual" (232-33), Jackson speaks into being her temporal self and experiences, simultaneously creating a manifesto for connection with other like-minded women.

The full title Humez appends to her edition of the writings of Rebecca Jackson—"black visionary, Shaker eldress"—connotes that this is a text overtly religious in nature and intent. Nonetheless, although *Gifts* does return repeatedly to the role of institutionalized religion in liberating spirituality, whether among A.M.E. congregations or Shaker communities, to conflate Jackson's spirituality solely with institutionalized religion is as reductive a reading as equating it exclusively with the "visionary." The text employs all the signs and wonders of conventional conversion, including the appearance of God (initially as a white man); the debilitation of the body as the spirit takes control; the use of highly metaphorical, often eroticized language (the conflation of spirituality and sexuality in black women's spiritual narratives a common one);[4] as well as numerous out-of-body, trance-like events. Jackson records that the many times when her "spirit left [her] body," she was "as sensible of it as I would be now to go out of this house and come in it again" (112). In her review of *Gifts*, Gloria T. Hull captures this particularized "vividness of [Jackson's] visionary scenes":

These are rendered with concrete precision and laced with a symbolic imagery which is spiritual/sexual/archetypal. Precious metals, shining light, geographical directionality, water and the sea, thunder, lightning and wind, blood and violence, snakes, flying, beautiful women, grapes, etc. all figure prominently in her iconography. (208)

Such spiritualized "iconography" is repeatedly unseated and tempered throughout the text by continuous juxtaposition to domestic parables (notably, the dream of the cakes, a loaves-and-fishes miracle; a dream of washing quilts) and doctrinal dreams (of healing, of judgment day), by which Jackson felicitously illustrates her spirituality and spiritual experience. Indeed, throughout her text, Jackson seems to take great delight in taking rhetorical liberties, describing the ineffable with "a decided preference for understatement" and a "baldness" of style (Humez 43); one of her "primary strengths as a visionary writer" is "precisely her ability to embed religious mystery squarely in the recognizable, commonplace reality in which we all live" (48). Jackson's literal journey to spiritual wholeness, however, was not so easily accomplished as her rhetorical one seems to have been. For although "free" and not slave, Jackson lived with constant reminders of her tenuous status as black woman, spiritual or otherwise. The early "dream of slaughter," for example, in which Jackson recounts her own literal evisceration by "a robber" and the 1850 dream in which the "men had killed all the women and children, and were dragging them like dogs through the street" (223) exemplify the mortal fears to which she was subjected by the historical realities of slavery and the Fugitive Slave Law.[5] Conversely, in a September 1862 entry, Jackson rejoices upon hearing "the Proclamation of President Abraham Lincoln . . . that on the first of January 1863, all the slaves in the United States shall be set at liberty," enjoining from "God Almighty . . . [a prosperous issue]" (282).

Such negotiations of individual power, via the voicing of individual authority and autonomy through dream visions and daily experiences, are indeed the hallmark of *Gifts of Power*. On the one hand, ever wary of "becoming a pharisee" (73), Jackson struggled against the hypocrisy and duplicity she feared within her own human nature[6]; at the same time, however, she remained unfailingly committed to naming her spirituality and her self on her own terms: "I might as well," she reasons in the face of social and familial disapprobation, "be hung for an old sheep as a lamb" (76). In this sense, *Gifts* echoes especially the voices of other black women writing spiritual autobiographies, particularly Jackson's contemporaries Amanda Berry Smith, Jarena Lee, Zilpha Elaw, and Julia Foote, each of whom evinced in her writing and her life an astonishing sense of "self-confidence, self-worth, and power" in her strivings toward the divine (Andrews, *Sisters* 15). Jackson, as she gained strength and confidence as an "instrument" of the Lord, wrote with delicious ambiguity and understatement of the "personal power" of which she came to make the most, ultimately diverting even divine providence itself in the service of her own, albeit spiritual ends: "I had in the beginning of my journey the gift of power given to me," she writes at one personal crossroads; "[and] I felt now was the time to use it" (140). Refusing throughout her life to take refuge in silence—instead "speaking in tongues," to adapt Mae Henderson's reading of black women's double-voiced discursive strategies across registers—Jackson bequeaths a self-determined text of a woman's self-will in shaping her subjectivity. "I have no language to describe my feelings" (71), she writes of that initial visionary encounter with God; but, of course, she does, with *Gifts of Power* itself standing as textual, experiential evidence thereof.

Manifesting simultaneously a humble account of sanctification and a revolutionary act of self-creation, *Gifts* reads familiarly across a range of literary genres and traditions—most notably those of African American slave narratives, spiritual autobiography, and American autobiography. The subjective particulars of Jackson's life, however, challenge the conventional boundaries of each. From its fearful, dramatic opening conversion via "thunder and lightning at the break of day," through numerous episodes of self-doubt and lengthy explications of church dogma, *Gifts* patterns the conventions of spiritual autobiography. The opening section, "Awakening and Early 'Gifts'" (1830-1832), charts Jackson's personal coming to spiritual consciousness, while "Breaking Away from Family and Churches" (1833-1836) and "Finding 'God's True People on Earth'" (1840-1843), the second and third sections, respectively, recount her explorations of spiritual and temporal ways of being. The last three sections of *Gifts*, comprising approximately one-half of the text,[7] are concerned primarily with painstaking and often tedious recountings of Shaker doctrine and the letter of that law. Jackson's text also voices the "talking book" tradition of slave narratives and African American autobiography identified by Henry Louis Gates, whereby authors' "representation of characters and texts finding a voice," especially during slavery, demonstrates "membership in the human community" (239, 128). Ostensibly an unembellished accounting of one dedicated to "do[ing] His will in all things" (*Gifts* 85)—"I am only," Jackson writes, surely with self-conscious sincerity, "a pen in his hand" (107)—*Gifts* provides a distillation of personal, everyday experiences not unlike the narrative of her contemporary the writer Harriet Jacobs,[8] which politicizes the personal in the service of larger social causes. Deliberately transcribing scenes from a woman's life in a woman's voice, Jackson demonstrates her will and her "ability to use her visionary gifts," as Humez notes, to "solve the most pressing problems in her outward life" (36). Foremost a meditation on the double-bind position of black women in antebellum America, *Gifts* both reflects and inflects a strategy similarly employed by African American writers of "makin a way outa no way."[9] Existing side by side with Jackson's project of self-definition and self-creation is the crucial, recurrent theme of being "useful to my people, either temporal or spiritual, . . . [those] held by their white brethren in bondage, not as bound men and bound women, but as bought beasts, and spiritually held by their ministers, by the world, the flesh, and the devil. . . . [I]f these are not a people in bondage, where are there any on the earth?" (181-92).[10] And against this backdrop where "persecution was raging" (158) on every side, Jackson's writings figure almost automatically as sacred, redemptive text of self-creation: "Next to the Bible itself," William L. Andrews notes, "autobiography was *the script*—the sanctified record and the directing text—that the victims of the African diaspora in America needed most to sustain them during their tribulation and to explain the reasons for their suffering" (*To Tell a Free Story* 14; emphasis mine).

Moreover, in keeping with the traditions of black women's activism and resistance, Jackson's narrative is grounded, like those of her nineteenth-century black spiritual sisters, in "a commitment to religious faith, human rights, and women's struggles" (Richardson viii). As a border figure between convention and radicality in issues of race and gender, family traditions, cultural heritage, and American history, Jackson occupies unique dialogic and experiential positions on "the borders of discourse" (Henderson 36). Because her text speaks to us "from the vantage point of the insider/outsider" (Henderson 36) in all things spiritual *and* temporal, other-worldly concerns simply do not exclusively preoccupy her. As Andrews notes of Jackson and her nineteenth-century spiritual sisters, "[C]onversion alone would not magically solve the problems inherent in their lives. They still had to come to terms with *the world outside and the self within* if their spiritual recovery was to proceed" (*Sisters* 12; emphasis mine). Indeed, everything Jackson did, as agent and author, registered this resistance to social and religious status quo, representing her desire for self-control over her life as individual and for membership in communities of like others. According to Humez, the primary impetus behind Jackson's text—far from mere self-effacement and social submission—is "how religious vision and ecstatic experience functioned for her and other women of her time as a source of personal power, *enabling them to make radical change in the outward circumstances of their lives*" (1; emphasis mine).

Jackson's particular balancing act—that of voicing personal authority and autonomy against patriarchal, racial, and even biblical mandates—reflects the paradoxical situation many women confront in their attempts to speak selves into being in their negotiations of the "inner source of strength"—"the 'still small voice' within" (Belenky et al. 54), deployed in the quest to know self and value individual experience. No matter what the role, Jackson continually found herself confronted by silencing, policing authorities—from her family, which ostracized her for behaviors "astrange" (85); to the church fathers, among whom her convictions "seemed to stir a continual fire" (138); to the Shaker leadership, whose practices of exclusion regarding "the colored sisters" (268) she challenged. Yet always, she found herself responding to and calling

forth that "still small voice" of her personal desires and politicized conscience: shaping doctrine, experience, and beliefs all in the service of
self and community; "authoriz[ing]," as Andrews notes, "through her
own example, an alternative role for women within communities of the
spirit founded on an egalitarian ideal" (*Sisters* 17). Jackson's roles as
church, family, and community member continually negotiated this condition of struggle, mediating "the world outside and the self within."
Her recorded prayers, for instance, frequently ask "the Lord" for guidance, "to show [her] all things that He would have [her] do, both spiritual and temporal" (92). Yet woven in among her deferential pleas is that
curiously autonomous theme: "Herein I saw at the beginning," she
declares in self-authorizing explanation, that "the mind I had would not
do" (85).

Through constant strivings to maintain the "balance of matter and
spirit,"[11] Jackson modeled a unique coming to terms with her own particular "encounters [with] the divine in the midst of historical realities"
(Cone 29) that was essential to her being in *this* world.[12] Hazel Carby's
pointed reminder that in nineteenth century cultural ideologies and practices "woman meant white" (36) speaks succinctly to the vastly different
race and class privileges that complicated Jackson's situation.[13] Her
struggles went beyond self-definition to survival—of body as well as
spirit—to a degree that arguably did not concern white female and
African American male writers of spiritual narrative autobiography. At
one point, for instance, early in her conversion, Jackson refrains from
praying for an ailing white woman even as she is "on the point of kneel-
ing": "I thought, 'Her husband is a Presbyterian and don't know you,
and if he comes in and sees an old black woman in his chamber praying
for his wife, he will push you into the street'" (81). Jackson also mediated a matrix of domestic responsibilities unique to her status as nineteenth-century black woman. She writes of her household duties, upon
which her livelihood—and her opportunities for writing—was contingent:

I had a great deal to do. . . . I sewed all day, having the charge of my brother and
his four children, and my husband to take care of, and see that the house was
keep in good order, done all their sewing, keep [*sic*] them neat and clean and
took in sewing for my living, held meeting every night in some part of the city,
then came home. And after Samuel [her husband] would lay down, I would
labor oft times till two or three o'clock in the morning, then lay down, and at
the break of day, rise and wait on the Lord, according to the covenant I made
January the 30, Friday morning. (82, 86)

Especially distressing were these obstacles set against her spiritual life by her family community, particularly her brother Joseph. As respected A.M.E. minister, Joseph was esteemed by his younger sister Rebecca "like a father" (87); as intractable head of the household, he represented to her many of the social and religious strictures against which she kicked. One entry records a time prior to Jackson's receipt of "the gift of reading" and literacy, when Joseph was "awriting a letter in answer" to one she had received. Jackson describes the incident in a passage resonant with her emerging narrative voice and resistant self:

I told him what to put in. Then I asked him to read. He did. I said, "Thee has put in more than I told thee." This he done [*sic*] several times. I then said, "I don't want thee to *word* my letter. I only want thee to write it." Then he said, "Sister, thee is the hardest one I ever wrote for!" These words, together with the manner that he had wrote my letter, pierced my soul like a sword. [As there was nothing I could do for him or his children that I thought was too hard for me to do for their comfort, I felt hurt, when he refused me these little things. And at this time,] I could not keep from crying. (107)

Her various spiritualist behaviors, from loudly calling on "the spirit" to experiencing trance-like dream states, alienated her from her beloved brother, whose "harsh words"—"She is a-going crazy"—and thoughtless treatment hurt her deeply, yielding a burden she seemed "unable to bear" (87). The cruelest irony, perhaps, was Joseph's refusal to accept the truth of Jackson's conversion, for in this he represented as well her ostracism among the larger A.M.E. church community.

Without question, it was within and against the confines of the institutionalized A.M.E. church community that Jackson most vigorously and visibly struggled for voice and self-definition. Originally founded in Philadelphia at the end of the eighteenth century by Richard Allen, an ex-slave and minister, the African Methodist Episcopal Church represented a free space in which black Americans could in part escape the racism and hypocrisy of dominant white Christianity, as well as exercise self-governing control in matters religious, social, and cultural. Consequently, as a collective manifestation of the kinds of religious/cultural practices that were essential to many black Americans' balanced, mediated world view, the A.M.E. church was in many ways more equitable than other social institutions concerning gender relations. Women played a relatively visible and participatory role, from female praying and singing bands, to women leading exhortations, to occasional church sanctioning of female itinerant preachers.[14] Yet even within this more generous religious community, Jackson's radical spiritual experiences and her insistent witnessing thereof "raised an opposition" (*Gifts* 86), especially among the male church authorities. She herself described the cumulative effects of both her means and her messages "as if I had opened a bottle of cayenne pepper among the people" (87). Jackson refused, for instance, to suppress the spontaneous sharing of her spiritual experiences, mistakenly assuming, as woman, the role of preacher rather than the more customary one of exhorter: "I would often have a gift in our public meetings, after souls would speak their feelings, before I was aware, I would be on my feet inciting them to the life of Jesus as our only waymark to God. . . . This made no small stir among the preachers" (105).

Even more than how she chose to speak out in the context of the church, what Jackson had to say regarding spiritual and physical connections in gender/domestic relations was the most radical and controversial element of her spirituality, both in preaching and in practice. For in her naming of "the sins and the nature of them," what so "offended" (86) was her preaching of celibacy. Guided to this conviction by the teachings of her "inner voice" and by her personal apprehensions of how fleshly beings might live in greater earthly happiness and truer spiritual harmony, Jackson vociferously and unequivocally names celibacy—"the condemnation of the flesh with all its ties and connections"—as "the foundation of my sanctification" (143), a curious and remarkably confident statement given both the uncertainty that marks early descriptions of her conversion and the wide range of human social relations she undertakes to understand and alter. Her insistence upon celibacy not only stood for Jackson as "the foundation" for her continued communion with "the spirit" and attendant gifts; it also justified an unprecedented step forward in her struggles for control over her person[15] and for a kind of autonomy in ordering her own life as a nineteenth-century, married, church-going woman that could situate her squarely within a community of like others. In an 1836 entry entitled "My Release from Bondage," following a spiritual mandate, Jackson separated herself "body and soul" from her husband of many years: "I was commanded," she writes, "to tell Samuel I had served him many years and had tried to please him, but I could not [any longer]" (147). Relating her history nearly thiry years after her conversion to an unknown woman "blessed with a weeping spirit," Jackson explains "what [her] faith is":

Twenty-seven years ago I was blessed. And in that blessing, it was made known to me that I must withdraw from my husband in all carnal pleasure—but I must be kind to him, keep him cleaned up, and prepare his victuals cleanly and neat, and do anything I could do to make him comfortable. (265)

This unprecedented, self-chosen process of withdrawal from her husband was both arduous and treacherous; Jackson records more than once that her "way was hedged" (135)—"my enemies," she writes, "increased like the hairs of my head" (149)—and that in his anger, "Samuel sought [her] life night and day" (147). Jackson's self-chosen path also marked, however, an unprecedented embrace of personal desires in the service of spiritual wholeness. In 1850, nearly twenty years after her espousal of celibacy, Jackson still counted her "virgin life" since her spiritual conversion with discerning judgment and contentment. An entry on her birthday records:

I am fifty-five years old today. . . . Nineteen years of this I have spent in the service of God, in obedience to my call to the Gospel. Thirteen years thereof, *I have dedicated my soul and body to the Lord in a virgin life*, for which I do this day lift up my heart, my thought, my mind, my soul, with all my strength, in thanksgiving to God, who in His unbounded mercy has looked upon me, the least of all His people, and has shown me such great things. (219)

With equal force as she exemplified in her life, Jackson also taught celibacy within her church as a means for all to come to a more holy, spiritual existence. Not surprisingly, her visionary understandings of this issue, not to mention her personal example, "parted a great many men and their wives" (149), resulting in particular sufferings of her spirit at the hands of those with whom she most desired community: family members and religious friends who accused her of "chopping up our churches" (103). Indeed, her way was also frequently hedged by those church elders, including her beloved brother Joseph, who tried to stop her "spiritual influence among the people and destroy [her] spiritual life" (95). Consequently, an intense, palpable loneliness permeates much of *Gifts*, and her entreaties to "the Lord" to justify "why it was that [she] was called to live a life that nobody lived on the earth" (137) eventually directed her to the Shakers, a people who similarly lived a kind of self-chosen exile within larger society and among whom Jackson at last recognized herself and began to find a home. Within the Shaker community, where what might be called feminist principles[16] grounded interpersonal as well as spiritual encounters, Jackson first glimpsed the possibilities for radical community which would accommodate all the threads of her identity as black woman, autonomous individual, community member, spiritual being. Her initial meeting in 1843 with the Shakers reveals her astonishment and pleasure in this physical space and spiritual place, among these people living the link between personal sovereignty and spiritual connection of which she was so desirous:

It was as much as I could do to keep my seat. They all took their seats. They all set [*sic*] alike. They all were dressed alike. They all looked alike. They all seemed to look as if they were looking into the spiritual world. For the first time, I saw a people sitting and looking like people that had come into a place prepared for the solemn worship of the true and living God, who is a Spirit and who will be worshipped in spirit and in truth. This people looked as though they were not of this world, but as if they were living to live forever. (139)

A reverent, celibate way of living that respected the personal rights of women and men alike; a simple embracing of the spiritual in social and familial relations; the foundational principle of "God the Father and God the Mother, who created Adam and Eve in their own likeness" (142)—these religious precepts of Shakerism reflected Jackson's own beliefs, those derived as much from personal experiences as from visionary teachings. And early in the 1840s, along with her soulmate and friend Rebecca Perot,[17] she fervently embraced Shakerism, living and practicing off and on among the thriving Watervliet, New York, community for the rest of her life.

Even among this people "living to live forever," however, Jackson rested uneasily; for despite the personal satisfaction she derived from their community, she was increasingly distressed by the social and political contradictions she witnessed in their religious doctrines and spiritual practices. In later years, her concerns for "her people" escalated, as evidenced by the several dreams she records beginning in 1843. An entry dated 1848 recounts her dream of "going south to feed the people" (213); one dated 1854 records her reluctant return from an out-of-body journey "to Zion," where she would have "stay[ed] forever" but for the knowledge of "a greater work [yet] to do in the world" (249). Moreover, the open, free-thinking society extended by the Shakers to herself and Rebecca Perot and to blacks in general notwithstanding, Jackson was increasingly troubled by the implicit racism exercised against particularly women of color, the mistreatment of whom she articulated through her dream of "the colored sisters"—overlooked and excluded—with "no [Shaker] caps on": "I thought mentally how strange it was—it must be because they were colored people" (268). And following much prayer and preparation, Jackson established in the 1860s with Perot and a coterie of "colored sisters" a separatist Shaker community, a women-created, women-directed space that represented the culmination of her years-long search for a welcoming, equitable place for human well-being, both individual and collective.[18]

Humez's observation, that to women like Rebecca Jackson "the spiritual fellowship with other black women, perhaps as much as the individual's own ecstatic experiences themselves, would have meant a great deal" (7), speaks with fitting understatement a truism that circulates throughout *Gifts*, surfacing again and again. The whole of *Gifts* reads, in fact, on one level as an extended invitation to friendship and connection via physical relationships and spiritual communion, setting the textual and experiential precedents for Jackson's version of Shaker community. Underlying the incessant proclamations of God's great love for her is Jackson's unconditional love for her "colored sisters"; and every instance of her self-creation through the telling of her experiences resonates with the reciprocal force of self- and other-awareness, with numerous incidents foregrounding the value of women's community and friendships for individuals' mediation of matters spiritual and temporal. Jackson's mother, although an "absent presence" throughout most of her life, forms an essential link in her understanding of this force. The 1834 entry "The Blind Receive Sight" records a poignant remembrance of how one woman, upon hearing Jackson singing "three heavenly songs," recognized Jackson's mother's voice: "My mother and [the woman] used to belong to a band meeting together when I was a child. It was my mother's voice she heard in me" (133). Such "band" meetings also were vitally constitutive to Jackson's vision of women's community. Within the A.M.E., for instance, women's praying bands—spiritual consciousness-raising groups," in Alice Walker's words (76)—nurtured a safer space for freer self-expression than that among those who voiced "opposition" to Jackson's gift of preaching. "I thought," she writes, "that we [women] had better hold a little meeting at our house and we would not feel so bad to speak and pray before us as we do before so many" (104). And not surprisingly, when Jackson begins pursuing Shakerism in earnest, it is a woman who emerges as her spiritual mentor and "lead": "[I]n this great struggle of fasting, praying, and crying to God to know His will concerning me from day to day, *all at once I saw a woman step before me. . . .* So I was strengthened, and my soul much comforted" (93; emphasis mine).

Variously—within these alternative, healing spaces; within a community of women who shared not just spiritual belief and religious conviction but also common desires and life-experiences—Jackson came closest to achieving the wholeness of spirituality and materiality that her faith in human existence and "divine encounters" convinced her was both possible and worth the pursuit. Finally, among the small band of Shaker women, black and white, with whom she formed a bond necessarily equally spiritual and temporal, there existed for Jackson a sense of connectedness, a kind of essential salvation-in-life. "Saturday evening, April 30, 1859. I held my first solemn meeting. We went forth and worshipped God in the dance. F. B. [Francis Bridge], A. F. [Anna Fisher], and M. J. [Mary Jones] and Rebecca Jackson. And we were noticed by our Heavenly Parents" (280).

The simple passage quoted above, which is tucked unobtrusively among the last pages of *Gifts*, serves as a striking, fitting end for the record of Jackson's life. This litany of individual women's names forming a community of spirit bespeaks the joys and pleasures—despite the trials and tribulations—of situating oneself among like-minded others. Jackson's final gift of empowerment is this portrait of wholistic selfhood with which she closes her life-writing: that of a woman at home among her friends, shaping herself and her community in conformity with the life she desired to live and the company she desired to keep. Alice Walker, in her tribute to Jackson, notes the historical legacy: "In 1878 eight black women, three black children, and three white women (one of them Jewish) lived in the Shaker commune, members of Rebecca Jackson and Rebecca Perot's spiritual family" (78); and Humez notes that the "little band" of 12 to 20 Shaker sisters survived 40 years after Jackson's death in 1871 (39). *Gifts* itself, which bears the sound of Jackson's voice and the impress of her will, bequeaths a more enduring spiritual legacy, one which models the saving graces of like-community moving across lines of generational and cultural and experiential difference.

Moreover, and of particular use to what Humez calls our "modern, secularized consciousness" (42), the impulses that pervade and distinguish Jackson's life-writing are decidedly feminist. For what is more personal than spiritual ecstacy and the moment of conversion? And what is more public than itinerant preaching and witnessed confession thereof? What is more political than the speaking and naming of spiritual belief and experience—the ineffable, intangible, mysterious; that which resists name and being, no matter when the time, what the milieu? Against these contextual ethics, autobiographical questions and the contingent issues of "truth" or believability become less central to making meaning, currently and historically, of a woman's life-writing. Although Jackson's text of spirituality and interior experience may indeed read as antiquated, even anomalous when filtered through contemporary "secularized consciousness," what Leigh Gilmore identifies as "autobiographics"—that is, "the *changing elements of the contradictory discourses and practices of truth and identity* which represent the subject of autobiography" (13; emphasis mine)—redeems Jackson's life and writing by repositioning them onto a field of narrative and experience which we contemporary readers may access, understand, adapt, and deploy in service of own lives and writings. So situated, *Gifts* offers, in Gilmore's understanding of women writing autobiography, "a way to re-cognize what one is otherwise unable to know" (7) that eclipses the limitations of personal experience and identity, historical time and place.

The writing of one woman's life, such as that of Rebecca Jackson, indeed remains exemplary within the traditions of American autobiography: revising conventional boundaries and expectations, marking a historical place of agency within the continuum of American women's experiences; giving us a way to name, to know, to make of use those experiences that outstrip theory, outstretch explanation, and overreach expectation, social convention, generic boundaries. Carolyn Heilbrun reminds us in *Writing a Woman's Life*, "Power is the ability to take one's place in whatever discourse is essential to action and the right to have one's part matter" (18). And in its resistant, unapolegetic telling of the particulars of one woman's life, Jackson's *Gifts* participates in the radical, "revolutionary" tradition of women's life-writing and self-creation: that "simple act of telling of a woman's [life] story from a woman's point of view" (Christ 7).

Notes

1. Humez's 1981 edition of Rebecca Jackson's *Gifts of Power* first brought Jackson's writing to publication. Other than a handful of book reviews and biographical entries, there has been relatively little critical work on Jackson and her text. See Alice Walker's "*Gifts of Power*: The Writings of Rebecca Jackson," in *In Search of Our Mothers' Gardens: Womanist Prose* and the citations from William L. Andrews's *Sisters of the Spirit: Three Black Women's Auto-biographies of the Nineteenth Century*.

2. Although, as Humez points out in her introduction, Jackson likely was familiar with the published autobiography of her contemporary spiritual sister Jarena Lee (first edition, 1836), it is unlikely Jackson began her journals with the intent to publish. The content and trajectory of her writings suggest that many of them were written in retrospect—i.e., entries from the earlier years reflect a knowledge of events from later years (e.g., her conversion to Shakerism.) "Most probably," Humez observes, "[Jackson] was . . . in the practice of making short, dated entries in a commonplace book or journal," to which she returned and reshaped into "a fully consecutive, narrative autobiography that would cover the perod from her awakening through her discovery of Shakerism" (43).

3. Jackson records in 1840, regarding her supernatural powers especially concerning the weather, "the people said I was a witch" (160). Humez notes also that in 1851 Jackson and her friend Rebecca Perot (cf. n 17) "took a very lively interest in seance spiritualism" (23).

4. I am indebted to the scholarly and conversational insights of Joycelyn Moody regarding nineteenth-century black women's spiritual narratives and autobiographies, especially "Black and Divine: Embodiments of Spirituality in 19th-Century African American Women's Autobiographies."

5. This argument is noted by Humez in a footnote to Jackson's dream-vision.

6. In this respect, *Gifts* reflects the central concern that, according to Daniel Shea, informs all American spiritual autobiography—"the question of grace." See *Spiritual Autobiography in Early America*, 11.

7. Humez has entitled the last three sections of *Gifts* "Shaker Doctrine and First Residence at Watervliet" (1844-1851); "Interim in Philadelphia: Experiments in Seance Spiritualism" (1851-1857); and "Second Residence at Watervliet: Establishment of the Philadelphia Shaker Community" (1857-1864). In her introduction, Humez discusses the narrative discrepancies, due to the recollected nature of the journals, that result when events occurring historically at one point in Jackson's life are recorded and interpreted at others.

8. Harriet Jacobs's *Incidents in the Life of a Slave Girl, Written by Herself*, Ed. Jean Yellin Fagan, first went to press in 1861, contemporaneously with Jackson's growth within the spirit and writing of *Gifts*.

9. The African American proverb tradition articulates this double consciousness dilemma and strategy—to "make a way out of no way" (Daniel 482); Ntozake Shange understands it thus: "bein alive & bein a woman & bein colored is a metaphysical dilema/i haven't yet conquered" (45). See Jack L. Daniel, Geneva Smitherman-Donaldson, and Milford A. Jeremiah, "'Makin a Way Outa No Way': The Proverb Tradition in the Black Experience" and Shange's *for colored girls who have considered suicide/when the rainbow is enuf*.

10. In the entry dated September 1862, in reference to the Emancipation Proclamation, Jackson makes explicit the connection between good works and "a prosperous issue": "My cries to Almighty God, both day and night, were a continual prayer for the deliverance of my people from both spiritual and temporal bondage. I have now lived to hear the Proclamation of President Abraham Lincoln" (282).

11. This worldview of "both/and" balance, which underlies much African American writing, finds epistemological foundations in a noncontradictory cosmology rooted in traditional African beliefs—particularly, as Johnnella Butler notes, in "the concept of *nommo*—humankind's harmony and oneness of matter and spirit as expressed through African culture." See *Black Studies: Pedagogy and Revolution*, 38.

12. Cone's description here refers to the "kinds of religious questions" that have been asked by African Americans and the consequent ways of seeing and being which are shaped according to such "encounters" with divinity "in the midst of historical realities." See *The Spiritual and the Blues*, 29.

13. Humez comments on the "relative prosperity and safety" of Jackson as "free" (not slave) black woman, "certainly . . . when compared with that of the majority of black women alive in antebellum America" (11).

14. See the documents collected in Humez's appendix, "Female Preaching and the A.M.E. Church, 1820-1852," including the 1889 narrative of Elizabeth and excerpts from the *Life and Religious Experience of Jarena Lee, A Colored Lady* . . . (1836, 1839) for parallel accounts of female itinerant preachers and women's roles within institutionalized religion. See also James Oliver Horton's "Freedom's Yoke: Gender Conventions Among Antebellum Free Blacks."

15. William L. Andrews singles out Jackson's story—that of "the converted black woman choosing a life of celibacy while still married"—as "the most extreme separation from the world" manifested by nineteenth-century itinerant black women preachers. See *Sisters of the Spirit: Three Black Women's Autobiographies of the Nineteenth Century,* 12.

16. The equitable doctrine of "the four-in-one Godhead—in which the Father and Son of traditional Christiantiy are balanced and completed by a Mother and Daughter in Deity" was certainly part of what attracted Jackson to Shakerism (Humez 37).

17. According to Humez, Jackson and Perot's friendship was instigated in the late 1830s; see Introduction to *Gifts* (especially 28) and Jackson's entries dated March 27, 1851 (255) and January 6, 1856 (260). Of particular interest is Alice Walker's response to Humez's suggestion that the two women shared a lesbian relationship; see *"Gifts of Power*: The Writings of Rebecca Jackson, in *In Search of Our Mothers' Gardens: Womanist Prose.*

18. Humez reads Jackson's "achievement in founding her Philadelphia Shaker family" on a par with Richard Allen's founding of the A.M.E. church, both "confronting perceived discriminatory treatment of blacks within a white-dominated religious institution . . . ultimately seeing the necessity of a separate, black-led church" (39).

Works Cited

Andrews, William L. *Sisters of the Spirit: Three Black Women's Autobiographies of the Nineteenth Century.* Bloomington: Indiana UP, 1986.

——. *To Tell a Free Story: The First Century of Afro-American Autobiography, 1760-1865.* Urbana: U of Illinois P, 1988.

Belenky, Mary Field, Blythe McVicker Clinchy, Nancy Rule Goldberger, and Jill Mattuck Tarule, eds. *Women's Ways of Knowing: The Development of Self, Voice, and Mind.* New York: Basic Books, 1986.

Butler, Johnnella. *Black Studies: Pedagogy and Revolution.* Lanham: UP of America, 1981.

Carby, Hazel. *Reconstructing Womanhood: The Emergence of the Afro-American Woman Novelist.* New York: Oxford UP, 1987.

Christ, Carol. *Diving Deep and Surfacing: Women Writers on Spiritual Quest.* 1980. Boston: Beacon, 1986.

Cone, James. *The Spiritual and the Blues.* Westport: Greenwood, 1980.

Daniel, Jack L., Geneva Smitherman-Donaldson, and Milford A. Jeremiah. "'Makin' a Way Outa No Way': The Proverb Tradition in the Black Experience." *Journal of Black Studies* 17.4 (1987): 482-509.

Gates, Henry Louis. *The Signifying Monkey: A Theory of African American Literary Criticism.* New York: Oxford UP, 1988.

Gilmore, Leigh. *Autobiographics: A Feminist Theory of Women's Self-Representation.* Ithaca: Cornell UP, 1994.

Heilbrun, Carolyn. *Writing a Woman's Life.* New York: Norton, 1988.

Henderson, Mae Gwendolyn. "Speaking in Tongues: Dialogics, Dialectics, and the Black Woman Writer's Literary Tradition." *Changing Our Own Words: Essays on Criticism, Theory, and Writing by Black Women.* Ed. Cheryl A. Wall. New Brunswick: Rutgers UP, 1989. 16-37.

Horton, James. "Freedom's Yoke: Gender Conventions Among Antebellum Free Blacks." *Feminist Studies* 12.1 (1986): 51-76.

Hull, Gloria T. "Rebecca Jackson and the Uses of Power." Rev. of *Gifts of Power: The Writings of Rebecca Jackson, Black Visionary, Shaker Eldress.* Ed. Jean McMahon Humez. *Tulsa Studies in Women's Literature* 1.2 (1982): 203-09.

Humez, Jean McMahon, ed. Introduction. *Gifts of Power: The Writings of Rebecca Jackson, Black Visionary, Shaker Eldress.* Boston: U of Massachusetts P, 1981.

Jackson, Rebecca. *Gifts of Power.* Ed. Jean McMahon Humez. Boston: U of Massachusetts P, 1981.

Jacobs, Harriet. *Incidents in the Life of a Slave Girl, Written by Herself.* 1861. Ed. Jean Yellin Fagan. Cambridge: Harvard UP, 1987.

Moody, Joycelyn K. "Black and Divine: Embodiments of Spirituality in 19th-Century African American Women's Autobiographies." Unpublished essay, 1995.

Richardson, Marilyn. Foreword. *Sisters of the Spirit: Three Black Women's Autobiographies of the Nineteenth Century.* Ed. William L. Andrews. Bloomington: Indiana UP, 1986. viii-ix.

Shange, Ntozake. *for colored girls who have considered suicide/when the rainbow is enuf.* 1975. New York: Macmillan, 1989.

Shea, Daniel. *Spiritual Autobiography in Early America.* Princeton: Princeton UP, 1968.

Walker, Alice. "*Gifts of Power*: The Writings of Rebecca Jackson." *In Search of Our Mothers' Gardens: Womanist Prose.* San Diego: Harcourt, 193. 71-92.

5

Silenced Stories:
May Sarton's Journals
As a Form of Discursive Resistance

Leah E. White

It is tricky business offering the world a story that does not fit into mainstream culture and yet has its own life, its own fragile right to exist.

—Carmela Delia Lanza

May Sarton could be considered one of the century's most prolific writers. Before her death in 1995, Sarton had written over twenty books of fiction, nonfiction and poetry. Despite the remarkable contribution she has made to the literature of the past century, Sarton's works have been largely ignored by major critics. Maureen Teresa McCarthy argues that Sarton's fierce independence may have contributed to her lack of recognition by critics. McCarthy describes Sarton as having "always marched to the beat of a different drummer, in defiance of a culture that has increasingly demanded conformity" (4). However, it is this defiance that makes Sarton's work attractive to feminist literary scholars.

Although Sarton's prolific career has offered many interesting texts for analysis, her published journals perhaps provide the best glimpse into who she was as a writer and an individual. Of particular interest is how Sarton discusses her experiences with depression. Because it can be very difficult for a woman to openly articulate her experience with depression, many women have turned to journal writing as a means through which one is able to articulate depression and attempt to regain emotional balance. Journals offer a safe place in which a woman is able to express her honest feelings and emotions. For Sarton, the journal is a place for accomplishing self-analysis. When describing the motivations behind women's autobiographical writings, Estelle Jelinek explains that many women attempt to articulate "their self-worth, to clarify, to affirm, and to authenticate their self image" (15). In a *Ms.* magazine interview, May Sarton describes her own journal writing as "my way to turn all that talking about myself into talking *to* myself. It separates what is important from what is not important" (Hershman 26). Sarton demonstrates that as a "feminine form" the journal offers a voice to women who may feel pressured to remain silent about aspects of their lives (Hogan 95).

The struggle with depression is clear in Sarton's journals. Jeanne Braham explains that all of Sarton's journals were written "on the heels of personal crisis, when self-assessment was crucial for restoring emotional balance and spiritual health" (153). Of additional importance is how Sarton releases her anger. According to Janice Wood Wetzel, in our society it is not acceptable for women to openly express their anger (91). She explains that women are socialized to value the relational aspects of life, rather than what might provide them with a sense of autonomy (91). Blatant expressions of anger could threaten a relational dimension and indicate a move toward autonomy, thus women are discouraged from such displays. Wetzel goes on to explain that women recognize the restriction of independence and consequently feel inadequate (95). These feelings of inadequacy can easily result in depression. Through the use of her journals, May Sarton violates the social assumption that she ought not to express such emotions. In fact, Carolyn Heilbrun lauds Sarton's *Journal of a Solitude* as a "watershed in women's autobiography" because it is one of the first published works to honestly discuss female rage (13).

Journal writing places a woman into a position of control over her own life. Female autobiographical writings, such as journals, are extremely valuable to women's resistance efforts. As Hélène Cixous advocates, "Woman must write herself; must write about women and bring women to writing. . . . Woman must put herself into the text—as into the world and into history—by her own movement" (875). Autobiography is perhaps the most powerful tool women have to help them accomplish this type of female centered writing. Through autobiographical texts, women are able to offer their own interpretations and reevaluations of the power structures that seek to control and silence them. Because the safety of the journal allows women to center themselves as subjects, journal writing functions as a form of discursive resistance.

One reason why the journal is especially effective in terms of resistance is that when it is made public, the journal emphasizes individual differences while simultaneously drawing others together as they recognize elements of commonality between themselves and the author. Because autobiographical writings enable women to recognize and value their differences, a mutual respect for such differences allows for the formation of powerful coalitions through which the oppressive ideological structures of society may be challenged (Lionnet xi). Thus, as the journal highlights an individual voice it also allows for the development of a community of others who recognize the fidelity of the life experiences expressed in the journal.

Because Sarton wrote her journals for publication, the journals illustrate her personal struggle with depression in a manner that is available to a wider audience than simply the self. Braham writes, "Sarton is increasingly conscious of moving from solitary experience into dialogue with a reader, making her experience available 'as a lens of empathy'" (163). While illustrating her personal struggle, Sarton's journals equip others with insight into how journal writing may be used to resist negative forces in their own lives. Carol Virginia Pohli explains this effect of Sarton's work writing, "Female readers take courage from her texts because they are convinced that Sarton writes out of her actual experiences as a woman who refuses to emulate behavior expected of women" (220). Sarton's public admission of this type of resistance, through her journal writings, encourages her readers to consider their own resistance efforts.

Journal writing unquestionably provides many women with a means through which they are able to make sense of and resist the oppressive dailiness of their lives. An analysis of how May Sarton uses journal writing as a way to confront her depression, will serve as an example of how journal writing functions as a powerful tool of resistance.

Not only do Sarton's journals offer her a means through which she is able to publicly as well as privately resist the oppressive forces in her life, they also provide her readers with a voice to which they can relate. Braham writes, "Though rooted in idiosyncratic experience, Sarton's journals seek to connect with a wide readership by revealing the need to create order out of chaos, reentry out of withdrawal, health out of illness" (153). A mutual sense of understanding concerning the difficulties of living with depression is developed between Sarton and her readers.

In order to explain how Sarton deals with her depression, three of her earlier journals, *Journal of a Solitude, The House by the Sea* and *Recovering*, will be discussed. Before illustrating how Sarton travels through a variety of stages of depression, I will show how her journals demonstrate her awareness of and desire to develop a female consciousness.

Initially, Sarton's journals clearly show that she was aware of the social pressures experienced by women. According to Bettina Aptheker, many women possess a distinct consciousness of social reality based on a sexual division in labor and institutional subordination to men. Because many women share the experience of living a life socially guided by prescribed female roles, they share a consciousness informed by their experiences. In some cases, such as Sarton's, depression becomes a part of that consciousness. Wetzel connects the threat of depression to the way in which labor is divided in our society (92). As women continually expend their energy on tasks that do not in return refuel them, they may become emotionally as well as physically exhausted, thus making them more susceptible to depression. Sarton's journals illustrate how her understanding of the social pressure experienced by women helped her to confront her own depression.

Although Sarton chose to live a life of solitude and personal artistic work, she did not escape the influence of social pressures. For example, in an early entry in *Journal of a Solitude* Sarton attempts to make sense of the conditions of women's lives:

When I said above that women were rarely as whole as men, I felt I must go back and think some more. It is harder for women, perhaps, to be "one-pointed," Much harder for them to clear space around whatever it is they want to do beyond household chores and family life. Their lives are fragmented . . . this is the cry I get in so many letters—the cry not so much for a "room of one's own" as a time of one's own. (56)

Sarton is also painfully aware of the pressures felt by the younger generation of women. Her willingness to mentor young female students provided her with insight into the conditions of their lives. In response to the news that two former students, who had set aside writing once they got married and had children, had begun to write poetry again, Sarton writes, "That news made me happy. It also made me aware once more of how rarely a woman is able to continue to create after she marries and has children" (*Journal* 70).

A few years later, writing in *A House by the Sea*, Sarton mentions two women she has agreed to advise while they are working on their master's theses:

These young women are determined to have children as a part of a fulfilled life and to do original work as well. I admire them wholeheartedly. But I am always up against my own hard view that it is next to impossible to lead a fulfilled life as a human being and do original work of the highest caliber, if one is a woman. (133)

Wetzel refers to this feeling of despair as a woman's sense of existential guilt, or the realization of one's inability to reach one's full potential, often leading to feelings of depression. Wetzel writes that "default on the task of becoming the self results in depression, represented by the absence of creative energy which blocks the way of the spirit" (101). A woman's feelings of depression may evolve from the realization that she is unable to reach personal fulfillment before she has even begun her journey. Thus, although Sarton attempted to surround herself in solitude, she was unable to avoid knowledge of, and experience with, the problems associated with the division of labor and women's subordination by men.

Sarton's journals also illustrate how she used journal writing as a way to communicate with her readers. Sarton's journals contain several references to letters she has received from readers. This type of response from Sarton helps to create a dialogue between her and her readers. Pohli writes, "In Sarton's world, author and reader are live, interdependent, talking moral entities whose mutual engagement with a clearly written work fertilizes a clearer sense of identity" (233). Susan Stanford Friedman argues that a "collective consciousness of self" is crucial to a woman's process of self-definition (56). She writes, "Instead of seeing themselves as solely unique, women often explore their sense of shared identity with other women, an aspect of identity that exists in tension with a sense of their own uniqueness" (44). Sarton's journals serve as one possible means through which people sharing similar experiences may find mutual understanding.

Frequently, Sarton responds to reader's letters in a manner that identifies and helps to develop a shared female consciousness. For example, in *Journal of a Solitude*, Sarton rewrites a portion of a reader's letter. The reader writes,

So much holds me back. My own inertia, the choice I made ten years ago to be second in marriage, the children, my background. . . . Just being a woman. It is difficult. Does one give up a measure of security, and whatever else is necessary, to develop? Can one *be* within the framework of a marriage, do you think? I envy your solitude with all my heart, and your courage to live as you must. (122)

To this Sarton responds, "It is not irresponsible women who ask that question, but often women with children, caring women, who feel deeply frustrated and lost, who feel they are missing their 'real lives' all the time" (122). Sarton continues with a lengthy journal entry that discusses many of the current issues facing women. This exchange of ideas between reader and author helps to build and promote an understanding for a mutually shared female consciousness. As one of Sarton's readers wrote, "You have helped me [recognize] a spiritual bond between myself and other women" (qtd. in Pohli 225).

The theme of journal writing as a way to accomplish emotional work is also frequently found in Sarton's journals. Sarton is quick to recognize that journal writing is a valuable tool in her life, especially when attempting to make sense of her experiences with depression. In a 1982 interview, Sarton explains that both *Journal of a Solitude* and *Recovering* were written "as an exercise to handle serious depression" (Saum 116). She opens *Recovering* writing, "I had thought not to begin a new journal until I am seventy, four years from now, but perhaps the time has come to sort myself out, and see whether I can restore a sense of meaning and continuity to my life by this familiar means" (9). A few days later she adds, "I am glad I decided to begin a journal again. It is a way of sorting myself out, that self that has been too dispersed for too long" (*Recovering* 15).

Often journal writers will return to old journals as a way to review past life events. Sarton occasionally looks back on the purpose of a previous journal. After several years of general happiness, Sarton reflects on *Journal of a Solitude*, writing, "The *Journal of a Solitude* had been a way of dealing with anguish; was it that happiness is harder to communicate, or that when one is happy there is little incentive even to try to sort out daily experience as it happens" (*House* 7).

Clearly Sarton uses her own journals as a way to help her work through the daily experiences in her life. For Sarton, as for other journal writers, journals are one of the best means through which one can make sense of a life. Margo Culley explains that many women turn to journal writing because it is "one place where they [are] permitted, indeed encouraged, to indulge full 'self-centeredness'" (16). The journal may very well be the only place where a woman is free from the social pressures that bear down on her. Whereas the labor of a woman's life rarely allows her room for her own endeavors, in a journal she becomes the "self as the subject," free to indulge whatever personal concern she may have (Culley 15).

With these base ideas in Sarton's journals explained, a closer look at how Sarton writes about her own depression may be taken. Depression itself can be fragmented, sometimes staying a few days and in severe cases lasting for months. Even when one has weathered an episode of depression, there is the underlying tension that a new wave may soon begin. Sarton's journals illustrate this cyclical nature of depression. In her work we can see the daily stress of the illness.

Sarton's journals show that she can sink into severe and lengthy depressions. Much of *Journal of a Solitude* articulates such an experience. Toward the beginning of this journal Sarton writes,

Cracking open the inner world again, writing even a couple pages, threw me back into depression. . . . I was attacked by a storm of tears, those tears that appear to be related to frustration, to buried anger, and come upon me without warning. I woke yesterday so depressed that I did not get up until after eight. (13)

Her experience while writing *Recovering* is similar. The following passage not only expresses a sense of despair, but also demonstrates a previous knowledge of this type of feeling: "When there is personal darkness, when there is pain to be overcome, when we are forced to renew ourselves against all odds, the psychic energy required simply to survive has tremendous force, as great as that of a bulb pushing up through icy ground in spring" (16). The sense that depression is a reoccurring event in Sarton's life becomes clear as one reads through her journals. Passages like the above are scattered throughout the works.

Sarton's journals also illustrate the frustration of having battled a bout of depression only to have another resurgence of emotion come rushing over her. This ebb and flow of depression is found in the later months of Sarton's *Journal of a Solitude*. After feeling fairly healthy for over a month Sarton writes: "The furies came to the window again two nights ago, and I had a frightful attack of temper, of nerves, of resentment against X, followed by the usual boomerang of acute anxiety. It is frightening to have regressed in this way" (82). This passage is discouraging evidence of the cycle of depression in a woman's life. Even when one believes she has conquered the sadness, she is not completely safe from another episode.

Because Sarton's battle with depression follows a cyclical pattern, the dailiness of the experience may be seen. Several times, Sarton writes of simply enduring the deep stages of her depression. She seems to recognize the bouts are not permanent, but rather can be weathered until happiness is restored. In *Journal of a Solitude* she writes, "The reasons for depression are not so interesting as the way one handles it, simply to stay alive" (16). Shortly after she adds, "Neurotic depression is so boring because it is repetitive, literally a wheel that turns and turns" (17). As the weeks of depression go on, Sarton observes, "There is nothing to be done but to go ahead with life moment by moment and hour by hour— put out birdseed, tidy the rooms, try to create order and peace around me even if I cannot achieve it inside me" (33).

Finally, this dailiness is articulated in Sarton's discussion of survival: "Is this the key? Keep busy with survival. Imitate the trees. Learn to lose in order to recover, and remember that nothing stays the same for long, not even pain, psychic pain. Sit it out. Let it all pass. Let it go" (*Journal* 34). Sarton's journals depict an understanding and acceptance of the daily process of enduring mental depression. It is perhaps Sarton's acceptance of the cyclical process of depression that provides her with the ability to utilize the journal as a tool to reconstruct happiness.

Sarton writes with enthusiasm as she feels her sense of peace return to her. Often she begins with tentative entries and then as she becomes more confident in her returned happiness she writes with more conviction. In *Journal of a Solitude*, when Sarton first realizes she may be climbing out of a depression, she hesitantly writes, "I don't know whether the inward work is achieving something, or whether it is simply the autumn light, but I begin to see my way again, which means to resume myself" (35). When the mood has not left her the next day, Sarton suggests with more clarity, "Has it really happened at last, I feel released from the rack, set free, in touch with the deep source that is only good" (37). A few more days after this entry, Sarton writes with confidence, "I can hardly believe that relief from the anguish of these past months is here to stay, but so far it does feel like a true change of mood —or rather, a change of being where I can stand alone" (39).

This series of entries illustrates the writing process Sarton uses to work through her depression and finally to position herself with a new sense of emotional balance. The journals function as a way to test thoughts, fears, and emotions. After an episode of depression, Sarton reflects on the entire experience. For example, at the conclusion of *Recovering*, Sarton uses one of her final journal entries as a way to put the whole experience into perspective: "I began this journal ten months ago as a way of getting back to my self, of pulling out of last year's depression, and now I am truly on a rising curve. What has changed in a miraculous way is the landscape of the heart, so somber and tormented for over a year that I was not myself" (224).

This type of reflection is also found in *The House by the Sea*. Although this journal is written during a positive time in Sarton's life, she does spend time looking back on the sadness she experienced while writing *Journal of a Solitude*. Through this reflection, Sarton is better able to appreciate the happiness she has reconstructed. She writes, "I come back to happiness here. I have never been so happy in my life, never for such a sustained period, for I have been in this house by the sea for a year and a half. I have not said enough about what it is to wake each day to the sunrise and to that great tranquil open space" (61). Such entries allow Sarton to reflect on the experience she has been through and ultimately value the life she leads every day.

When reading texts written by women, it is important to consider the "whole range of material conditions that have historically determined female subjectivity" (Costello 125). This is particularly true in understanding female depression. Attention must be turned to the social factors that make women susceptible to depression. A close reading of women's autobiographical works will provide the insight necessary to understand how daily oppression in a woman's life can lead her to psychological distress.

Analysis of May Sarton's journals has shown how one woman's voicing of her experiences with depression can help to develop a community of resistance against the oppressive environment that contributes to depression. When asked about her influence on her readers, May Sarton responded, "I've had many letters from people . . . who said, 'You've helped me to be able to understand myself and to not feel awful or rotten or wicked,' so there I think I've had value" (Carter 77). As one of the most prolific writers of the past several decades, May Sarton has much to offer, not the least of which is her individual voice. A voice inspiring in its honesty, challenging us to draw together as a community to better understand and manage experiences with depression.

Note

A version of this paper was presented at the 1996 Western States Communication Association Annual Conference, Pasadena, CA.

Works Cited

Aptheker, Bettina. *Tapestries of Life: Women's Work, Women's Consciousness, and the Meaning of Daily Experience.* Amherst: U of Massachusetts P, 1989.

Braham, Jeanne. "'Seeing with Fresh Eyes': A Study of May Sarton's Journals." *That Great Sanity: Critical Essays on May Sarton.* Ed. Susan Swartzlander and Marilyn R. Mumford. Ann Arbor: U of Michigan P, 1992. 153-66.

Carter, Nancy Corson. "An Interview with May Sarton." *Conversations with May Sarton* Ed. Earl G. Ingersoll. Jackson: UP of Mississippi, 1991. 74-84.

Cixous, Hélène. "The Laugh of the Medusa." *Signs* 1.4 (1976): 875-93.

Costello, Jeanne. "Taking the 'Woman' Out of Women's Autobiography: The Perils and Potentials of Theorizing Female Subjectivities." *Diacritics* 21.2-3 (1991): 123-34.

Culley, Margo. "'I Look at Me': Self as Subject in the Diaries of American Women." *Women's Studies Quarterly* 17.3-4 (1989): 15-22.

Friedman, Susan Stanford. "Women's Autobiographical Selves: Theory and Practice." *The Private Self: Theory and Practice of Women's Autobiographical Writings.* Ed. Shari Benstock. Chapel Hill: U of North Carolina P, 1988. 34-62.

Heilbrun, Carolyn. *Writing a Woman's Life.* New York: Ballantine, 1988.

Hershman, Marcie. "May Sarton at 70: 'A Viable Life Against the Odds.'" *Ms.* Oct. 1982: 23-26.

Hogan, Rebecca. "Engendered Autobiographies: The Diary as a Feminine Form." *Autobiography and Questions of Gender.* Ed. Shirley Neuman. London: Frank Cass, 1991. 95-107.

Jelinek, Estelle C. Introduction. *Women's Autobiography: Essays in Criticism.* Ed. Estelle Jelinek. Bloomington: Indiana UP, 1980.

Lanza, Carmela Delia. "'Always on the Brink of Disappearing': Women, Ethnicity, Class, and Autobiography." *Frontiers* 15.2 (1994): 51-68.

Lionnet, Francoise. *Autobiographical Voices: Race, Gender, Self-Portraiture.* Ithaca: Cornell UP, 1989. xi-xiv.

McCarthy, Maureen Teresa. "Introduction: In Our Mothers' Gardens." *That Great Sanity: Critical Essays on May Sarton.* Ed. Susan Swartzlander and Marilyn R. Mumford. Ann Arbor: U of Michigan P, 1992. 1-12.

Pohli, Carol Virginia. "Saving the Audience: Patterns of Reader Response to May Sarton's Work." *That Great Sanity: Critical Essays on May Sarton.* Ed. Susan Swartzlander and Marilyn R. Mumford. Ann Arbor: U of Michigan P, 1992. 211-38.

Sarton, May. *The House by the Sea.* 1977. New York: Norton, 1981.

——. *Journal of a Solitude.* New York: Norton, 1973.

——. *Recovering: A Journal.* New York: Norton, 1980.

Saum, Karen. "The Art of Poetry XXXII: May Sarton." *Paris Review* 89 (1983): 81-110. Rpt. in *Conversations with May Sarton.* Ed. Earl G. Ingersoll. Jackson: UP of Mississippi, 1991. 108-29.

Wetzel, Janice Wood. "Depression: Women-at-Risk." *Social Work in Health Care* 19.3-4 (1993): 85-108.

Retrospective Constructions and Negotiations:
Autobiographies/Memoirs

6

Gender, Sect, and Circumstance: Quaker Mary Penington's Many Voices

Linda S. Coleman

Historian Christopher Hill's description of mid-seventeenth century Britain as a "world turned upside down" might at first suggest only the individual despair and social turmoil created by the English Civil War. Out of confusion and chaos, however, arose revolutionary possibility. Those previously marginalized by gender and class grasped their opportunity to construct new identities and to speak out in previously unimaginable voices. In the life-writing of Mary Penington (1625-1682), a first generation Quaker, we read one woman's negotiations of the complex dynamic of gender construction during this particular and formative historical period. Against established feminine codes of behavior, Penington publicly asserted and defined herself under the Friends' imperative to break down the barriers between private spiritual conscience and public life. In rejecting the silencing norms for her gender, Penington sought truth and self-awareness through personal experience. Though the resulting isolation caused her both fear and initial failure in her youth and early adulthood, Penington ultimately found consolation and confirmation within Quakerism. And from these Friends, within the freely-entered-into community of saints, she gained confidence and trust in a shared external authority.

The stages in Penington's development parallel those found among many of the women interviewed by Mary Field Belenky, Blythe McVicker Clinchy, Nancy Rule Goldberger, and Jill Mattuck Tarule for their book *Women's Ways of Knowing*, a study of the sociology and psychology of modern gender roles.[1] They observe that women today often move among what they call voice positions, or ways of knowing. Personal and historical circumstances change or the development secured in one position enables movement to another.[2] Penington has left us evidence of her own shifting positions in the varied autobiographical forms she employed over the course of her life. Through her retrospective autobiography, as well as a diary and an autobiographical letter, we can listen

93

to the changing voices of Mary Penington, and through them come to a greater understanding of when our modern gendered ways of knowing first emerged and of what historical and personal conditions enabled and nourished individual women to move beyond silence and into self-knowledge.[3]

The 1640s, '50s and '60s, the years of Penington's youth and entry into middle age, encompass tremendous social and ideological shifts. Beyond the traumatic events of a Civil War and the Restoration were the underlying causes that we now recognize as the advent of modern culture and capitalism.[4] Perhaps most important for many women, changed opportunities for experience and expression were stimulated by the less hierarchical models of social organization suggested by the tenets of puritanism and by the emphasis on the individual and on process in emerging empiricism and capitalism. Puritanism, for example, rejected the role of priest as mediator between the individual and his or her God, which offered the possibility for reconfigured family relationships as well. Empiricism reached for the authority of the personal, giving at least theoretical importance to the daily, even domestic experience which was within the reach of every woman, regardless of class and education. More generally, new ideologies offered marginalized groups—and the culture as a whole—an opportunity to reconsider themselves, to consider/imagine their relationship to culture as mutable.

Theology and its practice in late sixteenth- and early seventeenth-century Britain increasingly supported and even created the need for private and public religious life-writing. Root causes included the Calvinist concept of election and the internalization of religious concern and responsibility. While public spiritual communities continued, many religious groups believed that an individual's spiritual status needed to be confirmed internally, regardless of class or gender. The potentially liberating effects of this changing spiritual hegemony, however, were contained by most mainstream Puritans through a paradoxical division: a spiritual equality against an equally important Calvinist emphasis on sin and evil. Inner freedom was limited by external assurances of inner frailty, and the resulting struggle came to represent one's standing among God's "elect" (Lerner 382). Complex religious personalities emerged from these paradoxical messages. Being free of the intermediary priest and having direct access to God, a woman or man might develop a distinctly independent personality. The built-in insecurities of the theory of election (only some were of the elect), however, worked to contain a feared social anarchy.

Puritans turned to both public and private forms of life-writing to explore and express their spiritual fates. In the diary or Puritan "confessional," as historian William Haller has termed it, the believer "could fling upon his God the fear and weakness he found in his heart but could not betray to the world" (38). Public autobiographies reflected more varied motives. While understanding and identification could be found only within and by oneself, writing about the process of conversion served two purposes: each autobiographer could act as a model to others in the path toward conversion; and, given the intangibility of election, writing about the struggle made public one's felt inner truth. A third and even more practical motive is possible: the public political debate over personal religious freedom necessitated public articulation of one's own faith/position.

Like other dissenting sects, Quakers defined themselves in opposition to the dominant Puritan and Anglican theologies and codes, at the very least attempting actually to practice some of the beliefs implied by Puritan theory. And among these practices was increased gender equality. As one of the more radical of the sects, at least during its first generation, Friends turned inward for spiritual insight and responsibility, in some cases rejecting even the final authority of the ministry and the Bible, where they found the "Inner Light," which is described as "'a spark of divine essense [sic]' which dwells in each human being, and . . . if obedience is yielded to this inner Light or word . . . man can be led to all Truth and thus possess a guide for the intricate problems of daily living and for the conduct of life" (Wright 7).

Significantly, the Quaker distinction or refinement that set it apart from the anarchy and pessimism of the Ranter and Seeker sects was the ability to hold together a "community of saints" while remaining true to internal authority. The mediation of the internal and external was based on the belief that conversion and religious life were part of a process, a "continuous revelation" (Wright 35).

Luella Wright, a modern Quaker historian, describes further the nature of the experience of the "Inner Light":

This Light . . . was not an abstract theorem to be perceived by means of the intellect or reason, but ideally a living and enduring personal experience. Acceptance of this Light, since it implied an introspective view of self, an examination of motives for action, and a surrender of the will to the leadings of the Spirit, frequently required a complete orientation in the convert's estimation of his former religious views and of the place that religion should hold in life. (29)

The evolving subjective process described contrasts markedly with the "sudden insight" of other radical Puritans (Barbour 26). For most women, used to daily tasks and goals and trained to trust experience rather than formal education in the execution of these tasks, such valued means to spiritual understanding were no doubt provocative and liberating. Even the Quaker emphasis upon the Holy Spirit metaphorically shifted the power of religious experience away from the Father and the Son to a more gender-neutral being. In fact, the Quakers experimented with the neuter, often using "It" (rather than the masculine pronoun) to describe the spirit (Barbour 110). These resulting shifts in emphasis often contributed to female followers being more directly and actively involved in their communities. The increase in authority and the balancing of individual understanding and community spirit are important to an examination of how these women's individual and collective voices came to be defined.

Like the Puritans, the Quakers turned to life-writing as an aspect of inward examination and outward identification. Within the community of saints, writing confessions was a common activity as early as the 1650s. What causes the earliest Quaker life-writing to stand out amidst their peers', however, is its genuine valuing of subjectivity, a result of the mystical, emotional element inherent in the experience of the Inner Light. The Quaker style, with its simplicity and its dependence upon plain and simple metaphor, seems to have come easily to the less educated female pen, as did its attention to domestic detail, a sign among the Friends of the "sacramental" quality of everyday life (Wright 173). The practice of Quakerism, especially as it grew, may not have been intended to promote full sexual equality (Barbour 132), but for justification of their participation in the political and religious activities of their sect, including preaching, public declarations, and confessions, Quaker women, like their Puritan peers, had a theoretical command to look inward and to confirm what they found outwardly.[5]

Belenky and her colleagues use as part of the base for their paradigm of knowing the moral framework established by Gilligan and others. In it, women, more generally—though not universally or exclusively—operate out of "notions of responsibility and care" (8). Such notions center on "the needs of individuals" which "cannot always be deduced from general rules and principles," and thus, "moral choice must always be determined inductively from the particular experience each participant brings to the situation" (8). This moral perspective, in turn, influences identity development:

the responsibility orientation is more central to those whose conceptions of self are rooted in a sense of connection and relatedness to others, whereas the rights orientation is more common to those who define themselves in terms of separation and autonomy [i.e., traditionally the male identity and moral viewpoint]. (8)

The existence of this division, which now falls largely along gender lines, is in large part a reflection of the parallel imperatives of modern patriarchy and capitalism which first emerged during the mid-seventeenth century.[6] We now expect a sexual division of labor and along with it an attempted or perceived division of public and private experiences, rights, and responsibilities; from this follows a constructed morality/ identity gap between the sexes. We can identify traces of the emergence of this polarization, as well as resistance to it, in the life-writing of mid-seventeenth-century Quaker women such as Mary Penington.

Mary Penington was born into the gentry class and orphaned at an early age. Her earliest writing focuses primarily on a youth and young adulthood plagued by religious doubt and wandering as she tried to understand her part in the "world turned upside down." As a consequence of an unusually strong desire for understanding and meaning, this girl/young woman broke the strictures of gender by insisting on independence of religious thought and action within her family and community. She thus simultaneously jeopardized her class privileges, becoming triply marginalized—by class, religion, and gender. She was baited by her more religiously conservative and conforming family and peers with accusations of violating both class and gender boundaries as she sought a personal faith in a variety of religious styles and communities: she was "proud and schismatic" and they said she could only be going "to those places to meet young men and such like" (24). She remembers becoming "a by-word and a hissing among the people of my own rank in the world" (28).

As Belenky and her colleagues assert,

We do not think of the ordinary person as preoccupied with such difficult and profound questions as: What is truth? What is authority? To whom do I listen? What counts for me as evidence? How do I know what I know? Yet to ask ourselves these questions and to reflect on our answers is more than an intellectual exercise, for our basic assumptions about the nature of truth and reality and the origins of knowledge shape the way we see the world and ourselves as participants in it. (3)

This is explicitly the task Penington set for herself as a very young woman. She learned in the established Anglican church, for example, that prayer "distinguished a saint from a sinner; that in many things the hypocrite could imitate the saint, but in this he could not" (19). This troubled her because, "I knew not what true prayer was; for what I used for prayer, an ungodly person could use as well as I, which was to read one out of a book" (19). Rather than remaining silent in her doubt and adhering to the external authority of the Church, Penington acted for herself and tried to compose her own prayers, though at that time she "could then scarcely join my letters" (20). There were, of course, limitations to her actions: to stand against the church, and to turn to her own creation, was not meant to claim authority for herself; her first prayer, for example, was to God, to request his guidance in prayer—i.e., she sought to obey her self-formed perceptions only as reflections of God's will.

While her shift to an internally driven faith satisfied Penington for a brief period, most of her youth was spent in spiritual isolation, from her family, her community, and from a secured understanding of religion: "I had none to reveal my distress unto, or advise with; so, secretly bore a great burden a long time" (21). Though in her early adulthood she was happily married twice and began a family, she "changed my ways often, and ran from one notion into another, not finding satisfaction nor assurance that I should obtain what my soul desired, in the several ways and notions which I sought satisfaction in" (28). She lapsed into complete doubt and "began to conclude that the Lord and his truth was, but that it was not made known to any upon earth" (30). Only after a series of visions/dreams, in which she experienced a visible and approachable Christ and his wife and received confirmation for her personal belief in the resurrection, did she open up to the invitations of the Quakers, of whom she had until this time been suspicious. Her desire was to be able "to feel" the truth of their way. And, in fact, "their solid and weighty carriage struck a dread over me" (42). Penington found the transition difficult: "The contemplation of those things [Quaker concepts] cost me many tears, doleful nights and days; not now disputing against the doctrine preached by the Friends, but exercised against taking up the cross to the language, fashions, customs, titles, honor, and esteem in the world" (44). Her family continued to bait her and yet, finally, she "happily gave up, divested of reasonings" because she "longed to be one of them" (44).

Women's Ways of Knowing sets up a paradigm of five epistemological positions.[7] The authors' first category, silence, is, of course, the traditionally privileged category for women—especially within certain Christian traditions. It is, however, according to Belenky and her colleagues, "an extreme denial of the self and a dependence on external authority for direction" (24). That it was the default position for women of Penington's period may be traced in the extended defenses among Quaker women (and other sectarian female speakers/writers) against the antifeminist use of the Bible, and especially St. Paul, to require women to be silent and obedient. Margaret Fox's "Women's Speaking Justified" is a fascinating verse-by-verse reversal of this repressive reading of scripture where she argues that only women who do not understand (that is, only

"Other" women) are required to be silent. Those with knowledge, and especially with confirmed internal experience of God, must and should speak. As Patricia Crawford believes,

The Bible provided women with a number of justifications for publication. Women cited the parable of the talents. . . . Elizabeth Bathurst, a Quaker, spelt out that this applied to women as well as men. The parable of the poor widow led women to conclude that each must contribute her mite. Quaker women used the Bible to justify their testimony. No one could hide her light under a bushel. (221)

The Puritan and especially the Quaker imperatives for self-examination created a gap within which women such as Penington could challenge existing norms through self-conscious ways of knowing. Penington never seems to have considered silence as an option, at least not as she retrospectively created herself in this autobiography.

Mary Penington's position on the historical timeline—at the transition into early modernism—caused her to be vulnerable to at least two different strategies for containing the voices of nonsilent women. As Michael McKeon argues, the earlier patriarchal model of gender, which sought to subsume women hierarchically under the authority of the state and then her husband, was replaced by Locke and others with modern gendered notions of a division between public and private, again relegating authority to the public male voice. The potentially liberating transition into liberal gender equality was quickly contained (296-97). And women who might have moved beyond silence were restricted to a new received authority. Today's "Listeners" are Belenky's second group of women, the received knowers. They operate out of a system of absolutes and, though they do reflect on their experience in ways that the silent do not, they still turn exclusively to authorities for a stable system of "truth." They are "intolerant of ambiguity" (42) and they conform to external demands, seeing an action for themselves as legitimate only when it primarily helps others, an ironic consequence, in part, of the female value for connectedness.

As a child, Penington consistently sought out a stable, externally determined truth. Her failure to conform to any of those which were available to her is linked to the gap in authority between old and new received ideologies. She observed the former to be in crisis and the new as lacking in stability. In their place Penington was forced to depend on her own independence of mind and as a result she rejected the subordination of self each system of authority would have demanded of her. Received knowledge is dependent upon the subject's perception of similarity to those to whom she is subordinate—a unified front of authority. The religious, class, and political strife of Penington's childhood revealed even to a child the reality and persistence of difference. According to William Perry, "With multiplicity, truth is no longer conceived as absolute and singular but multiple and infinite" (Belenky 62-63).[8]

Belenky describes the received position as "Conceiving the Selfless Self": "they must look to others even for self-knowledge" (48). Penington tried but failed to develop this belief in an encompassing external authority. Instead, within her life-writings, from the presentations of her early religious choices up to her marriages, Penington presents herself as acting primarily on her own will.

Unable to remain silent or to subordinate her voice to an external authority, the young Mary Penington speaks instead from the subjective voice position identified in *Women's Ways of Knowing*. And in her identification with the Quakers she found justification for the inner-directed will she had already developed. For the subjective knower, "truth [is] personal, private, and subjectively known or intuited" (54). As is the case for Penington, however, the subjectivist is "dualistic in the sense that there is still the conviction that there are right answers; the fountain of truth simply has shifted locale. Truth now resides within the person and can negate answers that the outside world supplies" (54). For all of the strength of character required of young Mary (a retrospective fortitude not atypical in conversion narratives, of course), she balanced any self-accusation of pride with her complete dependence on God for empowering her and providing the true way:

And He hath many times refreshed my soul in his presence, and given me assurance that I knew that estate in which He will never leave me, nor suffer me to be drawn from all which He has graciously fulfilled; for though various infirmities and temptations beset me, yet my heart cleaveth unto the Lord, in everlasting bonds that can never be broken. (46)

Belenky argues that for some women, subjectivism comes after a "crisis of trust in male authority in their daily lives" (58). Surely Penington's childhood, and the historical shifts in authority she lived through at an impressionable age, set the stage for her subjective position. Local churches literally had physical struggles for the pulpit and for followers, an evident crisis to the mind and heart of a young and bright child. Further, Penington's sometimes difficult to believe memory of her persistent rebellion against family and peers might be explained by Belenky's observation that subjective knowers "feel they can rely on their experience and 'what feels right' to them as an important asset in making decisions for themselves" (61).

Standing up for one's beliefs is especially challenging for women. For boys, according to William Perry's model of development, the multiplicity of truth which subjectivity creates becomes "a tool in the process of . . . separation and differentiation from others" (Belenky 64). But for a female subjective knower, assertions can create fear and a sense of isolation—she feels "vulnerable and unconnected": "Although she senses that she is free to control her destiny, she does not feel in control nor able to take the risks that experimentation entails" (65). That women of Penington's historical period would be vulnerable if isolated is especially evident in this observation by Keith Wrightson of every person's dependence upon connection/community during this time:

"Neighbourliness," unlike kinship, is a somewhat vague concept, lacking in precise definition. Yet it was a notion much employed by sixteenth- and seventeenth-century people. Indeed "good neighbourliness" . . . was a virtue which stood "perhaps first in the criteria by which the social and ethical standing of an individual in a community was measured" . . . neighbourliness [a]t its simplest . . . can be defined as a type of relationship between people established on the basis of their residential propinquity; but this too is inadequate. Two further characteristics of neighbourliness were that it involved a mutual recognition of reciprocal obligations of a practical kind and a degree of normative consensus as to the nature of proper behavior between neighbours. (51)

Penington's frequent reference to those who reject her choices helps us to understand the paradox of a woman who trusts in herself and yet who has been socialized to need confirmation from and connection to those whom she loves, respects, and depends on for her economic welfare. Wrightson helps us as well to understand Penington's later attraction to the Quaker community—an environment in which she is not asked to sacrifice herself but instead to collaborate in building connections.

Belenky refines our understanding of the style of subjective thinking by adding that it "distrusts logic, analysis, abstraction, and even language itself" (71). The silence of Quaker meetings, as the individual believer waits for her experience of the "Inner Light" together with her community of Friends, stands in bold opposition to the silent acquiescence of traditional women. Here we see, too, why the Quaker theology stood against the emerging received position: external authority originates in subjectivity and is many voiced. The Puritan theory of election valued the individual experience of salvation and privileged received authority, while the Quaker theory of grace encouraged, at least for that brief moment in history, a radical redefinition of authority.[9]

While "the voice of reason" that characterizes the procedural knower of Belenky's fourth category never comes completely to characterize the mature, converted Penington, her entry into the community of saints did allow her to return to a kind of external authority and thus to acquire many of the qualities of the "Connected" procedural knower: "Connected knowing builds on the subjectivist's conviction that the most trustworthy knowledge comes from personal experience rather than pronouncements of authorities" (112-13). Thus there is an advantage in "gaining access to other people's knowledge" (113). The later work of Penington, as she traces her long years as an important member of the Quaker community, offers ample evidence of the collaboration that is at the heart of connected knowing.

Procedural knowers are more "active" listeners (91) who live comfortably with fluid boundaries: "Each individual must stretch her own vision in order to share another's vision. Through mutual stretching and sharing the group achieves a vision richer than any individual could achieve alone" (119). Though early in her life Penington used private meditation, her mature mystical experiences came in her dreams. They are among the more interesting indications of how Penington negotiated shared vision. And tracing these dreams offers a concise overview of Penington's move through the subjective and into the procedural voice.

All three of Penington's dreams are described in very concrete and specific detail and recount vividly her emotional responses. In each she is an active participant who obtains insight into her own and Quaker life and belief. In addition, each reveals an increasing sophistication, paralleling the growth of the sect itself and her shifting ways of knowing. Of her first dream Penington testified,

I saw a book of hieroglyphics of religion, of things to come in the church, or a religious state. I thought I took no delight in them. . . . I turned from them greatly oppressed, and it being evening, went out from the company into the field, sorrowing, and lifting up my eyes to heaven, cried: "Lord, suffer me no more to fall in with any wrong way, but show me the truth." Immediately I thought the sky opened, and a bright light, like a fire, fell upon my hand, which so frightened me that I awoke. (32)

Making herself receptive to the Truth and receiving it in the form of Light foreshadowed the Quaker way of faith while reinforcing her subjectivity. In the second dream she could not find the solution alone but instead needed to discover it with others, although it continued to originate from within. In the dream she was awaiting the second coming, alone and unable to join either those in the crowd who rejoiced or those who lamented, but in her silence she was visited by "the Lamb" and his "bride," who appeared clothed in a fashion that she would come to know as the Quaker habit. After seeing both, she spoke with a man named Thomas Zachary, a Quaker, who suggested that they gather together as "seekers" in a new community, away from the wrongful believers. Immediately after this dream, Penington married her second husband, Isaac Penington: "My love was drawn towards him, because I found he saw the deceit of all nations, and lay as one that refused to be comforted by any appearance of religion, until He came to his temple, 'who is truth and no lie'" (38). In the dream that had preceded their marriage, Penington saw the Lamb and his wife "as a brother and sister" (37), alike in style and form. And in Isaac she found a brother, an equal, to struggle along with rather than against in the formation of a new faith. For the connected knower, "Authority . . . rests not on power or status or certification but on commonality of experience" (Belenky 118).

At the end of the first section of her life-writing, Penington's conversion was complete and her spiritual place secured, but the public experience of that private accomplishment was to include not just support from the community of saints but also societal victimization common among Quakers in the form of lost property and lowered social standing. Connected knowing came at a high price, too. In subsequent writings Penington was more explicitly class conscious, presenting herself as a woman who self-identified with the upper middle class and who thus remained painfully aware of the loss she had experienced to live according to her faith. For example, she feared leaving her home community after she and her husband were legally forced from their house for Quaker activity, partly because it meant leaving her Quaker meeting but also because,

The people in our neighborhood knew of our former affluence, and now pitied us for being so stripped; and did not expect great things of us, suitable to our rank in the world; but wondered how it was that we would still support a degree of decency in our way of living, and were able to pay every one of their own. We contently submitted to mean things, and so remained honorable before them. (55)

Penington's third dream and the spark for continuing her writing seems to have been Penington's creative and internalized way of reconciling the denial required by Quaker life and the tastes to which her class had accustomed her. In the dream, Christ and his bride returned. Penington and a few friends saw a great storm, blackness, which was soon cleared as they waited patiently to receive its meaning. The storm shifted into "one great vent of water" and then "clearness appeared" and then the upper torso of a man bearing "a long, green bough" that was a "signification of good." Amidst their celebration of this experience (characterized by inarticulate utterings, sounds rather than words) two realistic "resplendent" figures appeared. Penington recognized these two as the Lamb and his wife, but greatly changed, more "glorious" (49-51).

Having collectively experienced the loss of personal goods and social standing for the sake of their freedom of religion, Quakers of this period hoped that their great suffering had passed in that one great storm and that peace and prosperity were in their future. Personally, as Penington's subsequent descriptions convey, she felt her losses strongly and spent her time trying to maintain her new lifestyle while not losing her pride or economic security. Her dream offered hope that she might progress from suffering to stability. The imposition of the dream between her conversion and her stories of suffering formally unifies what Penington's personality implies indirectly in her storytelling.

The final cognitive position offered by Belenky, constructed knowledge, seems at first to unify many of Penington's experiences and voices: here, "women view all knowledge as contextual, experience themselves as creators of knowledge, and value both subjective and objective strategies for knowing" (15). A description by one of Belenky's subjects of letting "the inside out and the outside in" might have been used by Penington to describe her experience of the Inner Light (135). In contrasting this synthesizing perspective to the procedural knower's, Belenky observes that "women who are predominantly separate knowers describe looking for the 'pattern' of their selves, whereas connected knowers refer to the lost parts of the self" (136). For the early Quaker, the pattern is at once in the self and within the community. Yet the constructed point of view, more than the others, seems firmly grounded in our twentieth-century secular culture. For although Penington, too, might have felt that "[a]ll knowledge is constructed, and the knower is an intimate part of the known," she continued to believe that though her knowledge came from within, it came simultaneously from her God (137). Truth, as discovered from within, was God's eternal truth—not a relative or provisional truth of the moment.

The paradox of speaking in a voice that is at once dependent and independent is revealed in the fragmented language of Penington's final days. Only then, as she neared death, did she discover that none of her voices or experiences were sufficient to articulate her final fears:

but there remaineth still a deep sense of the passage from time to eternity, how straight, hard, and difficult it is; and even many times to those on whom the second death hath no power, yet subjected to such feelings as were our dear Lord's and Savior's, when in agony he cried out: "My God! my God! why hast thou forsaken me?" (70)

Widowed, near death, imagining herself into a space beyond her knowing, Penington placed her fate into the hands of another and allowed that other voice to speak for her. What she needed to know was beyond her knowing.

In her life-writings, Mary Penington has left us the complex tracings of an early modern woman's construction of self. To listen thoughtfully to the voices in which she articulates that self, it is essential that we remember her position in her world: that she was a woman of the seventeenth century, the historical moment when modernism emerged and patriarchy was thus required to transform its methods for containing women, creating a gap of power and in turn of opportunity for resistance; that she was a Quaker—a sect that loosened the radical potential of individual integrity and action inherent in protestantism, at least for a brief moment, and an ideology that brought individuals together in consensus; and that she was upper class—enabled by her money and social standing to negotiate at least some of the harsher penalties enacted by her culture against rebellious women. In short, if we read Penington through the lenses of feminist, cultural, and new historical analysis, we understand not only Penington but ourselves and our own voices in greater depth and to greater purpose.

Notes

1. Subsequent references to Belenky, Clinchy, Goldberger, and Tarule will use "Belenky" only.

2. Belenky has been criticized by anti-essentialist feminists, as have Carol Gilligan and Nancy Chodorow, authors whose work heavily influenced *Women's Ways of Knowing*. Although a thoughtful and rigorous critique of these writers is extremely important, much of the criticism seems not altogether fair or accurate. Belenky acknowledged the limitations of their study and offered their results as provisional only. In addition, they suggest that their paradigm is meaningful only when historicized and made receptive to, and reflective of, cultural and individual variation (15, 78). For further discussion of anti-essentialism, see the work of Elizabeth Spelman (especially 132-33 and 141-45) and of Margaret Ezell.

3. References to Penington's life-writing are from the Norman Penney edition, the most recent of four extant editions, and one based upon the first com-

plete edition published in 1821 (Blecki 25). The original, "An Account left behind by my dear Mother Mary Penington of her Exercises from her Child-hood, til her Convincement," was in her son John's hand. As both titles suggest, this is not an even, retrospectively shaped piece of autobiography; instead, it consists of various life-writing forms: journal, confession, epistle. Section one is a confession in the Quaker formulaic tradition which traces Penington's youthful trials, marriage, and discovery and acceptance of the Quakers. Her original motive was to preserve her conversion experience for "such as had a love for me" (47). Although there is no date attached, this confession was com-pleted sometime before 1668; that is, shortly after the Restoration. A brief post-script was added by Penington upon rediscovering the earlier manuscript in 1680; at that time she called for a new copy to be made and to be shared with her family and friends. In 1680 she again took up her pen, this time to relate a dream she had had and to convey the consequences of her conversion. From then into 1681 she intermittently kept a journal, to which she attached a long letter she had written to her grandson by her first marriage.

4. See Worden, Clark (especially her conclusion), and Thirsk.

5. For additional historical and theological context, see Trevett and Mack.

6. An especially helpful overview of this perspective is offered by McKeon.

7. The positions include silence, received knowing/listening, subjective knowing, procedural knowing (which breaks into separate knowing and con-nected knowing) and constructed knowing. Though Belenky attempts not to assign hierarchical value to the voices, they do progress from a position of con-striction to positions of increasingly relative freedom in action and thought. For additional insight into the value of Belenky's study for literary analysis of ear-lier texts, see Linda Lang-Peralta's essay in this collection.

8. Belenky set up her paradigm in response to the work of William Perry. The gendered experience of different moral and cognitive positions offered by their collective analyses is fertile ground for further exploration of McKeon's thesis on the development of modern gender codes.

9. Within a generation of their inception, Quakers formalized their practice and contained much of the radically subjective experience of their membership The Morning Meeting, for example, was a censorship board set up to control what was printed under the authorization of the Friends.

Works Cited

Barbour, Hugh. *The Quakers in Puritan England*. New Haven: Yale UP, 1964.

Belenky, Mary Field, et al. *Women's Ways of Knowing*. New York: Basic, 1986.

Blecki, Catherine La Courreye. "Alice Hayes and Mary Penington: Personal Identity within the Tradition of Quaker Spiritual Autobiography." *Quaker History* 65.1 (1976): 19-31.

Chodorow, Nancy. *The Reproduction of Mothering*. Berkeley: U of California P, 1978.

Clark, Alice. *Working Life of Women in the Seventeenth Century*. 1919. Boston: Routledge, 1982.

Crawford, Patricia. "Women's Published Writings 1600-1700." *Women in English Society 1500-1800*. Ed. Mary Prior. New York: Methuen, 1985. 211-82.

Ezell, Margaret. *Writing Women's Literary History*. Baltimore: Johns Hopkins UP, 1993.

Gilligan, Carol. *In a Different Voice*. Cambridge: Harvard UP, 1982.

Haller, William. *The Rise of Puritanism, or, The Way to the New Jerusalem as Set Forth in Pulpit and Press from Thomas Cartwright to John Lilburne and John Milton, 1570-1643*. New York: Columbia UP, 1938.

Hill, Christopher. *The World Turned Upside Down*. New York: Penguin, 1975.

Lerner, L. D. "Puritanism and the Spiritual Autobiography." *The Hibbert Journal* 55 (1957): 373-86.

Mack, Phyllis. *Visionary Women: Ecstatic Prophecy in Seventeenth-Century England*. Berkeley: U of California P, 1992.

McKeon, Michael. "Historicizing Patriarchy: The Emergence of Gender Differences in England, 1660-1769." *Eighteenth-Century Studies* 28.3 (1995): 295-322.

Penington, Mary. *Experiences in the Life of Mary Penington*. Philadelphia: Biddle, 1911.

Spelman, Elizabeth V. *Inessential Woman: Problems of Exclusion in Feminist Thought*. Boston: Hall, 1983.

Thirsk, Joan. Foreword. *Women in English Society 1500-1800*. Ed. Mary Prior. New York: Methuen, 1985. 1-21.

Trevett, Christine. *Women and Quakerism in the 17th Century*. York, England: Ebor, 1991.

Worden, Blair. *Stuart England*. Oxford: Phaidon, 1986.

Wright, Luella M. *The Literary Life of the Early Friends, 1650-1725*. New York: Columbia UP, 1932.

Wrightson, Keith. *English Society 1580-1680*. New Brunswick: Rutgers UP, 1982.

7

Mary White Rowlandson Remembers Captivity: A Mother's Anguish, a Woman's Voice

Parley Ann Boswell

> With troubled heart and trembling hand I write,
> The heavens have changed to sorrow my delight
> —Anne Bradstreet

> And when the baby died, the mother stood over the body, her wrinkled hands moving with animal grace, forming again and again the words: baby, come hug, Baby, come hug, fluent now in the language of grief.
> —Amy Hempel

Mary White Rowlandson's *A Narrative of the Captivity and Restauration of Mrs. Mary Rowlandson,* written sometime after her release from captivity in 1676 and published in 1682, was a bestseller during the seventeenth and eighteenth centuries in both the colonies and in England, and has continued to be a popular text in the United States, most especially with literary and feminist scholars, well into the twentieth century.[1] Because of the profoundly grim circumstances that led her to write this text, and because of the compelling narrative voice with which she told her story, Rowlandson's work has always been studied by American clergy, politicians, historians, and most recently, literary scholars, all of whom have been able to contextualize the *Narrative* to fit their differing needs.

We know that the seventeenth-century audience for whom she wrote this work read the *Narrative* as an indictment of the local native tribes and as a testament to the power of the Puritan faith, and that the text continued to be popular well into the nineteenth century. During the twentieth century, scholars of the Colonial American period have continued to acknowledge the value of her text; indeed, this text has been read as a captivity narrative, a spiritual autobiography, an anthropological study of Native American life, a case study of post-traumatic stress syndrome, an historical account of King Philip's War, and another glimpse into the Puritan mind. Rowlandson, about whose private life we know almost nothing beyond her own words, has been described by turns as a martyr, a propagandist, a saint, a victim, and a survivor.

Mary Rowlandson's text is worthy of all of these readings, and more. In fact, I suggest we add Rowlandson's narrative to another category of literary texts: narratives of the mother. Of all the ways in which her text functions, this aspect—Rowlandson as mother as storyteller— makes her text accessible to us in another valid way, and puts her narrative in context with other writings by American women. Read as a "mother narrative," this life-writing has a depth and complexity that we recognize in slave narratives, poetry, and much fiction written by later American writers. Rowlandson's recounting of her eleven weeks of captivity shares characteristics with Bradstreet's elegies to her grandchildren, Annie Burton's *Memories of Childhood's Slavery Days,* and Toni Morrison's *Beloved.* Like these works, Rowlandson's story is a mother's story, and her voice is a mother's voice.

Quite simply, Rowlandson's narrative represents an elegy to her children. Like so many other women of her century, Rowlandson succeeded in combining the personal sphere with the outside world in subtle yet significant ways: in this, a most public document, Rowlandson suggests a most private expression. She defines herself as a mother to her children, and expresses through her language, her rhetorical strategies, and her silences, her feelings of loss, anger, and grief, and ultimately, her loyalty to her children's captivity stories.

The introductory section of Rowlandson's narrative, in which she describes in graphic detail the massacre in Lancaster, Massachusetts, in 1676 by native Algonquians, allows us to glimpse the importance of family—mothers, fathers, children, babies—to her narrative. Within these six paragraphs, she identifies the victims not by using their formal, given names but by using their familial names: "There were five persons taken into one house; the father and the mother and a sucking child" (54).[2] These are generic family members who are being seized upon; these are "anyfamily." After describing several vivid scenes of violence and bloodshed, she writes a particularly simple, straightforward sentence in which she introduces herself and her children: "Then I took my children (and one of sisters, hers) to go forth and leave the house" (55). With this one sentence, she has introduced three aspects to her readers which will become increasingly important as she continues her story: she has defined herself within her family, she has distinguished herself and her family from the other "everyfamilies" she has mentioned, and she has begun to describe herself proactively.

Rowlandson continues to describe how she and her three children (a teenaged son, Joseph; a ten-year-old daughter, Mary; and a six-year-old daughter, Sarah), leave their burning home amid gunfire: "The Bullets flying thick, one went through my side, and the same (as would seem) through the bowels and hand of my dear child in my arms" (56). Within minutes she and her wounded youngest child become separated from the other two children, and all are taken captive.

Just before Rowlandson begins to narrate the story of her captivity among the Algonquians, she stops her narrative and adds a curious yet fascinating sentence to her opening remarks:

I had before this said that if the Indians should come I should choose rather to be killed by them than taken alive, but when it came to the trial, my mind changed; their glittering weapons so daunted my spirit that I chose rather to go along with those (as I may say) ravenous beasts than that moment to end my days. (57)

Rowlandson is describing a familiar adage to her readers: talking about a hypothetical trauma, and living through a real one, are two very different experiences. She admits that she used to talk about wanting to die at the hands of the enemy; when faced with that limited but real choice, she chooses to live. Why? She tells us that she chooses to live because the weapons of her captors frighten her, yet we also know, from her own descriptions, that the fighting has stopped and she knows she is to be spared. Her reason does not seem to follow from what she has described so far. Why, then, does she tell us she wants to live, and why does she give us an unclear reason?

Rowlandson has already given us enough information about herself to help us understand why she chooses to stay alive, not through overt description but by association. She has mentioned her children, their fates, and their actions more often in these first six paragraphs than she has mentioned any other persons. What remains on her mind by the time she is taken captive is not death but life—specifically the lives and survival of her family. We cannot read this final comment without identifying her decision to go with her captors instead of dying as an act to protect her children, especially the wounded youngest child. If Rowlandson was not daunted by the weapons of her captors, if she wanted to remain alive because her children were also alive, then why does she not tell us outright? Why does she not tell us directly that she chooses life over death for her children's sake? Why does she only suggest as much through her descriptions and emphases on familial relationships? Reading her narrative in the context of other Puritan writing might help us to explore these questions.

Rowlandson writes like other female Puritans of her generation: she uses rhetorical strategies taught to her by her clerical teachers (most probably Increase Mather), who themselves used rhetorical strategies based on Ramean logic and Biblical hierarchies.[3] To Puritan writers, the world is hierarchical and, within that paradigm, all of God's creations are ranked according to their "value"; the order among humans is, in its simplest form, men, women, children. Teresa Toulouse has pointed out that Rowlandson acknowledges this value system by ascribing titles to her captors ("my mistress," "the master," etc.) and by trying to find her own ever-shifting title while she is among the natives (658). Even among "heathens," Rowlandson defines her worth as less than her captors' because, although she is a Christian, she is a *female* Christian. Her worth, no matter in whose company, is ultimately defined by her sex.

Her children's worth, according to the Puritan hierarchical scale, is slightly less than her own.[4] So, when describing why she chooses life over death when faced with the enemy, to an audience of Puritan readers (all of whom would understand the same hierarchical system she does), of course Rowlandson would attribute her need to stay alive to the force of the native warriors around her, not to her commitment to her children. In the world in which she writes her story, she and her children are not so important nor their stories so compelling to Puritan audiences as a story of Christian vs. heathen or men-with-weapons vs. defenseless female. She states a reason for living that her audience would approve. She implies, however, by constant descriptors, that her allegiance is to her children.

This is only the first passage in which Rowlandson's words belie her emphases in the *Narrative*. Like other female writers in colonial New England, including Anne Bradstreet and Phillis Wheatley, Rowlandson employs a pattern of silences, implications, and encoded language in her text, which could, of course, mean different things to different reading audiences.[5] If we understand that she deemphasizes her relationship to her children in order to tailor her text to a Puritan norm, we might also understand that indeed her children are much more important to her narrative than we had thought. Much of what she narrates—a story full of Biblical passages, descriptions of the natives, memories of her trials—she does on behalf of those captives who had less value and less voice than she: her children.

Rowlandson's wounded daughter dies nine days into their captivity: "About two hours in the night my sweet babe like a lamb departed this life" (60). Once again, Rowlandson relates that she did what she had thought she could never do; although she could not "bear to be in the room where any dead person was," she spent the night lying with her "dead babe side by side all the night after" (60-61). She tells us that, once more, she has chosen to live instead of using "wicked and violent means to end my own miserable life" (61). Her reasons for wanting to stay alive at this low point become clear to us in the next paragraph: she wants to bury her child. For the second time in her narrative, she has associated her desire to live with the welfare of her child.

Beginning in the fourth remove and continuing throughout the twenty removes that make up her narrative, Rowlandson regularly mentions her dead child and her two living children: "Heartaching thoughts here I had about my poor children, who were scattered up and down among the wild beasts of the forest" (64); "[M]y spirit was ready to sink with the thoughts of my poor children" (71); "My son was ill . . . my poor girl, I know not where she was nor whether she was sick or well, or dead or alive" (71). Additionally, she reports on quite a number of other mothers and children, both English captives and natives, as she continues to survive among the Algonquians. "Here one [native woman] asked me to make a shirt for her papoose" (75); "Philip's [Rowlandson's native 'master'] maid came in with the child in her arms and asked me to give her a piece of my apron to make a flap for it" (76). She even mentions a "deer with a young one in her" during the fourteenth remove (80).

Rowlandson's accounts of mothers and children who are sick, dying, or dead are so numerous that they become an implicit "road map" for her reader. We can gauge Rowlandson's journey—both the literal and the spiritual—by the signposts she remembers to include. The most significant signposts she includes are not the Biblical passages nor the technicalities of her captivity; they are, quite clearly, her memories of the mothers and children she has encountered. She has led her readers on her journey most carefully by forcing us to pay attention to those details she thinks are most important. In this sense, she is an adept guide, one who masters the "wilderness" of her captivity narrative by using silent signals and linguistic codes to help her readers understand her most significant journey as that of an anguished mother.

The pattern of silence/implication/encoded language that Rowlandson uses is consistent and pervasive. There are so many stories of "dying babies and their mothers," according to Toulouse, that these stories help readers to understand Rowlandson's "feelings toward a God who ignores her desires" (662). Rowlandson's stories of mothers and their children allow her to express not just anger but a manifestation of her personal anguish as well. All Puritan texts reflect the writers' relationship to God; Rowlandson's use of Biblical quotations and reflections on how she reads God's will are quite traditional aspects of Puritan writing.

What is not traditional—especially in texts generated by male Puritans—is the constant mention of mothers and children in peril. In this sense, Rowlandson's is truly a "mother narrative." On her children's behalf, she identifies—however subtly—the violations against her children that they cannot articulate themselves: they have been devalued and abandoned by their own godly community. Near the end of the narrative, after she has been "redeemed" for twenty pounds, she describes her feelings about her freedom: "We were now in the midst of love, yet not without much and frequent heaviness of heart for our poor children" (95). Her happiness, near the end of the narrative, is always tempered by the memory of her dead daughter: "That which was dead lay heavier upon my spirit than those which were alive and amongst the heathen" (96).

Finally, after describing in painstaking detail the return of her daughter Mary from captivity, she concludes with a pointedly eulogistic passage: "Our family being now gathered together (those of us that were living), the South Church of Boston hired a house for us" (98). Rowlandson cannot forget that she has returned alive, but without the child who was wounded with the same bullet that wounded her. Nor does she want her readers to forget this child, either.

There are, of course, two Mary White Rowlandsons, the one who appears in this narrative and the historical one who wrote of her captivity and restoration two years after being released by the Algonquians. The first one is, in terms of narrative, the agent of her story, and the second is the voice who tells the story. The agent Mary Rowlandson has a story that concludes. She and her two living children all survive captivity and are reunited in the final remove of the *Narrative,* and she ends her story with a poignant, lyrical passage about her relationship to her faith and her God. "Affliction I wanted and affliction I had, full measure (I thought) pressed down and running over" (99).

About the writer of this text we know much less. We do know the external facts of her life after her captivity and publication of the *Narrative.* She was widowed two years after her release, remarried, and lived until 1710.[6] We also know that although she was the daughter of a wealthy colonist and the wife of a powerful minister, she lived modestly during the years after her release. Perhaps most significant to this study, we know that she published no other works beyond the *Narrative.* In the culture of the colonial Puritans, Mary White Rowlandson was considered a "goodwife," not a member of the clergy, nor a writer.

We do not know much about how this goodwife came to write this work, and yet her text is considered one of the most powerful testaments to Puritan faith ever written, and one of the most important historical documentations of English-Native relations during the colonial period. However she came to write and publish it—whether commissioned by an approving Puritan clergy, the colonial militia, or her husband—she must have known that her work was to be a public document.[7] She knew her work was likely to be edited, amended, and augmented by others, especially by the Puritan clergy. Like other female Puritan writers who truly believed in their faith and in the wisdom of their chosen leaders, Rowlandson must have understood that her work would be edited and shaped to conform to the Puritan narrative form, and she consented to it.

Consenting to remember and recount for the public a most private and horrific event as she did, Rowlandson found ways to embed within her text those aspects of her captivity that her Puritan community deemed less important than she did. Like the texts of other Puritan writers who were women, her text reflects how a woman writer dealt with textual compromise. Using the correct form, the appropriate rhetorical strategies, and the Biblical language with which her community was most fluent, she told two stories: the public allegory about the Puritan community's ongoing struggle with evil, and the personal story she kept reminding her readers to remember: her struggle to defend and tell her children's stories.

In his study of Rowlandson's narrative, Mitchell Robert Breitweiser makes the point that, writing only two years after her release, Rowlandson continued to grieve her experience: "[M]ourning is for Rowlandson incomplete at the time she writes, and the writing becomes a part of the work of mourning" (9). Remembering her eleven weeks with the Algonquians forced her to relive the nightmare of captivity, death, loss, and destruction. Writing, however, also allowed her the painful comfort of bringing her children out of relief, of bringing Sarah back to life, of controlling a world she would never control otherwise. Writing publicly, in formal Puritan rhetoric, might have seemed a small price to pay for the chance to tell one's own story.

The Puritans believed that human language, flawed as it was, was the most precious gift with which a wrathful God had left humankind after the Fall. Their respect for language is nowhere more apparent than in Rowlandson's *Narrative,* where she understands that some aspects of her captivity she can explain, and some must be understood not through language but through other means—through silence or subtlety. When we listen to her story, we hear a voice compromised by violence, by conformity, by grief. We also hear in goodwife Mary Rowlandson's voice a woman's story of grace and loss, delivered clearly as an elegy on mothers and their children.

Notes

1. There is a vast and fine body of scholarship on Rowlandson and her *Narrative.* Most useful as general works have been Breitweiser, Slotkin and Folsom, Slotkin's *Regeneration through Violence,* Vaughan and Clark, and Kolodny. I also found Ulrich's *Good Wives: Image and Reality in the Lives of Women in Northern New England* to be helpful. There are a number of recent articles on Rowlandson's work, many of which have contributed to my interest and understanding, most especially Burnham, Davis, Derounian, Downing, Logan, whose article "Mary Rowlandson's Captivity and the 'Place' of the Women Subject" was particularly valuable to me. Teresa Toulouse's "'My Own Credit': Strategies of (E)valuation in Mary Rowlandson's Captivity Narrative" has also been useful.

I dedicate this essay to Mary Kennedy Hutson.

2. All quotations from, and references to, Rowlandson's text are from *The Sovereignty and Goodness of God, Together with the Faithfulness of His Promises Displayed; Being a Narrative of the Captivity and Restoration of Mrs. Mary Rowlandson,* in Katherine M. Rogers, ed., *The Meridian Anthology of Early American Women Writers: From Anne Bradstreet to Louisa May Alcott* (New York: Penguin, 1991).

3. Ramean logic, named for the French logician Petrus Ramus, was, as Daniel Shea has described it, "the approach [to knowledge] of the educated Puritan in the seventeenth century" (96). Ramean logic collapsed the systemized rhetoric of Aristotle into two hierarchical, dialectical categories. A Puritan minister, trained to argue a sermon or treatise according to the rules of Ramean logic, would always move from general to specific in his argument, and always set up a series of opposites. The best readings on Ramean logic, and on its relationship to the Puritan way of knowing, are in Miller, Morgan, Ong, and Shea. See also Bercovitch, *The Puritan Origins of the American Self,* and *The American Jeremiad.*

4. See especially Logan and Greven, *The Protestant Temperament.*

5. See Martin, and Cowell and Stanford, eds., for critical essays and good bibliographies on Bradstreet; for critical essays on Wheatley, see Robinson.

6. See especially Greene, "New Light on Mary Rowlandson."

7. For a good discussion on the circumstances of the publishing history of the *Narrative,* see Derounian, "The Publication, Promotion, and Distribution of Mary Rowlandson's Indian Captivity Narrative in the Seventeenth Century."

Works Cited

Bercovitch, Sacvan. *The American Jeremiad.* Madison: U of Wisconsin P, 1978.

——. *The Puritan Origins of the American Self.* New Haven: Yale UP, 1975.

Breitweiser, Mitchell Robert. *American Puritanism and the Defense of Mourning: Religion, Grief, and Ethnology in Mary White Rowlandson's Captivity Narrative.* Madison: U of Wisconsin P, 1990.

Burnham, Michelle. "The Journey Between: Liminality and Diologism in Mary White Rowlandson's Captivity Narrative." *Early American Literature* 28 (1993): 60-75.

Cowell, Pattie, and Ann Stanford, eds. *Critical Essays on Anne Bradstreet.* Boston: Hall, 1983.

Davis, Margaret H. "Mary White Rowlandson's Self-Fashioning as Puritan Goodwife." *Early American Literature* 27 (1992): 49-60

Derounian, Kathryn Zabelle. "The Publication, Promotion and Distribution of Mary Rowlandson's Indian Captivity Narrative in the Seventeenth Century." *Early American Literature* 23 (1998): 239-61.

——. "Puritan Orthodoxy and the 'Survivor Syndrome' in Mary Rowlandson's Indian Captivity Narrative." *Early American Literature* 22 (1987): 82-93.

Downing, David. "'Streams of Scripture Comfort': Mary Rowlandson's Typological Use of the Bible." *Early American Literature* 15 (1981): 252-59.

Greene, David. "New Light on Mary Rowlandson." *Early American Literature* 20 (1985): 24-38.

Greven, Philip. *The Protestant Temperament: Patterns of Child-Rearing, Religious Experience, and the Self in Early America.* New York: Knopf, 1977.

Kolodny, Annette. *The Land Before Her: Fantasy and Experience of the American Frontiers, 1630-1860.* Chapel Hill, U of North Carolina P, 1984.

Logan, Lisa. "Mary Rowlandson's Captivity and the 'Place' of the Woman Subject." *Early American Literature* 28 (1993): 255-77.

Martin, Wendy. *An American Triptych: Anne Bradstreet, Emily Dickinson, Adrienne Rich.* Chapel Hill: U of North Carolina P, 1974.

Miller, Perry. *The New England Mind: The Seventeenth Century.* Cambridge: Cambridge UP, 1954.

Morgan, John. *Godly Learning: Puritan Attitudes Towards Reason, Learning and Education, 1560-1640.* Cambridge: Cambridge UP, 1986.

Ong, Walter, S. J. *Ramus: Method and the Decay of Dialogue.* Cambridge: Harvard UP, 1958.

Robinson, William H. *Critical Essays on Phillis Wheatley.* Boston: Hall, 1982.

Rogers, Katharine M., ed. *The Meridian Anthology of Early American Women Writers: From Anne Bradstreet to Louisa May Alcott, 1650-1865.* New York: Penguin, 1991.

Shea, Daniel B. *Spiritual Autobiography in Early America.* Madison: U of Wisconsin P, 1988.

Slotkin, Richard. *Regeneration through Violence: The Mythology of the American Frontier.* Middletown: Wesleyan UP, 1975.

Slotkin, Richard, and James K. Folsom, eds. *So Dreadfull a Judgment: Puritan Responses to King Philip's War, 1676-1677.* Middletown: Wesleyan UP, 1978.

Toulouse, Teresa. "'My Own Credit': Strategies of (E)valuation in Mary Rowlandson's Captivity Narrative." *American Literature* 64 (1992): 655-76.

Ulrich, Laurel Thatcher. *Good Wives: Image and Reality in the Lives of Women in Northern New England, 1650-1750.* New York: Oxford UP, 1982.

Vaughan, Alden T., and Edward W. Clark, eds. *Puritans among the Indians: Accounts of Captivity and Redemption, 1642-1836.* Knoxville: U of Tennessee P, 1981.

8

"Uncommon, bad, and dangerous": Personal Narratives of Imprisoned Confederate Women, 1861-1865

Judith Scheffler

Antebellum and Civil War personal narratives by Southern women richly reward literary as well as historical investigation.[1] Particularly intriguing among these autobiographical texts are the diaries and memoirs of three Confederate women prisoners—Rose O'Neal Greenhow, Eugenia Levy Phillips, and Catherine Virginia Baxley. Each of these women recorded her wartime incarceration in a personal narrative in which she constructed a self to suit her own purposes. These autobiographical selves simultaneously violated and affirmed prevailing social standards and female stereotypes. The conflict between the personal narratives of these imprisoned women and contemporary accounts of their stories reveals an intriguing puzzle about who each woman really was and contributes to discussion about the nature of women's autobiographical writing.

Sidonie Smith tells us that women's autobiography is subversive, and that the writer "rearranges the dominant discourse and the dominant ideology of gender, seizing the language and its power to turn cultural fictions into her very own story" (*Poetics* 175). "From [women's stories] erupt, however suppressed they might be, rebellion, confusion, ambivalence, the uncertainties of desire" (*Poetics* 176). Taking this assertion one step further, Margo Culley specifically examines the diary as literature, rejecting Robert Fothergill's statement that "the need to project an ego-image does not appear to be a leading motive in diaries written by women" (87). On the contrary, she claims that "women's diaries will be rich territory for study of the female construction of self and its literary representation" (17-18). An examination of personal narratives by Confederate women prisoners tests these theories, for in their works these three women construct selves that both subvert and uphold the image of the proper Southern lady.

Catherine Virginia Baxley (c.1810-?), of Baltimore, was imprisoned twice in Washington's Old Capitol Prison, where she was known as "the most defiant and outrageous of all the female prisoners" (Doster 84). Arrested first in December 1861 for "carrying information to Richmond" (*War of the Rebellion* [*WTR*], ser. 2. vol. 2: 271), she was said to have been conveying a commission as surgeon to her lover, Dr. Septimus Brown. Released in June 1862 on condition that she would not return North during the hostilities, she broke her promise and was again imprisoned in Washington in 1865. During this second imprisonment, lasting five months (Feb. 4-July 2, 1865), she kept a personal diary, clearly written with no thought of publication or outside readers. It is a raw, painful work, doubtless undertaken to pass the time and to help maintain the writer's stability under stress. Entries were recorded in a convoluted sequence within an interleaved copy[2] of Tennyson's recently published *Enoch Arden*, a gift from a Union officer. The poem's Victorian elegiac sentiment and nostalgia provide an unintended gloss on Baxley's entries, which record the death from typhoid (Lomax 147) of her wounded seventeen-year-old son, who, by coincidence, was imprisoned only a few yards away from his mother. Alternately mourning and moaning, Baxley gives full vent to her intense feelings of abandonment and her overwhelming physical discomfort in Washington's summer heat:

About 5 or half past five O'clock April 5—This confinement is very tedious very *very* irksome—I have exhausted every thing which could afford a few moments relief to the mind counted over and over again the small diamond shape lozenges in the India carpet the pains [*sic*] of glass in the window—one of the panes has been struck by a stone and rays strike out from the Centre like a halo I have counted the bars in the window blinds, two up and down down and up again There is an intolerable smell of whiskey in this room which annoys me exceedingly and at last I have discovered the cause my lamp. Some new fangled Yankee oil I suppose. The guards watch my every movement but are polite and even kind—for an hour I have been watching the movements of two spiders a large and small one they have finished weaving their web or *Snare* and are trying to trap or coax the unwary flies to enter three or four have been caught but some are wiser more politic not to be trapped I moralized as I watched and will profit in the future.

June 23rd. And still a prisoner is there none to help me I grow so weak my room is so close, so small the very walls seem pressing upon me—but—one window no ventilation over the door and no fireplace—the door fast I stifle Oh God have mercy upon me how I suffer how I have been goaded to almost insane acts what obliquy [sic] what infamous lies uttered against me.[3]

A very different woman, with a very different wartime prison experience, was Eugenia Levy Phillips (1819-1902), Washington socialite, mother of nine children, and wife of one-time Alabama senator Philip Phillips, a highly respected attorney in the capital. "How can a motherly soul with nine children be suspected of mischief?" wrote Mary Chesnut about this woman, whom she described as a "beautiful and clever Jewess" (176; 411). Nevertheless, Phillips was imprisoned twice: first in 1861 in Washington, for aiding the Confederate cause, and the next year on Ship Island, Mississippi, for violating Union General Benjamin Butler's infamous "Woman Order," which condemned Southern ladies who harassed the Union soldiers occupying New Orleans. Although unpublished, her diaries from each imprisonment and her memoirs, entitled "A Southern Woman's Story of Her Imprisonment," were intended to be read.[4] "Reflection," wrote Phillips, "is a thing rather unusual with me" (Aug. 8, 1861); her narratives were, to a degree, solicited by their audiences. "I shall send it home for the amusement of my Husband," she writes of her first diary. "Sent what I had made of my journal to P. as an offering on our wedding anniversary—" (Sept. 7, 1861). From Ship Island she writes, "A bright day for me—letters and papers. In one from My Dear Husband he requests me to keep a journal, which induces me to make another effort, if only to gratify him" (July 25, 1862). Likewise, Phillips composed "A Southern Woman's Story" twenty-seven years after the events, to fulfill a promise to her friends: "The journal I here send you has been an easy task—inasmuch as the scenes had made such an impression upon me, that it helped memory to sustain facts—which under my oath must claim for you all the reliability I assert" (Oct. 1889).

But other, more self-generated motives induced Phillips to write her narratives. Writing provided a diversion from the deadly monotony of imprisonment. Moreover, Phillips desired to justify herself and record her side of her story, for Butler had denounced her as an "uncommon, bad, and dangerous woman" (*WTR*, ser. 1. vol. 15: 510-11). Thus, her Ship Island diary is labeled "A Record of Inhumanity," and Phillips concludes "A Southern Woman's Story" with this forthright statement: "In many histories of the war, I have been shamefully spoken of. Been called a 'spy,' and imprisoned for it. Of course this is History—but I live in the hope of a truthful statement of facts, and in your little circle, doubtless you will all place the trust I here solicit."

Rose O'Neal Greenhow (c.1815-1864), the best known of these three imprisoned Confederate women, was also the most daring in her espionage for the South and the most relentless in her animosity toward the North. The widowed Greenhow, a socially and politically powerful Washington hostess, continued to send messages in cipher to the South, even while confined in the Old Capitol Prison with her eight-year-old daughter. Her prison journal, no longer extant, formed the basis for *My Imprisonment and the First Year of Abolition Rule at Washington* (1863), published in England, where it drew considerable interest during the war. These memoirs functioned openly as propaganda for a failing Southern cause, while simultaneously relating details of Greenhow's personal ordeal. Her primary purpose in writing was to secure English and French support for her beloved South:

> At all events, I have endeavoured in this sketch of my captivity to discharge a great duty. That duty was to contribute what I myself have seen and known of the history of the time. If the exposure therein made of the Yankee character, in the first year of its luxuriant and rampant development (after long compression in a condition of inferiority), shall add to the feeling of execration for such a race of people, and deepen the universal gratitude at the happy change which has severed us from them, and made it still more and more impossible that we can ever submit to any kind of political association with them again, then my poor narrative will not have been written in vain. (9-10)

In her work, the author's devotion to the Confederacy is equalled only by her pride in herself as a woman who had affected the course of the war by providing information leading to the Confederate victory at Bull Run. Condemned in Union accounts for her "almost superhuman power" and "almost irresistible seductive powers" (*WTR,* ser. 2. vol. 2: 567), Greenhow attempts to vindicate herself as a decent, civilized woman serving a just cause. She readily admits that her narrative violates confidences and destroys reputations of esteemed Northern officials whom she had once entertained at her table: "Instead of friends, I see in those statesmen of Washington only mortal enemies" (4). Likewise, she argues, her style may be criticized as "more bitterly vituperative and sarcastic, than in ordinary times, and upon ordinary subjects, would be becoming in the personal narrative of a woman" (7). Her explicit account of her ordeal, she is sure, will justify her actions to civilized readers.

Baxley, Phillips, and Greenhow were imprisoned because they presented a perceived danger to Union operations, but analysis of contemporary sources suggests that they were judged personally, as women, and not strictly on the basis of their political actions and statements. The nineteenth-century "cult of true womanhood" described the desired conduct of American women, with its credo of four "cardinal virtues—piety, purity, submissiveness, and domesticity" (Welter, "Cult" 152).[5] Anti-intellectualism (Welter, "Anti" 71) condemned a woman who strayed beyond her culturally ordained province of the heart to meddle in business and government matters. A vociferous, politically active woman obviously transgressed every one of these expectations. What was to be done about her?

The audacity of these three Confederate women made them easy targets for Northern critics. Their blatantly Secessionist views certainly gave offense, but more outrageous to the public, judging from newspaper accounts, was their brazen disregard of cultural standards of feminine decency. Following the arrests of prominent Washington women in 1861, the *Philadelphia Press* speculated:

When we consider what a scandalous mission that of secession is, we may well feel surprised to see it approved by "dear woman." What its attractions are to them, I am not magician enough to devise. . . . Is it offending the sanctities to write of these things? . . . When their husbands, and fathers, and brothers run off to enlist in the traitors' army, they leave behind these tender partners of their former homes; and if these latter become agents of discord and mediums of treachery, the law must take its course. ("Female Spies")

Similarly, a Washington journalist noted his "sad" emotions upon entering Greenhow's home, which had been converted into a temporary prison to house female political prisoners before their removal to the Old Capitol Prison:

That woman should, in the hour of our struggle, desert us, and side with our enemies, was more than we expected. And when the first traitoress was arrested in this city and confined in the Sixteenth Street Prison [Greenhow's home], we not only pitied, but in the longings of our hearts forgave her the offence that she had committed. ("Female Traitors")

Northern women, too, actively aided their cause and became involved in "unfeminine" escapades and espionage.[6] A comparison with loyal Northern females, however, made the treason of Confederate women all the more reprehensible:

While our Northern women have shown their devotion to the cause of their country by every description of feminine heroism, the fair ones of Secessia have signalized themselves by reckless disregard of the holiest instincts of their sex, characteristic of the criminality of the cause they serve. ("A Company of Fair Rebels")

The rhetoric of such passages clearly reveals the sexist grounds upon which these women were condemned. Like a beloved child gone astray, the Secessionist woman prisoner inspired a mixture of frustration, anger, and deep disappointment, for her actions threatened the very foundation of society. Perhaps her behavior was particularly threatening because it involved independent thought, considered unnatural in intuitive woman.[7] Her actions were scandalous, but she was an object of fascination nonetheless. Greenhow sarcastically describes the crass curiosity generated by her celebrated incarceration. One group of women "visitors" helped themselves to her child's cake and then launched into a verbal attack on Greenhow.

The superintendant told me that numbers daily came to the prison who would gladly give him ten dollars a-piece to be allowed to pass my open door, so as to obtain a view of the "indomitable rebel," as I was sometimes called in their papers. (230)

"This," dryly comments Greenhow, "was being 'damned to immortality'" (230).

Southern views of women, however, were more complex and ambivalent. The South exceeded Northern society in extolling feminine virtues; indeed, Woman symbolized the chivalric ideal at the heart of the Southern culture the rebellion swore to protect and preserve. Catherine Clinton lists the ideals exemplified by a proper plantation mistress in a patriarchal system: chastity, piety—particularly maternal piety, and absence of temper (90-96). In particular, women were expected to acquiesce to demands made by men and to refrain from complaints (Clinton 97; Wyatt-Brown 92). Recent studies of diaries of antebellum women, however, reveal the essential contradiction at the heart of Southern society: "the Southern lady's velvet glove," writes Suzy Clarkson Holstein, "covers a fist of steel" (115). Plantation mistresses took considerable responsibility for managing their estates, yet they joined in perpetrating the myth of helplessness that defined them (Scott 21; Gwinn 4-5).[8] In reality women were the backbone of a society that was losing increasing numbers of men to war.

Socially advantaged women like Mary Chesnut may have harbored genuine reservations about women's position in society, but their protests were "undercurrents of discontent" (Holstein 114; 121), expressed in diaries and letters, rather than openly raised during the war as subjects for debate (Jones 24). Baxley, Greenhow, and Phillips, unlike Chesnut, did not criticize women's socially ordained role in their public comments *or* in their private writings. Their assertive and daring *actions*, however, conflicted with the accepted female model. Greenhow's biographer, Ishbel Ross, cites Confederate news articles that praised her heroic actions and power "as representative of the feelings of every true Southern lady" (235). The response of her compatriots was not always so positive, however. Those dedicated to traditional roles made indirect, catty comments on the unorthodox, albeit patriotic, actions of Greenhow and Phillips. Chesnut describes the criticism of socially prominent Southern women:

Our party of matrons had their shot at those saints and martyrs and patriots, the imprisoned Greenhow and Phillips. . . . Mrs. Lee punned upon the odd expression "Ladies of their age being confined." These old Washington habituees say Mrs. Greenhow had herself confined and persecuted, that we might trust her the more. She sees we distrust her after all. (Chesnut, Aug. 29, 1861: 171-72)

The narratives of Baxley, Phillips, and Greenhow respond to these criticisms by constructing personae that both contradict and affirm cultural stereotypes and expectations. Each uses recurring themes that reinforce her narrative persona and that structure her text. These are "metaphors of self," to use Culley's term for the "accumulation of selected detail, particularly in the repetitions, preoccupations, even obsessions of the diarist" (18).[9] All three women were mothers whose writings indirectly challenge critics by stressing their loyalty to the Confederacy and dedication to maternal duty as basic values underscoring their decency. Each professes fundamental principles of courtesy and civility; their writings, moreover, implicitly affirm appropriate behaviors for men and women as dictated by Southern culture and definitions of good breeding. Beyond this common foundation, each woman creates a text that constructs the self that suits her individual purposes.

Readers may ask whether Phillips and Greenhow, at least, consciously shaped their works to reflect the images they wanted to project to readers, reconciling their unconventional actions with the prevailing code of conduct for Southern ladies. They presented themselves as exceptions to cultural standards, but excusable because of their intense patriotism. In doing so, they avoided addressing directly the criticisms against themselves, instead justifying their "unfeminine" conduct indirectly by showing their adherence to unquestionable values of motherhood, country, and good breeding. Accounts by their contemporaries often complicate the picture by contradicting the self-presentations of Phillips, Greenhow, and even Baxley, leading the reader to question which story to believe. Applying Sidonie Smith's theory that nineteenth-century female autobiographers could function as "agents of contestation" ("Resisting" 84) helps to resolve this question. She explains, "At any historical moment, women are influenced by heterogeneous, contradictory forces of culture rather than only those discourses and practices specifically defining their selfhood and life scripts. And even the latter discourses and practices are riddled with contradiction" ("Resisting" 104, n14).

Baxley presents an intriguing example of apparent contradiction. She had been imprisoned less than one week when she wrote to Secretary of State Seward to request her release on the grounds that she was a silly, innocent woman, incapable of dangerous espionage: "I carried with me nothing in the world but a few friendly letters packed it is true in my bonnet. I was not trusted with state papers. I am not fitted to be, being very nervous, impulsive and frank; in other words I never calculate. . . . Liberate me, for God's sake . . . I shall die here. Reason is even now tottering" (Jan. 3; 5, 1862; *WTR,* ser. 2. vol. 2, 1316-18). Some external accounts seem to confirm this self assessment. One journalist in Washington noted, "She is, as she represents herself, a very 'explosive' woman" ("Female Traitors" 21).

Baxley's diary, written from the Old Capitol Prison during her second imprisonment, seems to have served as the private audience to which she expressed her feelings. Its distressed tone and images of hopelessness, entrapment, and abandonment suggest that the writer was fragile and emotionally volatile. Her situation had become extremely stressful, for she was coping with the shock of her wounded son's imprisonment and death. The structure of Baxley's diary is a byzantine web of random associations, focused upon her mood and her mind's wanderings. She seems guileless and unconcerned about her public image. The ability to release her pain in writing had become her solace and support:

June 24th And so terribly warm this room is filled with insects and bugs of every description. I am so weary so tired this dull weary monotony is terrible my head is so giddy from weakness I can scarcely stand I have no appetite nor desire for food how true it is that mans [*sic*] inhumanity to man makes countless thousands mourn.

Who was Catherine Virginia Baxley? Descriptions of Baxley, including her own, are almost always pejorative in tone and content. Her letters requesting release from her first imprisonment and her diary written during her second imprisonment describe an imprudent but well-intentioned and politically naive woman. While her diary expresses a consistent and even forceful contempt for the North, it gives no hint that she engaged in overtly aggressive actions. War records, however, label Baxley "the strongest kind of secessionist," having bragged of sending 200 guns South (*WTR,* ser. 2. vol. 2: 1315). Her letter written from prison to her alleged lover, Dr. Brown, likewise provides evidence of a strong side to this woman. Encouraging him to risk an escape from his own prison, she writes, "They ascribe to me a marvelous power and capacity of mischief. I'll be even with them yet. . . . Whilst my condition is pitiable in the extreme I almost wish that death would come to my relief, but these devils shall not have the pleasure to know how much I feel. I tax every power and nerve to bear up, but 'tis indeed a terrible tax" (March 14, 1862; *WTR,* ser. 2. vol. 2: 1320). The intensity that characterizes her diary also marks this letter, but without the diary's frequent use of hyperbole. Perhaps she used the diary to release feelings pent up by the "terrible tax"; outside sources suggest that, for whatever reasons, Baxley presented a different public face, even among her compatriots.

Greenhow herself held Baxley in contempt, despite their shared political sympathies; in her estimation, Baxley had overstepped all limits of acceptable female conduct. Although her loyalty to the South was unshakable, Greenhow's code of good breeding and appropriate conduct was perhaps even more basic to her value system. "Unladylike" daring in defense of the cause was to be applauded, but was also to be carefully distinguished from "unladylike" *manners*; propriety had to be maintained at all costs. Greenhow stated that she considered Baxley "*non compos mentis*" (*My Imprisonment* 169). Her ravings "from early morn till late at night, in language more vehement than delicate," made Greenhow fear for her young daughter's ears (169-70). An incident recounted by Greenhow in her prison memoirs sheds light upon the tension between these two women, and serves to enrich our understanding of each:

The guards were at this time often extremely insolent, and questioned the slightest rule of privilege, so that it was necessary to make constant appeals to the officer on duty. One day, on going down, the guard very rudely placed his musket before me, and said, "You shall not go down that way," and ordered me to go by a dirty back stair, which was not the usual route. I immediately sent for the officer of the guard, Lieutenant Miller, who passed me down. Some time after the woman Baxley, and the one *calling herself Mrs. Morris,* or *Mason,* attempted to go down, and were also stopped by the guard, with whom they entered into an angry contest, and resolved in defiance to force their way through them. Morris was pushed into a corner, and held there by a bayonet crossed before her, whilst the more daring of the two, Baxley, seized on the musket that obstructed her passage, and attempted to pass under it. The guard cursed her. She struck him in the face, which caused his nose to bleed, and he knocked her down and kicked her. Attracted by the commotion, I went up, under escort of Lieutenant Miller, when this statement was given to me and to the officer by the women, amidst sobs and cries—the guard, also, who witnessed it, giving substantially the same account. Thus it will be seen that I must have suffered much from this humiliating association. Captain Higgins came up to speak with me on the subject, greatly mortified at the occurrence, and said that he would punish the guard if he could have any justification in doing so. I told him that I thought it was a case which he could not take cognisance of, as he could only regard it as a fight between a prisoner and a guard, in which the prisoner was the aggressor. (291-92)

Virginia Lomax, imprisoned with Baxley during her second incarceration, offers the most fascinating of all portraits in its contrast with the Baxley of diary entries.[10] She notes that Baxley "said and did pretty much what she pleased. She was very witty, and quick at repartee. Nothing seemed to damp her spirits, and to fear she was a stranger" (142). In Lomax's narrative, Baxley figures as a prominent prisoner, constantly vexing the administration with her sarcastic pranks and flagrant violation of rules. Lomax claims that Baxley's complaints about her son's treatment caused officials to restrict her visits to him in the prison hospital.[11] Despite the diary's painful passages written upon the death of Baxley's son, Lomax claims that Baxley "seemed to recover in a few days her usual spirits, but every night, before retiring, she would fold the torn and faded 'jacket of gray,' worn by the youthful soldier, and place it tenderly beneath her head" (147-49). Baxley, it seems, was quite a complex and strong woman, whose diary self contrasted in a vivid and fascinating way with the Baxley as perceived by her contemporaries.

Unlike Baxley's diary, Eugenia Phillips's diaries from Washington and Ship Island are far more structured and rational; Phillips envisioned an outside reader from the start, and this may partly account for the effect of a linear progression in her writing. Hers is a more balanced persona than that of either Greenhow or Baxley; she appears to the reader as a likeable, fun-loving woman with considerable courage and self-respect. Her self-congratulatory passages are much more moderate than those in Greenhow's political tract, as were her actions in support of the Confederacy. Writing for an audience of friends and family, the diarist balances self-praise with liberal references to her thankfulness for Divine assistance and even frank recognition that individual Union officers and soldiers have treated her kindly.

Phillips's recurring theme is outraged innocence and irreverent opposition to an odious authority that persecutes her "for political opinions" (Aug. 28, 1861). Her first imprisonment, with her two daughters and sister, was in Washington in the Greenhow house. The Washington narrative is filled with references to her "harmless" antics rather than with complaints: "A saucy disposition seizes me" (Aug. 28, 1861); "Today, being somewhat in the diabolical vein" (no date, 1861); "To night we mutinied against authority. Tired of our rooms, we seated ourselves at the head of the stairway" (Sept. 12, 1861). An entry after long silence begins, "Great despondency and illness have marked the interval since I last wrote in my journal," yet it concludes with her defiant, "But I determined to live to plague mankind a little more and in the hope of seeing a few of these 'detectives' hung" (Sept. 5, 1861). At Ship Island, however, the tenor of the narrative changes, for here she encountered physical and emotional hardships that challenged her mind's "natural tone" (July 7, 1862).

Although she, too, transgressed the rules of conduct for a proper Southern lady, circumstances led Phillips to become the epitome of outraged Southern womanhood, the very symbol of the Union desecration of Southern culture. New Orleans women deplored Butler's occupation of their city and openly insulted Union soldiers. Order No. 28 (May 15, 1862) of "Beast Butler," giving his men license to treat any offending woman in New Orleans as "a woman of the town plying her avocation," made him the most hated of all Yankees, caused Jefferson Davis to order his immediate execution by any Confederate who could capture him, and led to his denunciation in the British Parliament (*WTR,* ser. 1. vol. 15: 426, 906).[12] Phillips violated the order when she allegedly laughed at the funeral procession of a Yankee officer as it passed beneath her balcony. She was banished by Butler to Ship Island "until further orders," to be fed on soldier's rations and denied communication with anyone but one female servant (*WTR,* ser. 1. vol. 15: 510-11).

The persona of her diary written from barren Ship Island is that of a proud woman whose civilized standards of conduct are sorely tested. To fellow Confederates she was a victim, but to her Union jailers she was a "dreadful Secessionist," and she writes of her initial fear that the label of "bad woman" would jeopardize her safety with the soldiers. Phillips took pains, she claims, to destroy that negative reputation during her imprisonment. The rule against communication served to her advantage, "for with my experience among these Yankee officers, I should hardly be able to behave with that propriety which alone makes a woman superior to such wretches" (July 24, 1862). In her diary she records her suffering in a frank, rational manner, starkly contrasting with that of Baxley. She consciously filled letters home "with gay nonsense and forgetfulness of my surroundings" (July 24, 1862). Like many who write during imprisonment, Phillips used her diary to provide mental exercise and defeat despair, even launching upon a satiric description of the "costumes of the Isle" to stimulate her diary's "muse." Throughout her writing, references to her sufferings are always in the past tense, written when she had regained control of the situation and could look back from a position of relative strength. Phillips no doubt took care about the image her diary was projecting to family, whose concern for her during her imprisonment was great, just as she took care about the image "A Southern Woman's Story" projected to friends, whose good opinion she endeavored to maintain, even years after the war had ended.

With Phillips, as with Baxley, outside evidence at times contradicts the writer's own account of her experience. The picture is less complex than with Baxley, however, since Southern accounts consistently defend and sympathize with Phillips. But Northern accounts differ dramatically from her own, even allowing for the distortions and prejudices of partisan writers. Butler, of course, considered her one of New Orleans's "she-adders, more venomous than he-adders" (Butler 421), but so much infamy surrounds Butler's own name that he can hardly be considered an objective witness. *The New York Times,* however, directly contradicts Phillips's account of her behavior during her Washington imprisonment. With her two daughters and her sister, a proud Phillips began her confinement: "We immediately prepared with courageous heart inspired with the thought that we were suffering in a noble cause, and determined so to bear ourselves, as not to shame our southern countrywomen" (Aug. 28, 1861). A week later she notes, "We certainly are four very amicable and patient women" (Sept. 8, 1861). Front page newspaper articles report a different story, criticizing Phillips for her alleged complaints about ill treatment:

During their stay in prison, the Phillips' continued to utter the most violent secession sentiments, and to express their antipathy to the Government. (Sept. 25, 1861)

. . . whatever may have been their station in life, the conduct of Mrs. Phillips, her daughters and her sister, was such as would indicate women of depraved character. Their language was violent, profane, and sometimes even obscene. . . . (Sept. 28, 1861)

The reports condemn her on grounds that she violated standards of appropriate female behavior, which, she claims, she took the greatest pains to observe.

The narratives of Baxley and Phillips illustrate the range of responses to the trauma of imprisonment recorded in Confederate women's diaries. How they endured rigorous treatment and severe environmental conditions are recurring themes in the narratives of both. Baxley's diary is especially interesting in this respect, for her theme of incipient madness imposes an ironic order upon the otherwise haphazard text. Unlike Phillips's controlled passages recording her pain in the past tense, Baxley writes from the center of her despair, almost using her diary as a life support to prevent her from drowning in her emotions. Readers cannot know whether personality differences account for the dramatic contrast between these diaries or, on the other hand, whether Phillips's intention to write for an outside audience explains the difference. One of Baxley's keenest laments, after all, is that she is totally abandoned; she cannot envision any support person in her life, much less a reader for her text: "I am sick—weary heart-broken where are you Willie my child had they not—murdered you there would be one to love one to help who would not fail me." The diaries of both women, however, project the immediacy of the prisoners' lived experience and pain.

In Rose Greenhow's *My Imprisonment*, on the other hand, the prison experience has been carefully processed and edited to achieve a desired effect on the reader. Greenhow's approach is blatant celebration of herself in her prison memoirs; she refuses to apologize to anyone for her patriotic actions. Page after page of *My Imprisonment*, which the author claims was based upon her prison journal, disproves Fothergill's assertion that "one does not find in past centuries women diarists who strut and perform and descant on their own singularity" (87).[13] Consider Greenhow's description of events during the evening of her arrest by Union officials:

I knew that the fate of some of the best and bravest belonging to our cause hung upon my own coolness and courage. (54-55)

Had he advanced one step, I should have killed him, as I raised my revolver with that intent; and so steady were my nerves, that I could have balanced a glass of water on my finger without spilling a drop. (61)

She exults in her own remarkable talents in espionage:

I was in Washington, as the Indian savage in the trackless forest, with an enemy behind every bush. My perceptive faculties were under a painful tension, and every instinct was quickened to follow the doublings and windings of the ruthless foe who was hunting my race unto death; and, of course, no word or indication was lost upon me. (229)

With characteristic lack of humility, Greenhow makes recurring allusions to her predecessors among famous persecuted women: "The story of the hapless Queen of Scots was most feelingly called to my recollection" (69). "The words of the heroine Corday are applicable here" (123).

"The apartments of the unfortunate Marie Antoinette were not more roughly scrutinised" (168). Greenhow is not introspective; she reserves analysis for political commentary, with an eye toward presenting her views to the reader and promoting her cause.[14] Always on stage, she exemplifies Sidonie Smith's descriptions of women's autobiography as "eccentric and alive," "theatrical" (*Poetics* 176).

Even Greenhow, however, was not above using stereotypes of feminine weakness and delicacy to her advantage.[15] She clearly expected preferential and respectful treatment as a *female* spy, and bitterly denounced Union crudity during her house arrest:

An outrage was now perpetrated, more foul, more galling to me as a woman, than any which had preceded it. A woman of bad repute . . . was brought to my house, and placed in the chamber of my deceased child adjoining mine. For what object I know not, but this woman was allowed unrestricted intercourse with me, the order being given that our meals should be served together. (102-03)

Baxley, Phillips, and Greenhow to some extent all refer to their inherent feminine weakness and to the obligation of any gently bred man, even an enemy jailer, to behave with due respect.

Rose Greenhow's narrative, however, offers a most intriguing contrast between a self-portrait and outside contemporary accounts. Postwar memoirs of Union officials who knew her confirm that Greenhow was "reputed to be the most persuasive woman that was ever known in Washington" (Keyes 330) and "the most adroit of the Confederate emissaries" (Perley 111).

Greenhow's unfeminine arrogance, together with this powerful public image, doubtless fueled the criticism against her. The September 28, 1861 cover of the satirical weekly *Vanity Fair* pictures a soiree in which elegant Southern ladies each wear a ball and chain. Prominently seated in the foreground is Greenhow herself, and beneath is the caption, "Probable effect on the mode, of certain recent arrests in fashionable circles." Provost Marshall of Washington William Doster's memoirs dwell upon this impressive woman: "Her carriage was graceful and dignified, her enunciation too distinct to be natural, and her manners bordering on the theatrical" (79). Even from the safe vantage point of 1915, when he wrote his memoirs, with Greenhow long since dead, Doster clearly is still fascinated with her. He proceeds with his amateur analysis of her career, presenting her as "an intermeddler with politics" whose "object was to be made a Southern martyr" (81-82). He outlines her rise from obscurity to social and political prominence, postulating that, as war approached, Greenhow aspired to acts of heroism in order to compensate for her fading beauty and to secure her social position among a Secessionist aristocracy that "laughed at her pretensions" (81-83). Doster's comments agree with earlier criticisms printed in the *Philadelphia Press*: "[S]he glories in her martyrdom, and will doubtless look forward to being duly commissioned as one of the saints in the rebel calendar" ("Female Spies").

Echoing this Northern sarcasm were Southern skeptics, as seen in Chesnut's allusion to the comments of catty Confederate ladies. Fellow Confederate prisoner Augusta Morris also complained of Greenhow in her correspondence: "In my letter I also spoke of the cabal formed against me by Mrs. Greenhow . . . she is drowned by mean ambition of being known [as the only one] in the good work and jealous of everything that surpasses her in loyalty and courage" (Feb. 24, 1862; *WTR*, ser. 2. vol. 2: 1349). "Greenhow enjoys herself amazingly," is Morris's sardonic comment (Feb. 19, 1862).[16]

Whatever the truth about the extent of Greenhow's self-promotion in her actions or her memoirs, there is no doubt that she intended *My Imprisonment* to serve as propaganda for the South. As such, her book exemplifies Robert Sayre's theory that "American autobiographers have generally connected their own lives to the national life or to national ideas" (146-50) and have tended to tell their personal stories as a discussion of the nation's goals and beliefs. Sayre's statement that Frederick Douglass "used his life as an instrument of persuasion" (166-67) ironically applies to Greenhow as well, though her energies were directed toward a very different cause. Ross states that Greenhow's memoirs sold well in England and "made her a center of discussion in 1863. The literary set took her up. Rose swiftly established herself with Thomas Carlyle" (256). Nevertheless, her book failed to accomplish her goal of securing much needed British support for the Confederacy.

Reviews of *My Imprisonment* reveal that Greenhow could not escape readers' tendency to "care more about the ideologue than the ideology," illustrating Thomas Doherty's theory of American autobiography and politics (107-08). Autobiography, Doherty asserts, is the wrong genre to choose for propaganda. Indeed, Greenhow found that she, rather than her cause or her book, was the subject of many reviews. The prestigious *Examiner* gave quite a favorable review, condemning Federal cruelty and "tyranny," but focusing comments on Greenhow's suffering and noting that ladies who persist in such dangerous actions have "no right to complain" (743). *London Review of Politics, Society, Literature, Art and Science* echoed the verdict that the author "deserved her imprisonment," but concluded with admiration: "Wives and mothers like Mrs. Greenhow must make a nation of heroes" (656-57). However, the new weekly periodical, *Reader: A Review of Literature, Science, and Art*, blasted the book and its author: "It is a very silly book; but, then, ladies in towering passions very seldom speak, and still less write, sensibly; and even the most ardent friends of the North can hardly be afraid of Mrs. Greenhow doing much damage to their cause" (660-61). Reviews were especially personal in Greenhow's case because of her gender and the inevitable public interest in an imprisoned woman's story.

The personal narratives of these three Confederate women prisoners illustrate how women's autobiographical writings, meant to varying degrees for public review, can be a radical force by which a writer constructs her own version of her life and outward events. Their "attempt to reconcile sometimes irreconcilable readings of the self, to sustain and to subvert comfortable fictions" (Smith, *Poetics* 176) constitutes their lasting interest and value to readers, who may learn from them how prevailing cultural expectations affected women's lives, from a woman's point of view. Who, actually were these women? Somewhere at the intersection of their personal accounts and contemporary evidence lies the multifaceted truth of the lives these women led. The pride that inspired and sustained them underscores Phillips's parting comments to the commanding general of Ship Island: "[M]y entire conduct was an effort to show you what a southern woman was capable of under the most atrocious outrage of the war" ("A Southern Woman's Story," 8: 127).

Notes

1. For further discussion of Southern women's personal narratives from the antebellum and Civil War period, see Clinton, Gwinn, Holstein, Jones, Scott.

2. An interleaved copy of a book includes blank leaves inserted between the pages of text. Baxley wrote, often in random sequence, upon these blank pages, as well as in margins of the text.

3. Baxley uses very little punctuation in her diary.

4. For a discussion of the theory that nineteenth-century diaries were intended to be read, see Culley 3-4 and Bunkers.

5. See also Baym 27 on the Cult of Domesticity.

6. Examples are Pauline Cushman, Union spy and scout, and Dr. Mary Edwards Walker, medical volunteer and briefly assistant surgeon in the Union army. She later became noted for her "eccentricity" in promoting dress reform.

7. Smith in "Resisting" 82 discusses the harsh view taken of nineteenth-century women who, in the act of reasoning, violated their irrational nature:

"The woman who would reason like a man becomes 'unwomanly,' a kind of monstrous creature or lusus naturae."

8. Scott 29 comments that a few "urban great ladies," like Mary Chesnut and wives of Congressmen in Washington, led a life of comparative ease. They were exceptions to the rule.

9. Culley refers to Olney's phrase, "metaphors of self," in James Olney, *Metaphors of Self: The Meaning of Autobiography*. Princeton: Princeton UP, 1972.

10. In her book, Lomax uses pseudonyms for all names but Mary Surratt's; Baxley is "Mrs. Johnson."

11. Baxley's place as nurse for her son was taken by Mrs. Mary Surratt, later hung for complicity in Lincoln's assassination. Lomax 148 writes that "he died in Surratt's arms—his mother being allowed to see him just at the last." Lomax gives a very sympathetic account of Surratt's stay in the prison, describing her selfless and voluntary role as nurse to the wounded and sick among the prisoners.

12. For a discussion of Butler's infamy in the South, see Chesnut 378-79, and West 142-43. For Butler's side of the story, see *Butler's Book* 414-21, and Parton 322-45; 438-43.

13. Greenhow's example also opposes Spacks' s assertion 112-13; 118-19; 132 that most public women are reluctant to assert themselves in their autobiographies and discuss their identity apart from a group.

14. Wilson's discussion 438-44 of the myth of the Old South and his reference to Mark Twain's criticism of the South's "inflated speech" (*Life on the Mississippi*) shed light on Greenhow's own inflated rhetoric. See also Wyatt-Brown's discussion 31-32 of Southern traditions of oratory.

15. Jones 14 notes how Southern women exploited their divided image. For a discussion of nineteenth-century attitudes toward women's bodies, see Smith-Rosenberg, "The Female Animal."

16. Morris also suspected that Baxley was a counterspy, placed in prison by the North to extract information from Greenhow. See *The War of the Rebellion*. ser. 2. vol. 2. 1347. It appears that the rivalry among Morris, Baxley, and Greenhow was considerable, and that, political affiliations notwithstanding, they disliked each other quite a bit. There is no documented evidence of their cooperation to advance their cause.

Works Cited

Baym, Nina. *Woman's Fiction: A Guide to Novels by and about Women in America, 1820-1870*. Ithaca: Cornell UP, 1978.

Baxley, Catherine Virginia. Unpublished autograph diary and notebook. 14 Feb. 1865 to 2 July 1865. Rare Books and Manuscripts Division, New York Public Library.

——. Letters to William H. Seward, Secretary of State, and Edwin M. Stanton, Secretary of War, and others, January-April 1862. *The War of the Rebellion: A Compilation of the Official Records of the Union and Confederate Armies.* Ser. 2. Vol. 51.2. Washington, DC: GPO, 1897. 1316-21.

Bunkers, Suzanne L. "Diaries: Public and Private Records of Women's Lives." *Legacy* 7.2 (1990): 17-26.

Butler, Benjamin F. *Butler's Book: Autobiography and Personal Reminiscences of Major-General Benj. F. Butler; a Review of His Legal, Political, and Military Career.* Boston: A. M. Thayer, 1892.

Chesnut, Mary. *Mary Chesnut's Civil War.* Ed. C. Vann Woodward. New Haven: Yale UP, 1981.

Clinton, Catherine. *The Plantation Mistress: Woman's World in the Old South.* New York: Pantheon, 1982.

"A Company of Fair Rebels." *Frank Leslie's Illustrated Newspaper* 9 Aug. 1862: 318.

Culley, Margo, ed. *A Day at a Time: The Diary Literature of American Women from 1764 to the Present.* New York: Feminist P, 1985.

Doherty, Thomas P. "American Autobiography and Ideology." *The American Autobiography: A Collection of Critical Essays.* Ed. Albert E. Stone. Englewood Cliffs: Prentice-Hall, 1981. 95-108.

Doster, William E. *Lincoln and Episodes of the Civil War.* New York: Putnam, 1915.

"Female Spies." *Philadelphia Press.* No date given. *The Rebellion Record. A Diary of American Events.* Ed. Frank Moore. Vol. 2. New York: Putnam, 1862. 32.

"Female Traitors in Washington." No newspaper source given. 15 Jan. 1862. *The Rebellion Record: A Diary of American Events.* Ed. Frank Moore. Vol. 4. New York: Putnam, 1862. 20-22.

Fothergill, Robert A. *Private Chronicles: A Study of English Diaries.* London: Oxford, 1974.

Greenhow, Rose O'Neal. *My Imprisonment and the First Year of Abolition Rule at Washington.* London: Richard Bentley, 1863.

Gwinn, Minrose C. *Black and White Women of the Old South: The Peculiar Sisterhood in American Literature.* Knoxville: U of Tennessee P, 1985.

Holstein, Suzy Clarkson. "'Offering up Her Life': Confederate Women on the Altars of Sacrifice." *Southern Studies* 2.2 (1991): 113-30.

Jones, Anne Goodwyn. *Tomorrow Is Another Day: The Woman Writer in the South, 1859-1936.* Baton Rouge: Louisiana State UP, 1981.

Keyes, E. D. *Fifty Years' Observation of Men and Events, Civil and Military.* New York: Scribner, 1884.

[Lomax, Virginia]. *The Old Capitol Prison and Its Inmates. By a Lady, Who Enjoyed the Hospitalities of the Government for a "Season."* New York: Hale, 1867.

The New York Times 25 Sept. 1861: 1.

The New York Times 28 Sept. 1861: 1.

Parton, James. *General Butler in New Orleans. History of the Administration of the Department of the Gulf in the Year 1862.* 4th ed. New York: Masin Bros., 1864.

Phillips, Eugenia Levy. Phillips-Myers Papers. No. 596. Vol. 2, 3, 5, 6, 8. Southern Historical Collection, U of North Carolina at Chapel Hill.

Poore, Benjamin Perley. *Perley's Reminiscences of Sixty Years in the National Metropolis.* 1886. Vol. 2. New York: AMS Press, 1971.

Rev. of *My Imprisonment*, by Rose Greenhow. *The Examiner* (London) 21 Nov. 1863: 743.

Rev. of *My Imprisonment*, by Rose Greenhow. *London Review of Politics, Society, Literature, Art and Science* 19 Nov. 1863: 656-57.

Rev. of *My Imprisonment*, by Rose Greenhow. *Reader: A Review of Literature, Science and Art* (London) 5 Dec. 1863: 660-61.

Ross, Ishbel. *Rebel Rose: Life of Rose O'Neal Greenhow, Confederate Spy.* New York: Harper & Bros., 1954.

Sayre, Robert. "Autobiography and the Making of America." *Autobiography: Essays Theoretical and Critical.* Ed. James Olney. Princeton: Princeton UP, 1980. 146-68.

Scott, Anne Firor. *The Southern Lady: From Pedestal to Politics 1830-1930.* Chicago: U of Chicago P, 1970.

Smith Sidonie. *A Poetics of Women's Autobiography.* Bloomington: Indiana UP, 1987.

——. "Resisting the Gaze of Embodiment: Women's Autobiography in the Nineteenth Century." *American Women's Autobiography: Fea(s)ts of Memory.* Ed. Margo Culley. U of Wisconsin P, 1992. 75-110.

Smith-Rosenberg, Carroll, and Charles Rosenberg. "The Female Animal: Medical and Biological Views of Woman and Her Role in Nineteenth-Century America." *Journal of American History* 60 (Sept. 1973): 332-56.

Spacks, Patricia Meyer. "Selves in Hiding." *Women's Autobiography: Essays in Criticism.* Ed. Estelle C. Jelinek. Bloomington: Indiana UP, 1980. 112-32.

Vanity Fair 29 Sept. 1861: 145.

The War of the Rebellion. Ser. 1. Vol. 15. Washington: GPO, 1886.

The War of the Rebellion. Ser. 1. Vol. 51. 2. Washington: GPO, 1897.

The War of the Rebellion. Ser. 2. Vol. 2. Washington: GPO, 1897.

Welter, Barbara. "Anti-Intellectualism and the American Woman 1800-1860." *Dimity Convictions: The American Woman in the Nineteenth Century.* Athens: Ohio UP, 1976. 71-82.

——. "The Cult of True Womanhood: 1820-1860." *American Quarterly* 18 (Summer 1966): 151-74.

West, Richard S., Jr. *Lincoln's Scapegoat General: A Life of Benjamin F. Butler, 1818-1893.* Boston: Houghton Mifflin, 1965.

Wilson, Edmund. *Patriotic Gore: Studies in the Literature of the American Civil War.* New York: Oxford, 1962.

Wyatt-Brown, Bertram. *Honor and Violence in the Old South.* New York: Oxford, 1986.

9

I Was Re-Elected President:
Elizabeth Keckley as Quintessential Patriot
in *Behind the Scenes, Or, Thirty Years a Slave*
and Four Years in the White House

Lynn Domina

During the fall of 1862, in response to Washington's influx of slaves assuming their freedom, Elizabeth Keckley with several anonymous others created the Contraband Relief Association, "contraband" being the designation for AWOL slaves who had made their way to Union territory. In her autobiography, *Behind the Scenes, Or, Thirty Years a Slave and Four Years in the White House,* Keckley presents the genesis of this organization as a moment of inspiration: "If the white people can give festivals to raise funds for the relief of suffering soldiers, why should not the well-to-do colored people go to work to do something for the benefit of the suffering blacks?" (113). Her idea is greeted with enthusiasm, in an apparent moment of solidarity, both by powerful whites and by the colored residents of several major cities. Keckley concludes her description of this event with an appeal to the most powerful, the most revered, the most mythic of all: "Mrs. Lincoln made frequent contributions, as also did the President" (115). If the President contributed, her cause must have been both legitimate and unitary, for surely Abraham Lincoln would not have supported an organization whose purpose was divisive. Yet Keckley does not stop quite yet; she adds one further sentence: "In 1863 I was re-elected President of the Association, which office I continue to hold" (115). Writing in 1868, Elizabeth Keckley, a former slave who has become dressmaker to Washington's social elite, has out-Lincolned Lincoln, who had also been reelected but who had been assassinated early in his second term.

This passage, and surrounding statements I will discuss further, reveals Keckley's complicated status in terms of her potential membership in any given community. If we accept Benedict Anderson's implied description of community as "a deep, horizontal comradeship," Keckley

139

seems in this passage to be oddly displaced (7). In a text marketed as a slave narrative (despite the fact that Keckley's "thirty years a slave" occupy only a small section of her narrative), one might hastily assume that she would identify her community as among former slaves. Since, however, Keckley introduces class distinctions among the members of her race, identifying herself if only by association with the "well-to-do colored people" rather than with "suffering blacks," she clearly subverts any notion of undifferentiated unity among former slaves. And although her passing reference here to Mary Todd Lincoln reveals little, other points in the narrative expose the tension between them—despite Keckley's frequent assertion that she writes in part to defend Mary Todd Lincoln against their nation's unjust accusations. Keckley's (and Lincoln's) membership in a community of women is hence no less problematic than is her membership in a community of former slaves.

The Lincoln for whom Keckley demonstrates the greatest comradeship is not Mary Todd but Abraham. Throughout the text, Keckley represents herself as a mimetic example of the dead heroic president. In doing so, she claims her community as the nation and her identity neither as black nor as woman but as American. Paradoxically, such national identity erases its internal differences; in claiming her community as America, Keckley is apparently able to disregard the possibility that she belongs wholly to none of the American subcultures that comprise the nation. Indeed, acknowledging her membership in these particular communities—former slave and woman—could preclude her identity as American, for an American was implicitly if not always explicitly white and male.[1] Since "nation" is frequently assumed to consist of a community of peers "regardless of the actual inequality and exploitation that may prevail," Keckley uses her status as American to elide her lack of membership in other American communities (Anderson 7). In this case, the whole is not greater than the sum of its parts; rather, the whole remains whole only to the extent that it refuses to acknowledge its composition. To retain its power as a "symbolic force," a nation must achieve a perception of itself as an "impossible unity" (Bhabha 1). To the extent that Keckley can plausibly represent herself as an American, she need not—indeed, perhaps, must not—address the conflicted composition of such an identity. The national community, to function efficaciously as an identity, must subsume all others.

Because Keckley published her narrative in 1868, when the concern of the nation was reunification (of white citizens) rather than abolition, she could not reasonably appeal to white readers by stressing either the horrors of slavery or continuing racial inequality. To the mind of Americans still recuperating from the war, slavery had been abolished and was hence neither a problem nor an issue of continuing interest (Foster 60). Keckley, therefore, could not rely exclusively on the genre of slave narrative to create her audience. Her access, however, to the sanctum sanctorum of the Lincoln White House permitted her to individuate her life by—ironically—attaching it to the lives of the slain President and his economically stricken widow. Because Americans continued to mourn Abraham Lincoln and continued to be scandalized by Mary Todd Lincoln's apparently profligate habits, Keckley's audience would read her book in order to see what she had seen rather than to experience what she had experienced.

At times Keckley presents this synoptic possibility by virtue of her access to significant personalities rather than through her direct experience. In the court of autobiography, fortunately, hearsay is seldom stricken from the record. And although Keckley occasionally appears to be an omniscient narrator, she generally reveals the source of her information (and hence establishes her credibility). Yet in his introduction to this volume, James Olney suggests that "memoir" is the appropriate class for Keckley's narrative:

After the first three chapters, the book could best be described as "memoirs"— i.e., the sort of narrative that is grown out of personal experience but that does not focus on the personal element and describes instead external events and figures who occupy some important place in the affairs of the world. (xxxiii)

Although Olney's definition of "memoir" certainly suits Keckley's text, I will continue to use "autobiography" since I am arguing in part that Keckley's relation to the public world establishes her primary textual identity as American and her community as Americans. Lincoln occupies an important place in her world as well as in "the world"; hence to the extent that Keckley's desired self is constituted through her interactions with the nationally powerful and famous, her public role permits her both to evade and to establish revelations of a private self.

Following Lincoln's second inauguration, a "grand levee" is held; all of the invitees are white: "Many colored people were in Washington, and large numbers had desired to attend the levee, but orders were issued not to admit them" (158). Keckley's sentence structure, obviously, evades the question of the origin of those orders, though the story that follows attempts to redeem Lincoln of responsibility. Among the crowd of colored people is Frederick Douglass, until an apparently naive "gentleman, a member of Congress" spots him and asks why he isn't inside shaking Lincoln's hand (158). Douglass responds, "The best reason in the world. Strict orders have been issued not to admit people of color"

(159). This particular congressman intervenes with Lincoln, who issues an invitation to Douglass—but not to the hundreds of other individuals outside; Douglass—by virtue of his eloquence or his fame or his general exceptionalism—is apparently granted the status of honorary white. Although he is invited in because he has spoken *for* black people, slave and free, he is not invited in *as* a black man. But Lincoln is especially gracious to Douglass, and Douglass in subsequently narrating the event is "very proud of the manner in which Mr. Lincoln received him" (160). Neither Douglass nor Keckley overtly critiques the situation, though other slave narrators frequently have expressed dismay at the segregation and injustice they find in the north, especially those who write after the passage of the Fugitive Slave Law.[2] Of course, however, Keckley is not writing as a slave to would-be or could-be abolitionists but as a free American to other free Americans.

In fact, Keckley is much more likely to criticize the assumptions and behavior of recently emancipated blacks, implicitly positioning herself as, if not not-black, then at least as not-recently-freed (Keckley had purchased herself in 1855), and hence complicating any black-white dichotomy. When she speaks for these blacks, she situates herself as mediator rather than as representative:

you [emancipated blacks] were not prepared for the new life that opened before you, and the great masses of the North learned to look upon your helplessness with indifference—learned to speak of you as an idle, dependent race. Reason should have prompted kinder thoughts. Charity is ever kind. (112)

By her choice of pronouns, Keckley reveals her uncomfortable detachment from this crowd, though earlier in the passage she acknowledges their apparent bond: "Poor dusky children of slavery, men and women of my own race—the transition from slavery to freedom was too sudden for you!" (112). Keckley is syntactically both a part of and apart from this class of people, and her vocabulary emphasizes her ambivalence. When she refers to "my own race," the others are "men and women," while earlier in the sentence these same people are "Poor dusky children." Keckley may be in the class of "free blacks," but she is determined not to be perceived as of it. Throughout this section, her narration is tentative as she attempts to offend neither the North nor the South while simultaneously arguing that a translation of "slave" into "free" will not occur simply because a geographic border has been crossed or because a document promises to acquire the status of law. The act requisite to acknowledge borders or laws seems less imaginary than the act of creating a self and subjectivity that are free. Paradoxically, to assume the responsibilities of freedom, slaves must eventually constrain their desire for freedom:

> They came with a great hope in their hearts, and with all their worldly goods on their backs. Fresh from the bonds of slavery, fresh from the benighted regions of the plantation, they came to the Capital looking for liberty, and many of them not knowing it when they found it. Many good friends reached forth kind hands, but the North is not warm and impulsive. (111)

The plantation is not evil, merely benighted; the North is not heartless or even indifferent, merely nondemonstrative; ex-slaves are not lazy or ignorant, merely too hopeful and naive. Keckley, however, is not naive, and hence not among the class white northern citizens have termed "an idle, dependent race" (112). She can use the terminology she does to explain each group to the others because she understands herself to be a member of none; she apologizes for everyone rather than advocate anyone.

At times, however, Keckley's condescension toward other former slaves becomes more overt. In a rare and perhaps even unique statement from a former slave, Keckley declares,

> Thousands of the disappointed, huddled together in camps, fretted and pined like children for the "good old times." . . . they would crowd around me with pitiful stories of distress. Often I heard them declare that they would rather go back to slavery in the South, and be with their old masters, than to enjoy the freedom of the North. (140)

From a former slaveholder, this last statement might seem resentful or embittered; from a former slave, it is shocking, especially as Keckley otherwise herself expresses some longing for the past, as I will discuss. Since Keckley only infrequently presents conversations with other former slaves, this statement must be taken as representative of her views, at least in terms of the relationship she is constructing between her represented self and her imagined audience.

To confirm the idea that these former slaves need enlightenment first and foremost, Keckley describes the misunderstandings of an elderly woman:

> She had never ventured beyond a plantation until coming North. The change was too radical for her, and she could not exactly understand it. She thought, as many others thought, that Mr. and Mrs. Lincoln were the government, and that the President and his wife had nothing to do but to supply the extravagant wants of every one that applied to them. (141)[3]

Such an interpretation on the part of former slaves is understandable, since the law, especially subsequent to the Dred Scott decision, had previously equated itself and government with the slave's master, and since the master had generally been exempt from legal repercussions in his treatment of slaves. The law had previously been literally embodied in the will of the master; it would be only logical to assume that government was analogously embodied in those who governed. Keckley's greatest amusement in this situation, however, emerges not from the woman's inability to abstract "law" from the person of its symbolic representative, but from the woman's expectation that the government should fulfill her modest desires in the way of attire: "Her idea of freedom was two or more old shifts every year" (141-42). Such condescension places this woman in the realm of character and Keckley in the realm of audience; by exploiting tone to distance herself from this woman, Keckley shifts herself in the direction of her own audience—those white readers for whom this passage would serve as entertainment rather than as a call to conscience.

Although Keckley does not interrogate her own response here, she is less able to laugh when ignorance is displayed on the part of a white boy in a situation that might otherwise be analogous. Tad Lincoln is unable to read, insisting that A-P-E spells "monkey" since the word in his book is accompanied by an illustration resembling a monkey. At the time, Keckley says, "I could not longer restrain myself, and burst out laughing," but in the retelling she is much more circumspect (218). Tad Lincoln, being white, is racially unmarked and hence relieved of the responsibility of representing his race with his every act; his illiteracy makes no comment on the potential of other white boys. Tad Lincoln is ascribed a level of individuality that would have been unthinkable for a black companion, a fact Keckley recognizes:

[H]ad Tad been a negro boy, not the son of a President, and so difficult to instruct, he would have been called thick-skulled, and would have been held up as an example of the inferiority of race. . . . If a colored boy appears dull, so does a white boy sometimes; and if a whole race is judged by a single example of apparent dulness [sic], another race should be judged by a similar example. (219-20)

If a colored boy appears dull, his dullness embraces Keckley, who has struggled throughout the text to establish her own individuality, her own ability to enflesh the great American characteristic of self-reliance.

Keckley has demonstrated herself to be particularly self-reliant through her success in purchasing herself in 1855, and in her determination to live separately from her husband after he reveals his pronounced attraction to alcohol. In stark contrast, Mary Todd Lincoln identifies herself entirely according to her relationship with her husband, having confessed that "from her girlhood up [she] had an ambition to become the wife of a President," and she is utterly unable or unwilling to function without the significant attention and good will of others (228). Although Keckley claims to have written this narrative in part to exonerate Mary Todd Lincoln from the disparagement she has suffered in newspaper articles and other sources of innuendo following Abraham's death—when Mary Todd is revealed to owe $70,000 in clothing debts—Keckley is so unsuccessful at eliciting the reader's sympathy that one cannot but notice her ambivalence. In an attempt to settle these debts, Mary Todd offers her gowns and jewels for public sale, a decision that garners her more scorn than income.

A substantial portion of Keckley's narrative consists of an explanation of this decision and the role Keckley had in its execution. To defend herself against potential accusations of impropriety in revealing the details of these events, she asserts, "Had Mrs. Lincoln's acts never become public property, I should not have published to the world the secret chapters of her life" (xv). If, as William Andrews argues in a slightly different context, "the 'lies, secrets, and silences' of women can deliver them into community or alienate them from it," Keckley inverts this process, revealing to the nation the secrets Mary Todd Lincoln has shared with her, delivering herself into the national community from which Mary Todd Lincoln has been alienated (*To Tell* 255). By declaring her information to be not secret, Keckley ironically creates the reader's desire to interpret it as secret; by revealing and hence destroying the secret, Keckley inserts herself into the community of readers who will be privy to this secret, as this same secret has initially created her communal relationship with Mary Todd Lincoln. Simultaneously, in going public with another woman's life, Keckley is able to retain proprietary control over her own private life. If autobiography in being the public revelation of private events undermines any distinction between public and private, Keckley surreptitiously reinforces that distinction, revealing the private decisions of a public figure who then functions to shield Keckley's own private life from the public gaze. Since slaves, in being private property, could not own private property, Keckley would have had no private life until 1855; having converted herself into a free woman, she is determined not to treat her own life as public property, not to invite speculation on the propriety of her own decisions.

Had Mary Todd Lincoln been a national favorite at the time of the President's death, her subsequent security might have been better ensured. She had, however, already acquired a reputation for being somewhat snobbish and even indecent. When Keckley delivers the first dress she makes for her, Mary Todd's reaction is initially petulant, then more conciliatory. By the time she actually enters the levee for which the dress has been made, she becomes actually gracious, to Keckley's surprise: "I had heard so much, in current and malicious report, of her low life, of her ignorance and vulgarity, that I expected to see her embarrassed on this occasion" (89). On her husband's arm, she is able to appear regal, though one wonders if even then her response didn't elicit disapproval—for when her dresses are eventually displayed for public sale, Keckley quotes a newspaper article: "The peculiarity of the dresses is that the most of them are cut low-necked—a taste which some ladies attribute to Mrs. Lincoln's appreciation of her own bust" (305). Keckley cannot apparently protect Mary Todd from the consequences of her own vanity.

Keckley does, however, attempt to protect Mary Todd from her impulsivity. While the two are in New York arranging for the sale of the gowns, Mary Todd travels under the pseudonym of Mrs. Clarke. When the manager of the hotel in which they stay refuses on racial grounds to serve Keckley in the dining room, Mary Todd indignantly prepares to go out to a restaurant, despite the late hour. Keckley urges her to tolerate the hotel's lack of consideration: "You came alone, and the people already suspect that everything is not right. If you go outside of the hotel to-night, they will accept the fact as evidence against you" (283).

Such poor judgment is typical of Mary Todd Lincoln as Keckley presents her in this text. At the time of Lincoln's assassination, Mary Todd has few friends in Washington, and she chooses to grieve alone until her departure, when "the wife of the President was leaving the White House, and there was scarcely a friend to tell her good-bye" (208). Mary Todd frequently claims that Keckley is her closest friend and urges her to accompany the Lincoln family back to Illinois, apparently oblivious to the fact that Keckley has no means of support outside her dressmaking business. Mary Todd's proclamations of friendship for Keckley are apparently not reciprocated, however, as she writes toward the end of her narrative:

Mrs. Lincoln's venture proved so disastrous that she was unable to reward me for my services, and I was compelled to take in sewing to pay for my daily bread. My New York expedition has made me richer in experiences, but poorer in purse. During the entire winter I have worked early and late, and practised the closest economy. Mrs. Lincoln's business demanded much of my time, and it was a constant source of trouble to me. (326)

Presumably, some of Mary Todd's $70,000 debt is owed to Keckley. It is most ironic, of course, that thirteen years after Keckley has purchased her freedom and three years after slavery has been abolished in the United States, she is nevertheless performing significant unpaid labor for the widow of the man who had issued the Emancipation Proclamation.

Mary Todd's view is that the people of the United States owe her financial support, since they also owe "*their* remaining a nation to my husband!" (352). And as Keckley presents him, Abraham Lincoln valued nothing if not empathy and reconciliation—although Mary Todd frequently criticizes the members of his cabinet and commanders of the Union army, Abraham Lincoln speaks highly even of Confederate soldiers. Admiring a portrait of Robert E. Lee, Lincoln tells his son Robert, "I trust that the era of good feeling has returned with the war, and that henceforth we shall live in peace" (138). After the fall of Richmond, Lincoln requests the military band to play "Dixie," celebrating rather than denigrating this symbol of southern culture, though southern listeners might have interpreted the act less positively.

The text Keckley has written mimics this act of Lincoln's, functioning more to mute than to amplify the violence of slavery, a choice perceived as necessary if former slaves were to participate in the American Dream. If former slaves were to believe that a history of progress would continue into the future, they could only also believe that the South would progress morally (Andrews, "Reunion" 12).[4] As Lincoln speaks highly of Lee, Keckley speaks highly of Jefferson Davis: "[H]e always appeared to me as a thoughtful, considerate man in the domestic circle" (69). And for his political views, she extends forgiveness: "[E]ven I, who was once a slave, who have been punished with the cruel lash, who have experienced the heart and soul tortures of a slave's life, can say to Mr. Jefferson Davis, 'Peace! you have suffered! Go in peace'" (74).

In part because she does not devote substantial space to her life as a slave, Keckley does not emphasize the "cruel lash," though she does refer to other episodes of violence. As a four-year-old, Keckley has the responsibility of caring for an infant. When the baby falls out of its crib through Keckley's too-vigorous rocking, she is whipped for the first time, though she devotes only two comparatively neutral sentences to the experience: "The blows were not administered with a light hand, I assure you, and doubtless the severity of the lashing has made me remember the incident so well. This was the first time I was punished in this cruel way, but not the last" (21). She does devote considerably more space to a series of beatings she receives as a young woman; they are administered by a Mr. Bingham, and she is disturbed in part because of the sexual impropriety involved: "Recollect, I was eighteen years of age, was a woman fully developed, and yet this man coolly bade me take down my dress" (33). Keckley fights against these beatings, attaining and displaying a sense of self-determination in the process. The passage ends not only with her victory, but with Bingham's conversion: "[H]e asked my forgiveness, and afterwards was an altered man. He was never known to strike one of his servants from that day forward" (37). Bingham here functions as a synechdochic example of Keckley's hope for the future South.

In contrast to these passages, Keckley devotes significant space to her reunion with her former owners and to her justification for her affection for them. This reunion is apparently one event that prompts her disconcerting prefatory statement: "If I have portrayed the dark side of slavery, I also have painted the bright side" (xi). Her concern for and desire to visit her former owners are also disconcerting to her northern acquaintances, to whom she offers an explanation:

You forget the past is dear to every one, for to the past belongs that golden period, the days of childhood. . . . To surrender it is to surrender the greatest part of my existence. . . . These people are associated with everything that memory holds dear, and so long as memory proves faithful, it is but natural that I should sigh to see them once more. (241-42)

Perhaps the past is dear to Keckley, but to her the future is also dear, and her nation's survival depends significantly on its citizens' ability to decline vengeance. She again attempts to explain the South to the North, and the peculiar feelings of those involved in its peculiar institution: "You do not know the Southern people as well as I do—how warm is the attachment between master and slave" (242). To northern ears, this statement would clearly echo southern paternalistic justifications for slavery, and it could tend to confirm former slaveholders' assumption that affection shared between slaves and slaveholders negated any problematic aspects of slavery (Fox-Genovese 131). As Keckley presents her reunion with her former owners, mutual affection is the predominant emotion. She is told that she is "needed to make the circle complete," and her membership in this circle is paradoxically more authentic than is her membership in the circle of former slaves, northern women, or northerners in general (245-46). Like many former slaveholders, her former owners' attitude toward slavery appears to have shifted dramatically. Throughout this scene, they treat Keckley as a peer, and one visitor insists that since peace has been achieved, all will soon be well: "[T]he change is an evidence of the peaceful feeling of this country; a change, I trust, that augurs brighter days for us all" (254).

Keckley's status as an American depends to some extent on the existence of an America that is one united nation. Her body with its dark skin and her legal status as a manumitted slave cannot be the site at which the nation dissolves. Slavery itself becomes an odd historical event, which in hindsight no one who participated seems to have supported: "By the end of the century, those who wrote of their lives before the war—loyal though they might be to their people and their region—were likely to present themselves as having always opposed slavery" (Fox-Genovese 346). Former slaveholders, then, claimed allegiance to their local community rather than to the economic structure under which it had defined itself. Keckley attributes the persistence of slavery not to the determination or inhumanity of slaveholders but to the law, specifically as it is situated in the Constitution of the United States:

They [slaveholders] were not so much responsible for the curse under which I was born, as the God of nature and the fathers who framed the Constitution for the United States. The law descended to them, and it was but natural that they should recognize it, since it manifestly was their interest to do so. (xii)

That slaveholders would have acted according to their self-interest, she seems to say, is only logical.

Keckley's understanding of the power of the law is reflected in her determination, slave and free, to be obedient to it. Although she does occasionally critique laws regarding slavery, especially as they apply to mulatto children, she declines to oppose civil law to any more cosmic moral law. She obtains her freedom not by simply taking it, by becoming a new woman with a new name in the North, but by purchasing it according to the legal and economic options provided for such occasions. Addressing her master, she says, "By the laws of the land I am your slave—you are my master, and I will only be free by such means as the laws of the country provide" (49). It is the law, apparently, that grants or withholds freedom and a free subjectivity, rather than a free subjectivity that grasps freedom from a legal structure designed to prohibit it. And when she does purchase her freedom, she does not simply assert it in the text but includes the substantiating legal documents.

For Americans live under the authority of the law, and if Keckley is to define herself as an American, she cannot simultaneously present herself as an anarchist or legal relativist. When she realizes that she cannot remain in Washington as a free black without a permit, "such being the law," she does not express outrage but instead relies on the influence of sympathetic friends to see that the fee for such a permit would be suspended (65). As Keckley exhibits herself in this text, she is not merely obedient. Rather, she is the quintessential patriot whose character incorporates significant American virtues. Having purchased her freedom in part through loans provided by white acquaintances, she works first to free herself from this debt: "I went to work in earnest, and in a short time paid every cent that was so kindly advanced by my lady patrons of St. Louis" (63). So she is law-abiding, frugal, and honest—and ironically she attributes her ability to raise herself up to her experience of slavery itself: "Notwithstanding all the wrongs that slavery heaped upon me, I can bless it for one thing—youth's important lesson of self-reliance" (20). Rather than determining that she will become a member of that "idle, dependent race," slavery teaches her diligence and independence (112).

When her former owners ask whether she harbors any resentment regarding their treatment of her, Keckley cites another one-time American value: "I have but one unkind thought, and that is, that you did not give me the advantages of a good education. What I have learned has been the study of after years" (257). Presumably, more formal education would have increased her self-reliance and made her even more suited to the role of responsible businesswoman that she filled.

By establishing the Contraband Relief Association, she determines that freed slaves will become race-reliant and assumes that self-reliance will soon follow. Although her significance as an American in this text might seem to occur primarily through her association with other significant Americans—Abraham and Mary Todd Lincoln, Jefferson and Varina Howell Davis, Stephen Douglas—her significance as a public figure occurs not only through the acts she witnesses but also through the acts she performs. She establishes and raises funds for a national organization; she enlists the aid of interested others; and she finds herself re-elected president. She becomes an interesting national figure not merely because she knew Abraham Lincoln but because she mirrors him. She writes her narrative not simply because she has observed America and can tell about it, but because she demonstrates the character of the nation in the character of herself.

Notes

1. Although I am writing here in past tense, one could easily argue that present tense is equally appropriate. For the term "African American," for example, designates in the United States not national allegiance or membership (or dual citizenship) but race—though outside the United States the term designates both race and national citizenship; a white immigrant to the United States

from an African country is generally not included in the term. To the extent that the United States remains a racist culture wherein access to power occurs through whiteness, the first half of that term, "African," could be said to confound the second half, "American," creating an oxymoron.

2. See Harriet Jacobs (375, 451, 503); Louisa Picquet (41).

3. Harriet Jacobs relates a similar incident regarding a slave woman who believed the President of the United States was himself governed by a queen (376).

4. Frances Smith Foster also addresses the attraction of the American Dream for slaves, though her discussion focuses around antebellum slaves who choose to run away in order to pursue it rather than postbellum slave narrators who urge forgiveness for the South as their only hope.

Works Cited

Anderson, Benedict. *Imagined Communities: Reflections on the Origin and Spread of Nationalism.* New York: Verso, 1991.

Andrews, William L. "Reunion in the Postbellum Slave Narrative: Frederick Douglass and Elizabeth Keckley." *Black American Literature Forum* 23.1 (1989): 5-16.

——. *To Tell a Free Story: The First Century of Afro-American Autobiography, 1760-1865.* Urbana: U of Illinois P, 1986.

Bhabha, Homi K. "Introduction: Narrating the Nation." *Nation and Narration.* Ed. Homi K. Bhabha. New York: Routledge, 1991. 1-7.

Foster, Frances Smith. *Witnessing Slavery: The Development of Ante-Bellum Slave Narratives.* 2nd ed. Madison: U of Wisconsin P, 1994.

Fox-Genovese, Elizabeth. *Within the Plantation Household: Black and White Women of the Old South.* Chapel Hill: U of North Carolina P, 1988.

Jacobs, Harriet. *Incidents in the Life of a Slave Girl. The Classic Slave Narratives.* Ed. Henry Louis Gates, Jr. New York: Mentor, 1987.

Keckley, Elizabeth. *Behind the Scenes. Or, Thirty Years a Slave, and Four Years in the White House.* New York: Oxford UP, 1988.

Olney, James. Introduction. *Behind the Scenes. Or, Thirty Years a Slave and Four Years in the White House.* By Elizabeth Keckley. New York: Oxford UP, 1988. xxvii-xxxvi.

Picquet, Louisa. *Louisa Picquet, the Octoroon: or Inside Views of Southern Domestic Life. Collected Black Women's Narratives.* Ed. Henry Louis Gates. New York: Oxford UP, 1988.

10

Fatal Pie and Drops of Frosting:
Anne Ellis's Acts of Community Building
in *The Life of an Ordinary Woman*

Jennifer S. Brantley

Throughout her life, Anne Ellis faced grinding poverty and hard, financially unrewarding labor. Before she could even "remember much," she had crossed the plains three times from Missouri to Colorado in an ox team (13). She moved from shanty to shanty, among men in search of the quick riches of mining. She lost two husbands and one very dear daughter. Near the end of her life, she grew sick with asthma and during this "enforced leisure," she was encouraged to write about her life, and so began her autobiography, *The Life of an Ordinary Woman*, a story of life in mining camps in Colorado in the late 1800s, published in 1929.

In this narrative, Anne Ellis is able to build multiple communities—with herself as child, herself as writer, and ourselves as readers. Through her matter-of-fact, detailed approach, we become an ideal audience able to lay aside our inconveniences and remembered injustices that become small beside Anne as a starving child or grieving adult. Anne uses her writing in the present moment to overcome her feelings about her past isolation.

According to Elliot West in his foreword to the 1980 edition of *The Life of an Ordinary Woman*, this book is exceptional in many ways, but especially for its point of view. Most books reflecting this time "were written by and for adult men" (ix). Little attention was given by these writers to women and even less to children. Breaking from this male, adult-centered tradition, Anne Ellis writes both about her time as a child and her time as an adult. Through her eyes, we see the daily lives of these remarkable pioneers. Also according to Elliot, the few books that were written by women "have come from the pens of those who arrived in the West well educated and reasonably secure financially" (xi). Anne Ellis writes of different women; of her mother who could neither read nor write but was a source of indomitable strength and goodness; of prostitutes whom she neither condemns nor turns into Miss Kittys of *Gun-*

153

smoke fame; of saloons and town drunks; of dances and fist fights. Anne Ellis looks at this world with a clarity of vision and honesty of voice.

In part, Anne's clarity of vision and her creativity are due to the profound influence of books in her life. She writes, "The greatest influence in my life has been books, good books, bad books, and indifferent ones" (122). As a child, she devoured books. She read the popular writers, such as Bertha Clay and Ella Wheeler Wilcox, but she also read Charles Dickens, Emile Zola, George Sand, and Victor Hugo. Mostly, these books were borrowed. Anne Ellis could escape her isolation through reading, but also in the act of borrowing.

Anne Ellis's self-education contributes to the success of the writing of her own memoirs. Through her writing, she is able to cross the barriers of isolation in her history, creating a sense of community among her readers. In the first half of the book, when she writes of herself as a child, she is able to do this through her powers of observation and through her connections with her distant, always pregnant mother. Her mother becomes for Ellis the definition of pioneer: "Always, when I think of pioneers, I see my mother, a baby on her arm, working, working, ever hopeful, seeing something to laugh at, cooking for the men, feeding the cattle at night, doctoring both the men and cattle" (12).

In the second section of the book, Ellis writes of overcoming the barriers of isolation through her cooking and making of homes. In her history and her shaping of history, she seeks her strengths within her limitations as female, yet she redefines these limitations. As Ellis remembers, "Thus it is, some of the noblest things we do we are ashamed of, and sometimes are proud of such little, piffly things" (13). Ellis gives her own definitions of noble and little. Cooking was for her something noble. At one point, she recalls, "Give me . . . a well-cooked, well-served meal, a bouquet, and a sunset, and I can do more for a man's soul than all the cant ever preached. I can even do it without a sunset!" (xiv). She also claims, "I am never so happy as when I have plenty to cook, and enjoy this being outdoors by the side of the streams, among the trees, and living in the tents" (294).

Ellis did not, however, cook simply to please men, but more to satisfy her artistic sensibilities in a world with few outlets. She later writes that during this time she even thinks she may want to write, "but writing seemed impossible to me then" (247). Thus, her writing of remembrance, an artistic act, becomes a connection to her cooking, her only artistic outlet in the past. With this act of writing, her words and her vivid description of the meals, we, as readers, feel as if she is recooking these meals. The two artistic outlets have merged. She was too busy in surviving her life to record it; now she relives as she remembers.

This desire to record her life, repressed until she becomes sick and has time to write, created in her an imagination ripe with the intricate details of daily living. She speaks so directly to us that as readers and members of her present community, we become part of her past community, a community that at the time often excluded and judged Anne Ellis and her family. At times in the book, Anne Ellis's remembrance of isolation in the midst of this rush for riches in mining towns is painful and cold, but never self-pitying. Both within and without the covers of the book, Anne Ellis builds a sense of community among poor women who usually have no voice at all. In fact, this book is being told by a woman poor even at the time of the writing of the book. She is poor at the beginning of the book, poor at the end of the book, poor while writing the book, and poor at the time of publication. In fact, according to Elliot West in *Growing Up with the Country*, when Anne Ellis was given an honorary master of letters degree by the University of Colorado in 1938, she had to borrow money for the train trip to receive her degree (49).

Poverty adds a depth, a dual perspective, to Anne's writing, as both subject of the narrative and condition of the writer. At one point in her book, she writes, "If it were not for poor people writers would lack a lot of material" (15). At the same time, however, that she builds this sense of community among the "ordinary," poor women, she seems to disregard the possible judgments of her life by the community within the book, challenging her community of readers outside the book, as well. Often, the effects of this are to bind together the reading community, so we can rise above the community of the book. In other words, Anne Ellis often reminds us to look at any possible hints of hypocrisy within ourselves.

One example of her disarming honesty concerns her childhood friendship with Si Dore, a man who lived with "fast" women (prostitutes) and was a drunk. The community voiced many objections to her friendship with him, but Anne "did it anyway—he was generous with his nickels and dimes, and always asked me to eat—good codfish and mackerel, and biscuit over which he folded a very dark white cloth on taking them from the oven" (31). As readers, we may want to dislike Si, to see him as a rough drunk, a woman chaser, but Ellis gives us the positive side of his character. Suddenly, as readers, we feel a part of this remembered community and yet Ellis makes us see him more clearly than if we lived solely within that community: we like Si Dore in spite of ourselves. He is generous; he is careful with his biscuits; he loves his dog; he tells great stories; he makes Anne a sled. Anne Ellis makes us see him more clearly than if we lived among the community of Anne and Si, thus privileging the community of readers. Through Anne Ellis's eyes, we become more careful and considerate observers of humanity.

Another childhood friend we are tempted to prejudge is Picnic Jim. He was a drunkard, a gambler, a haunter of saloons. Anne writes, "Mama was often brought to task by her neighbors for letting us children be with Picnic so much" (33). Picnic would take the children camping and be gone for days. Anne tells of a time when he took them berrying, went into town, proceeded to drink a great deal, and promptly forgot them. The children are left alone in the dark mountain woods and burn a mattress for light. After long into the night, Picnic remembers them and comes yelling through the woods.

As readers, perhaps we are at first tempted to think of Picnic as a horror, a neglecter of children. Anne, once again, refuses to allow us this judgment. Later that night, after Picnic has cooked for them, Anne recalls, "After we ate, Picnic said, 'Annie, before you get in bed, don't you want to go and look at the stars?' I did. (And he was supposed to be, and was a drunken bum!)" (102). Anne, through her attention to detail and her clear-sighted vision, teaches the reader tolerance and understanding, but is never didactic. She makes us see both sides of characters; we feel that we know them and we like them, faults included. We become a community of the past, sharing the stars and the fire with Picnic and Anne. In fact, Ellis's recollection of the past seems so immediate that, as readers, we exist in several layers of time: Anne's past, Anne's present time of writing, our present time of reading, and our recollection of reading. The combinations within these layers are many and varied, creating a community of readers that is timeless and multifaceted.

To further enrich our understanding, she remembers of Picnic, "[B]ut in spite of the fact that he was as bad as painted, and put in lots of his time at the sporting houses, all we ever learned from him was worth while; stories of cities; how to pack a jack, and all the tricks of camping" (33). Suddenly, we, as readers, rise above the remembered community of the book. Through Anne Ellis's vision, we allow Picnic into our world, accepting him with his faults, with his knowledge.

According to Elliot West, bachelors were very important: "More than any specific lessons, these men gave children a sense of being cared about" (*Growing Up* 166). West specifically addresses the issue of community response to these men:

Uncle Pomp, Picnic Jim, Mr. Howell, and Jimmy Anderson were not, as some parents and social critics feared, simply corrupters of the young. More often they gave boys and girls what parents found most difficult to provide—the time for attention, sympathy, and affection—and children often credited them with teaching values that parents professed to promote. In their own way, these adults were among the most determined preservers of childhood and staunchest defenders of traditional upbringing. (166-67)

Anne Ellis has made a remarkable contribution to our understanding of these men who are far more complex, more involved in traditional women's roles than our television westerns would like us to think.

Not only does Anne show great sensitivity to these colorful men, but she also creates rich pictures of colorful women. As a child, Anne's mother does washing to help make ends meet. Anne delivers the wash, and some of the customers are the women of the "fast-house." Anne knows she is not supposed to enter the house, but with typical Ellis curiosity to see all of life, she does:

And this is what I remember: first a strong sweet smell (strong perfume always brings back the fancy-girl smell), several pretty girls with lots of lace on their clothes, which were long loose affairs. One is sitting on the floor in a mess of pillows, two men (we wash for one of them), dressed and seemingly in their right minds, are sitting there laughing. They give me candy and I leave after having a very pleasant time. I tell Mama, and she is so interested in all the details she forgets to whip me, but next time we go, she has me take a bouquet of wild flowers to pay for the candy they gave me. (41)

With clarity and simplicity, Anne Ellis allows the reader to enter a community we may in our own lives reject or ignore. We smell their smell, see their lace, taste their candy. Like Anne, we have a "very pleasant time." And with a deft stroke of paint, we also clearly see Anne's mother. She, too, like the reader, becomes so wrapped up in Anne's story that she does not judge or punish through whipping. Instead, she has Anne take a bouquet to them to repay their generosity. As with the dual function of poverty, here Anne's imagination has a dual function. At the time of the events of the book, she used it with her mother to escape punishment. In her writing, she uses the gift of imagination to recreate her life and to gain her reader's sympathy.

The vision inside the fast house becomes even sweeter and more heavenly when contrasted with the scene at Anne and her family's cabin. The ceiling is covered with canvas that sags and drips. Once her mother sees a mountain rat in the canvas and plunges a fork into it. Anne writes, "I cried, not because I was sorry for the rat, but just at the sordidness of it all" (42). Juxtaposed against the scene at the whorehouse, dirty becomes clean, clean becomes dirty. Anne Ellis creates in her community of readers a sense of relativity, a notion to judge each incident separately. In other words, those fast women, "dirty" women, were good to give candy and a few moments of sweetness to a little girl whose ceiling dripped rat blood.

All of this occurs well before Anne is seven years old. For a child she has seen so much, endured even more. At one point, Ellis writes of a time when she considered suicide:

Once, when things had gone worse than usual, I decided to commit suicide, my plan being to crawl into a big snowdrift, and die there. I thought how sorry they would feel in the spring when the snow went off, and I was found. I hoped I would not look like a cat we had found early one April!—but—Mama had just made two custard pies, the frosting sweating huge drops of gold, and had put them on the cupboard shelf to cool. So I put off the dreadful act till they were eaten, and always since then, there has been something, if not a pie to save me. (37-38)

This passage is pivotal to the connections and acts of community building Anne engages in. As readers, we feel appalled at the untold agonizing poverty and despair that would bring a young girl to such thoughts, strong enough to be remembered in great detail years later. At the same time, however, we want to laugh as she compares herself to a cat she found one spring. As with the childhood friendships with Si Dore, Picnic Jim, and the fast women, we feel both repelled and drawn into Anne's story. Her strength and courage, her ability to find "drops of gold" amid poverty and fear, bring us into her life without sentimentality. For Anne as child, we may feel pity, but in Anne as writer and recorder, we find courage.

The passage concerning suicide also connects strongly with Anne's ways of overcoming barriers in her recalled past, in her present time of writing, and in the immediate present of our reading. Her powers of observation are quite evident here; as readers, we can also taste the sweating custard pies that saved Anne as a child. In this passage, we see the connections to food, which will become for Anne her way to cross boundaries and create community through her adult life. For Anne, food will always be her salvation as she cooks both for survival and for her community and family; the description of the food will later be Anne's salvation as a writer of these events. In the passage, we also see the connections to her mother, distant yet another source of salvation for Anne as a child and Anne as a writer.

In another passage, we see also the triumvirate ways (remembered history, present writing, immediate present of reading) in which Anne crosses boundaries and creates community. Times become tough again in Anne's childhood when she remembers that, despite Mama's being "a fine manager . . . each day our meals are slimmer until things get desperate" (30). Anne, with her acute childhood powers of observation, recalls a butcher shop being broken into and someone stealing all the meat: "A great to-do follows, and Mama wonders who 'had the gall to do it'; and Henry would like to know 'who in blazes did do it.' There is talk of searching each cabin, and Mama points out to us the dreadful punishment which comes to thieves" (30). As a "canny youngster" who "kept it to [her]self," Anne knew that "rolled in a piece of canvas, and pushed far back under the bed, is a quarter of black frozen meat" (30). She also knew that her stepfather, Henry, "didn't have a hand in it; he hadn't the nerve" (30).

Again, salvation and connection to community come through observation, food, and mother. In fact, Si Dore and Picnic Jim have helped her mother steal this meat. And again, Anne presents the reader with a dilemma; do we sit at a distance in our seats of judgment or do we join into her text, her memories, and hold dear the secret of black, frozen meat? As readers, I am convinced we join as a community in her life and writing. Anne, the child, is no longer hungry and alone; she has her mother, Si, Picnic, and us. Anne, the adult, is no longer alone in her memories because she creates and connects through writing.

Anne is probably never more alone than when she first attends school, a place where "[n]ice little girls sat on these steps with their arms around each other, and whispered; I never sat there, or if I did it was alone" (49). School is a place where she is humiliated for her manner of speaking, her manner of dress. She remembers that "no girl ever made a companion of me or put her arms around me, and even now when a woman shows any feeling toward me it embarrasses and thrills me" (50).

Here Anne is also humiliated for what is in other contexts her connection with the world—food. One day a young girl finishes her lunch and leaves a sandwich on her desk. The sandwich is "a luscious-looking one, the red jam showing with little pink streaks where it had soaked in" (50). Anne's powers of observation, her imagination, and her starvation create barriers of isolation in her immediate world; she steals the sandwich and is caught: "I never heard the last of it—of starving and stealing to eat" (50). Anne Ellis, the child, is isolated from her peers, teased, because she dared to starve and steal.

At the same time, however, that Anne, the child, experienced barriers of isolation in her immediate world, the adult creates connections with her outside world, the world of her readers. We despise the little girl with the jam sandwich and identify with the thief—not the first time Anne does this. In fact, we, as readers, become companions to Anne and place our metaphorical arms around her, embracing her exactly for what created barriers, embracing her exactly for what dissolved those barriers—her writing and recording of events.

Anne Ellis presents a parade of life, filled with hard, big-spirited pioneers, described in often poetic, lush ways, giving us, yet again, the compelling paradigms that draw us closer to people we may never know in our own lives. She writes of miners "coming off night shift, primroses in the buttonholes of their jumpers, on their faces yellow pollen mixed with powder smoke, coal dust, and dirt" (62). She and her family were, at times, part of this community yet always somehow separate from it, too independent to fit in.

This community, this parade of life, includes people like Lil, "a cheerful, happy sinner" who could not say no to men, yet "did far less harm than some of her more virtuous sisters" (58); or J. Frazier Buck, a gentleman with a violent temper, who once when thrown by his horse, jumped up and down on a box of blasting powder, screaming, "Christ, blow me into a million pieces, put four legs on each piece, so I can run down that damned horse" (71); or Eli, a bachelor who kept an immaculate cabin, was a wonderful cook who decorated his food and gave presents to Anne and her family. These folk march through Anne's writing with such detail and vividness that they seem to whisper in our ears as we read. Anne writes that she once thought, "Too bad these glimpses of another's inside workings come so seldom" (75). Luckily for us, Anne's glimpses do not come seldom but often.

At one point, Anne subtly gives to a thinking reader a metaphor for these glimpses: "In those days you never held a dress up so that your friends could see the outside, oh, no! It was the wrong side which was turned outward and examined to the smallest detail. How it was lined, and interlined; how bound; how the seams were finished; the smallness and evenness of the stitches, how the steels were put in" (90). Anne is never simply satisfied to look on the outside of people, but at the seams and darts that comprise them. She looks at both the largeness and smallness of their souls. She also manages to turn the reader inside out, reaching from the past into the present community of immediate readings and responses. She seems to know how we, even in the late twentieth century, may judge or respond to some of these characters. Then she turns our possible self-righteousness back on us, teaching us tolerance for the very communities in which we live today.

One example of a lesson in tolerance is the episode with Nellie Smeltzer, the town dressmaker whose product is turned inside out, as is her character. Nellie comes to town with education and breeding and goes into a decline. She is very isolated, except for her frequent visits from Anne: "She has no intimate friends, neither women nor men, and never seems to feel the want of them. No relative ever came to see her" (91). Later she is brought up on insanity charges because she has kissed a cow. Nellie's response was, "She's the only creature who loves me; why not kiss her?" (94). At the end, Nellie dies proud and alone with only the things that loved her—the cow and her chickens, who lived with her in her house. Anne Ellis turns Nellie Smeltzer inside out for us and we look at her fine seams, her stitching. Yet Anne does more than this. She gives to Nellie a community denied to Nellie while she was alive; she gives us to Nellie, an unforgettable character. Anne Ellis finds her community with outcasts and with us, her readers.

Ellis ends her section on Nellie Smeltzer with a lovely piece of writing describing the dressmaker's window: "But, even to the end, there was a sign creaking above the door, 'Fashionable dressmaking'; and ladies, yellow and fly-specked, dressed in beautiful colors, with tiny waists, big sleeves, and long trains, looked and smiled at you from the fashion sheets in the bay window" (94). Like this bay window, the parade of life in mining towns has been captured for us. Some of the characters may be fly-specked but they are always beautiful and richly textured.

Despite these depictions of isolation within her early community, Anne Ellis did experience incidents of community in her own world. When Anne makes her move into the adult world with the horrible death of her mother one Christmas, the neighbors, so quick to condemn and isolate Anne and her family, become a source of strength. When the doctor is sent for, "After ages he does come, and many others with him. (Nowhere on earth are neighbors so good as in mining camps)" (167). These neighbors bring clothes for the funeral, they cook, they dress the mother.

At first, it may seem difficult to reconcile these opposing views of Anne's community. How can these be the same neighbors so quick to judge Anne and her family? Once again, Anne asks the reader to partici- pate directly in the text. The reader is made to resist the dualistic approach to humanity and instead asked to judge each incident sepa- rately. For those of us who have experienced both the cruelty and the compassion of small-town life, these seemingly polarized incidences are closer to reality than we may at first assume. The petty concerns of daily life place petty obstacles between us; the great tragedies of life make us bake casseroles and lay aside our hatreds.

However, this community, it must be remembered, is comprised of poor miners. They have little room in their cabins and even less food. Anne Ellis's mother is dead at the age of thirty-nine. Anne's immediate community may be able to reach out in times of great tragedy, but in the essentials of daily living, they have little to share. Their day-to-day existence is tragedy, so Anne is the sole caretaker of six children until she marries her first husband, George. Once again, Anne's poverty has a dual function as subject of the narrative and condition of its writer. Anne, the "ordinary" (poor) woman becomes emblematic of other "ordinary" women, while at the same time, informing the readers of a history of courage and fortitude.

At this point in the narrative, Anne's acts of community building in her past become cooking and making homes, never leaving behind her keen powers of observation. Anne is a very poor bride who strongly desires material things to make her home. When her first baby, Neita, is born, she has a bed made of a soap box. Anne writes:

Many times I would look at it, longing for a real baby bed, consoling myself with the thought that one day when we are rich and great, it will be something to tell—"My baby's first bed was a soap box." We have become neither rich nor great, and this is the first time I have mentioned the soap box. It seems things of this sort are only a virtue when you rise above them; otherwise they are a disgrace. (185)

The reader is smitten with the voice of this "common" woman. Again, her act of writing is an act of community building; she has never mentioned the soap box bed before. We share her secrets, and we feel she is correct in her practical wisdom: soap boxes as baby beds are only virtues if you now sleep in presidential suites. Ironically, however, despite the fact that Anne Ellis remained poor all her life, through her act of writing, her act of sharing secrets, she has, without the aid of dollars and luxury gilded four poster beds, made the soap box a virtue.

Even the coffin boxes of death must be made into virtues when Anne's husband, George, is killed in a mining accident. She becomes a young widow with two children, one only six months old. As the miners who have come to tell of the death stand around, Anne writes, "Now I dress and prepare breakfast for us all. These everyday duties are the saving of one in trouble" (205), as they have been Anne's entire life. After the miners leave and Anne is alone, she describes her feelings: "I am alone and glad of it. I go in the yard and a spirit of rebellion at fate comes over me" (205). Once again, as in the time of her mother's death, the neighbors file into the house. This time, however, Anne has no good words and few feelings of connections with this community so stricken by poverty: "[H]ow can they comfort this silent, dry-eyed creature who doesn't act like any woman would . . . and I am glad when they leave" (206).

However, no matter how tired or alone or grief stricken, Anne Ellis always seems to see beyond the moment into a community of some sort, if only a community of one woman and the larger unknown and unseen world. A "big Irishwoman" comes in, bringing a small bundle of cloth for the baby. This woman lost her husband in a mining accident only a month ago. Anne writes: "I, too, at this, open up and we cry together, for ourselves, for each other, and for all sorrowing womanhood" (206).

Life is tough for Anne Ellis, but she is a tough woman, able to find comfort in small things, like the golden drops of custard as a child. For her grief, she finds comfort at a community dance. At first, she feels bad dancing, with "George being dead such a short time, but I do so want to go that finally I compromise by going, but wearing a black dress" (211). For Anne, the main event of the evening is the supper, which she remembers and lists in careful detail: "boiled ham, turkey, cranberries, celery, salad, sandwiches, pickles, bread, pies, several kinds of cake and ice-cream, also huge cups of boiling hot coffee" (211). Anne finds comfort and common bonds in the details of food, in the food itself, and in the writing and recollecting of the food. This careful attention to detail brings her readers to the feast.

Perhaps her memories of such feasts are vivid because at that time, her life was so incredibly bleak, as she moves herself and her two small children from mining camp to mining camp, finally returning home to Bonanza.

In Bonanza, Anne begins to run a boarding house, creating and tending to her own small community through making a house and cooking. At times, however, even this act of community building has its limitations. Two old friends visit, well-dressed and "carefree" women. Anne writes: "I, so tired, rushed, and worried, am trying to get a meal ready for fifteen or eighteen men, I will own up a feeling comes over me, 'Why is it always thus? Why can other people have a good time while I must ever work?'" (221). These well-dressed women bring into Anne's world the sense of a different world, a different community; they make Anne's mode of survival, thus her sense of self, seem subservient. Anne admits her tears fall into the dinner. She does not tell the reader how long she cried, and she does not linger on the tragedy of her life.

Perhaps at this point, the reader feels compelled to join the community of the well dressed women and is shut out from that memory as Anne moves quickly in the following paragraph to a series of funny stories about miners and the first telephones. But if we are shut out, Anne the writer, places herself with us and also shuts herself out, moving quickly from the scene of a woman, tired and alone, crying into a dinner not cooked for herself.

If Anne Ellis of the past did too often cook for others, she "cooks" in the present time of her writing, now preparing a feast that both she and her readers can share. Anne explicitly reminds the reader of her sense of connection through writing. As she lived through these past hard times, often alone, she had the eye of a writer; in retelling these memories she is never alone. She has herself as writer, herself as woman remembered, and her readers. Anne Ellis moves smoothly within this community, and luckily for us, we, as readers, never feel alone and find ourselves befriending both writer and woman remembered.

At one point, Anne Ellis even finds herself to be a knowledgeable writing teacher. Her daughter, Neita, wants to become a writer: "Like most writers, she wished to write of something else than what she knew, and of some other place; then I would tell her: 'Oh, Neita, there is so much to write of here. Can't you see it? Why, there is a story in every house. If I could only write!'—never thinking I would try it after over twenty years!" (235). Even during her times of isolation, Anne would find her connections in the knowledge of the stories in every house.

When she writes of wanting to write, Anne Ellis is able to see her old self with a sense of admiration and pride without bravado. Her memories have prepared her for her present task. At one point, she is close to picking up a pencil as she sits in a busy train station with very few women and her children the only ones "in this adventuring crowd" (247). In her isolation, Anne again turns to thoughts of writing: "That day as I sat there I thought, 'I wish I could write about these people and describe their actions, faces, and clothes'; and I considered getting a pencil and doing it, but writing seemed impossible to me then" (247). She thinks "[B]ut there was no time for writing in this mad but thrilling search for gold" (248). Anne Ellis was too busy living her life and trying to survive it to write.

Instead of picking up the pencil, Anne reaches for a frying pan. Without the sense of connection through writing, Anne was forced to turn to her old standby, her companion, cooking. This was survival but also art. At this point, she has married Herbert, and they are living well on his three dollars a day. She writes that if men were fed better, they would drink less. She feels that part of the craving for alchohol is hunger. Here I believe she means hunger in a literal and metaphoric sense, and her writing and cooking arts merge. These lonely miners hunger for food and the comforts of food cooked in a home. Anne, a "good cook and manager," takes pride in being sure Herbert's lunches are better than other men's. She writes in meticulous detail about the food, as careful a writer as she was a cook:

So in my home there was a hearty breakfast, fruit, a cooked breakfast food, meat, potatoes, and usually hot biscuit, coffee-cake or cookies, and coffee. The lunch was always good home-made bread, meat, fruit, cake, and pie, always a change each day. Then a big supper at night consisting of a salad, two vegetables, meat, bread, and two kinds of dessert always. Each day I baked pie and cake. Miners did and do live well, when they are working. (233)

This was Anne Ellis's act of creation at a time when writing was not available for poor women. But like her menus, she carried these stories in her head until she could write.

Seemingly, when times were flush, as they were during the dinners described above, women had time for community building. Such a time occurred during the marriage of Teddy Roosevelt's daughter, Alice, highly publicized in the newspapers. Anne writes, "You see this was Romance, and having none of our own we took part of hers" (241). The women of the town wanted to do something special, so they held a meeting, decided on a gift, and each contributed fifty cents, paying a woman to do a centerpiece of Battenberg lace which they sent to Alice as a wedding gift.

Every day the women would gather when the stagecoach brought the papers and would read lists of all the other gifts folks had sent Alice. The women waited and read every day for "long, long weeks . . . the papers never mentioned any 'lovely gift from the West.' We never heard a word. Alice, how could you?" (242). This question reverberates beyond the book as a question from a community of isolated women reaching out, who have Anne Ellis as spokesperson. Here, in a rare moment in the book, we have an extended community. We, the readers, join the women, waiting in the dust each day, and indeed, even today, we may ask, "Alice, how could you?"

This seems to be the last time Anne Ellis and her family are financially well off and can spare time and worry for such things. She and her family continue to move, Anne making her home in each camp. The ultimate blow, however, is the death of her daughter, Joy, from diphtheria. Even in this most horrible event, Anne shields herself from both her own pity and ours: "I crouch beside the grave, and when I arise am a better woman than ever before, more human, more lenient toward faults in others, with more feeling and understanding for people, seeing now that money isn't everything" (267). This description of sacrificial cleansing, much like the question, "Alice, how could you" reaches into the lives of the readers. By writing of this terrible time, perhaps Anne Ellis makes us better women, more human, more lenient. This seems to be the consummate union of reader and writer: I do not need to lose my daughter to feel your pain; I am a better person for having shared your loss through the act of reading. Indeed, Anne Ellis's writing about this loss is an exceptional act of sharing, of allowing us to become her community of grievers. We become those women who bring casseroles and bolts of cloth to the houses where a death has occurred.

At the end of Anne's book, she poises herself amidst a disaster, yet with characteristic aplomb. Anne emerges from the details of pain, rising from the pages of the book—pen in one hand, apron clenched around her waist, the other hand extended to her reader. One day after Anne has cooked "four large cakes . . . a fleet of deep, rich, brown, fragrant pumpkin pies, and a huge pile of bread," a terrible storm comes (295). Everything is destroyed. Anne writes that she "always kept the day's menu. This day's report is: 'Aug. 18 - 69 meals, steak, string beans, potatoes, fried rice, cookies, pumpkin pie. Fatal pie.' The fatal pie was underscored; that was all the time one had" (294-95). This passage is only a few pages from the end of the book, when Anne's husband, Herbert, dies and she is, once again, alone. Here we have a culmination of the book: Anne's attention to details, which she will later transmit into the community building act of writing, details recalled by underlining fatal pie,' and her act of community building through food, born in her childhood when the golden drops of custard frosting saved her.

In fact, Anne Ellis's entire autobiography, too long ignored, becomes golden drops of custard frosting, sights and smells reaching out to modern readers, asking us to notice small things, to celebrate our histories. Her book becomes the fatal pie, an underscoring of a life long gone but remembered in careful detail. We need to remember the lives of women as seen through the eyes of women. They may be able to help us remember our own strengths, help us to single out the battles truly worth fighting, and help us find connections in a history from which too many women have been omitted.

Anne Ellis's *The Life of an Ordinary Woman*, published in 1929—very well received but too soon forgotten—is a book that will do just this.

After having read *The Life of an Ordinary Woman*, I remembered Anne Ellis as I waited in Granby, Colorado, for a three-hour late Amtrak train to Lincoln, Nebraska, growing more and more irritated with each passing moment. I paced, I slapped mosquitoes, I stared down the tracks into a sinking sun. Suddenly, Anne Ellis seemed to appear on the horizon like a mirage, a reflection to remind me of the oasis-life I lived. My self-pity lessened; my anger dissipated.

As I look back on that sweltering day, what I remember most are not the mosquitoes nor the dust nor my exhaustion. I am reminded of railroad tracks converging in a distance, connecting me with a group of women long ago, waiting for a newspaper report of their gift of Battenburg lace. Anne Ellis has made me reconsider my own memories.

Works Cited

Ellis, Anne. *The Life of an Ordinary Woman.* 1929. Boston: Houghton Mifflin, 1990.

West, Elliot. Foreword. *The Life of an Ordinary Woman.* By Anne Ellis. Lincoln: Nebraska UP, 1980. ix-xxii.

——. *Growing Up with the Country: Childhood on the Western Frontier.* Histories of the American Frontier. Albuquerque: U of New Mexico P, 1989.

11

Testament of Youth:
Vera Brittain's Literary Quest for Peace

Elizabeth Foxwell

British feminist and pacifist Vera Brittain (1893-1970) is remembered mainly for her haunting autobiography *Testament of Youth*, first published in 1933. Currently in its nineteenth edition and inspiration for a 1979 BBC production and PBS *Masterpiece Theater* presentation, it remains the best-known book of a woman's World War I experience, heartbreaking in its account of love, wrenching loss, and ultimate renewal from the ashes.

Testament of Youth, which helped set a new standard for autobiography in its accessible style and established Brittain's literary reputation, reconnected Brittain to life, after she had lost fiancé, brother, and two close friends and witnessed countless deaths as a Red Cross, or Voluntary Aid Detachment (VAD), nurse in World War I. *Testament of Youth* depicts Brittain's redefinition of self and quest for purpose through her commitment to feminism and a growing dedication to pacifism, and her need for the "earnest, independent labor" that the author she much admired, Olive Schreiner, had earlier articulated. Most of all, it underscores Brittain's sense of obligation to others—to speak for and serve both the dead and the living.

Testament of Youth was both personal catharsis and voice for the lost souls and survivors of her generation, although Brittain was ridiculed for thinking that her life—a woman's life—was interesting enough for a book. "Didn't women have their war as well?" she asked in answer to the preponderantly male war memoirs by Siegfried Sassoon, Robert Graves, Ernest Hemingway, and others that sought, equally with Brittain, to overcome the personal sense of fragmentation of the postwar world (*Testament of Experience* 77).

Brittain also wrote fiction and indeed most often identified herself publicly as a novelist, but her real strength lay as observer in her autobiographies. Although she was to write three others, the 1940 *Testament of Friendship* (about the short life of her great friend, novelist Winifred

Holtby), the 1957 *Testament of Experience*, and the unpublished *Testament of Faith*, *Testament of Youth* is generally regarded as her best and most universal work.

Through *Testament of Youth*, Brittain endeavored to 1) come to terms with the past and search for personal purpose in the alien postwar world; 2) educate others on the hard lessons of her youth in the hopes of avoiding their repetition; 3) remember and honor the dead, and inspire and find connections to the living; 4) claim a place in the literary world through a self-identified and -defined form of literature; 5) provide a vivid record of women's active participation and suffering in war, disputing its perception and appropriation as a solely masculine arena; 6) explore and interpret the relationship of the private individual to national and international events. In doing so, Brittain used autobiography as a powerful tool for both political and personal expression and illustrated both a quest for enlightenment for herself and others.

Coming to Terms

Overcoming the war's "strange, neurotic revenge." (*T of Y* 475)

I detached myself from the others and walked slowly up Whitehall, with my heart sinking in sudden cold dismay. Already this was a different world from the one I had known during four lifelong years, a world in which people would be lighthearted and forgetful. . . . And in that brightly lit, alien world I should have no part. (*T of Y* 462)

With these sad words, Vera Brittain described her alienation and isolation at the Armistice. Others wanted to forget; she could not, her memories of World War I and the men she had lost seared into her consciousness.

The bare outline of her story is simple. Brittain, after a long struggle with her parents, won an exhibition to Oxford (a type of scholarship) and re-met about the same time her brother Edward's friend, Roland Leighton. Despite conventions that dictated a constant chaperone, they fell in love. With the outbreak of World War I, Roland was called to the front, followed by Edward and his two friends, Geoffrey Thurlow and Victor Richardson. Brittain left Oxford to volunteer as a nurse, first in England and then in Malta and France. While Roland was on leave from France, he and Brittain became engaged. He was killed by a sniper's bullet in December 1915, followed by Thurlow's death in April 1917, Richardson's blinding and subsequent death in June 1917, and Edward's death in action in June 1918. After the war, Brittain returned to Oxford, graduated, and took up journalism and lecturing work. *Testament of Youth* ends with her approaching marriage to political scientist George Gordon Catlin in 1925.

The main reason for Brittain's writing of her own experiences in *Testament of Youth* was catharsis. The work simultaneously illustrated her place as the Outsider in the postwar world, and her claiming a place through its publication in the present of the 1930s. Her chapter 10 heading, "Survivors Not Wanted," expressed her sense of being alone and rejected by her Oxford contemporaries immediately after the war. She elaborated on this theme: "I had been, I suspected, largely to blame for my own isolation. I could not throw off the war, nor the pride and grief of it; rooted and immersed in memory, I had appeared self-absorbed, contemptuous and 'standoffish' to my ruthless and critical juniors. . . . until I left college, I never publicly mentioned the War again" (493). Brittain described here her isolation as a result of grief and a painful generation gap between herself and the younger, uncomprehending, and often disdainful students. "No doubt the post-war generation was wise in its assumption that patriotism had 'nothing to it,' and we pre-war lot were just poor boobs for letting ourselves be kidded into thinking that it had," Brittain wrote bitterly (*T of Y* 490), expressing the younger generation's benefit of hindsight, its unfair condemnation of her generation for their lack of such an advantage, and its estimation that their sufferings and service in the war meant nothing.

In her groping for identity, Brittain recalled its near dissolution, in the nervous breakdown that was narrowly averted; her "mind groped in a dark, foggy confusion" (*T of Y* 470-71). At Oxford, she avoided mirrors because she believed she was growing a beard "like a witch" (*T of Y* 484). She detailed a fearful, recurring series of mental images including "the German ward and the sharp grey features of a harmless little 'enemy' dying in the sticky morass of his own blood" (490). Thus, Brittain vividly described a 1919 manifestation of today's post-traumatic stress disorder, which would have been expected in a soldier rather than someone in an ostensible "sidelines" role.

Although the entire *T of Y* could be defined as a quest for reconciliation with the past, Brittain addressed this most directly in her post-graduation pilgrimage to the graves of Roland and Edward, what she called "one of the strangest, saddest, and most memorable of all my adventures" (523). She wept during the writing of the visit to Edward's grave (*Chronicle of Friendship* 87)—clearly a cathartic event. As she recounted planting a fern and rosebuds at the grave, she mused:

How trivial my life has been since the War! . . . How mean they are, these little
strivings, these petty ambitions of us who are left, now that all of you are gone!
How can the future achieve, through us, the sombre majesty of the past? Oh,
Edward, you're so lonely up here; why can't I stay for ever and keep your grave
company, far from the world and its vain endeavours to rebuild civilization?
(*T of Y* 526-27)

In this somewhat melodramatic scene, Brittain blended past, present, and
future. The reconciliation with the dead and the questioning of purpose
are suggested both by the woman of 1921, and the writer of the 1930s.
Accompanying her thoughts, Brittain, with the planting of the flowers,
signaled new life and personal rebirth.

The book also served to reconcile Brittain with her dead fiancé, in
exploring her courtship and ultimate decision to marry Catlin and her
fear of new psychological ties and abandonment of the dead. "I did not
wish to live, emotionally, any more," she wrote, "for I was still too tired;
I wanted only to stand aside from life and write" (*T of Y* 615). Brittain
thus described persistent physical and mental exhaustion into the 1920s,
holding herself aloof from the world out of a sense of self-preservation.
In her examination of marriage, she revealed mixed emotions of fear,
guilt, and hope:

There remained only now the final and acute question of loyalty to the dead. . . .
Up and down the solitary roads through Regent's Park, or round and round the
proletarian paths of Paddington Recreation Ground, I walked pondering this
ultimate uncertainty. . . . Roland—you who wrote in wartime France of "another
stranger"—would you think me, because I marry him, forgetful and unfaithful?
. . . So long as I am in the world, how can I ignore the obligation to be part of it,
cope with its problems, suffer claims and interruptions? (655)

Brittain described her anguish and inner debate over the men of past and
present, of keeping faith with the dead versus the duty to her own life
and others. She illustrated the demands of the world and her need for
closure and personal fulfillment against the compelling and painful pull
of the past. She fully developed this theme in *Testament of Youth*'s final
scene, describing a frantic search in a crowded train for Catlin:

Quite suddenly he saw me and started eagerly forward, his hands outstretched
and his face a radiance of recognition beneath his wide-brimmed hat. As I went
up to him and took his hands, I felt I had made no mistake. . . . I found it not
inappropriate that the years of frustration and grief and loss, of work, and conflict and painful resurrection, should have led me through their dark and devious
ways to this new beginning. (661)

Through the metaphor of betrothal, Brittain described a reconnection to life, to hope, and to the future, in her choice of a husband and a companion in life after enduring so much death.[1]

Brittain viewed *Testament of Youth* as "the final instrument of a return to life from the abyss of emotional death" (*Testament of Experience* 76), articulating how the book finally enabled her to cope with her memories. She told novelist Phyllis Bentley much later, "How close I was to total insanity at that time . . . because by writing about the First War, I had to relive it, and if the book had not got published, the reliving of it would never have ended" (Brittain letter to Bentley, May 31, 1961).[2] To fit in at Oxford, Brittain had remained silent on the war; over 10 years later, through *Testament of Youth* she reclaimed her voice to carve out a niche in the present.

Educating Others

My object . . . is to challenge that too easy, too comfortable lapse into forgetfulness which is responsible for history's most grievous repetitions. (*T of Y* 12)

In the book's foreword, Brittain indicated her effort to "rescue something that might be of value, some element of truth and hope and usefulness, from the smashing of my own youth" (11). She told a reader in 1934, "I gave [private facts] to the world in the hope that they would persuade those who come after to do all in their power to prevent the recurrence of such a catastrophe as the one that laid waste my generation" (Brittain letter to M. A. Goucher, June 6, 1934). Thus, through *Testament of Youth,* Brittain hoped to learn, instruct, and heal; give new hope to her contemporaries; and unite what she perceived to be a scattered and depleted generation.

One lesson she seemed to convey was the irony of war. This point of view was especially evident in her discussion of nursing German prisoners in France:

A badly wounded boy—a Prussian lieutenant who was being transferred to England—held out an emaciated hand to me . . . and murmured: "I tank you, Sister." After barely a second's hesitation I took the pale fingers in mine, thinking how ridiculous it was that I should be holding this man's hand in friendship when perhaps, only a week or two earlier, Edward up at Ypres had been doing his best to kill him. The world was mad and we were all victims; that was the only way to look at it. These shattered, dying boys and I were paying alike for a situation that none of us had desired or done anything to bring about. (376)

In this passage, Brittain noted the inherent absurdity of caring for the "enemy"—clearly not her perception—while her compatriots, and her brother, were killing the very soldiers she nursed. She demonstrated both the compassion of the war nurse and the perspective of the older woman and emerging pacifist in portraying the "enemy" as a human being and the situation as insane.

She also conveyed much anger and disillusionment over the war in her estimation of the Treaty of Versailles:

The Big Four were making a desert and calling it peace. They did not seem to me to represent at all the kind of "victory" that the young men whom I had loved would have regarded as sufficient justification for their lost lives. . . . I was beginning already to suspect that my generation had been deceived, its young courage cynically exploited, its idealism betrayed. (470)

Brittain provided a double perspective of immediate postwar disillusionment and a more entrenched view of wasted human life. She turned her anger into a more constructive purpose by changing her major after the war—from English to history—at Oxford, and explained her rationale in *T of Y*. "It's my job, now, to find out all about it," she wrote, "and try to prevent it, in so far as one person can, from happening to other people in the days to come" (471). In studying history, she indicated a need to be useful and a sense of obligation to pass on her hard lessons to society.

Through her experiences, she learned of the hazards of isolation. She wrote that "no life is really private, or isolated, or self-sufficient" (*T of Y* 472), noting how individual lives had an impact on society, and vice versa. Seeking insight about the war for her own sanity and the preservation of other lives, Brittain believed that a connection to others was necessary to avoid another war. "We should never be at the mercy of Providence, if only we understood that we ourselves are Providence," she noted, thus declaring a disbelief in Fate, and the power of the individual to seize the initiative, educate him- or herself, and thus save the world from chaos (*T of Y* 472). This belief was manifested in Brittain's approach to autobiography, which endeavored to show meaning and significance in an ordinary rather than prominent life.

"[F]or better, for worse," Brittain wrote, "we are now each of us part of the surge of great economic and political movements, and whatever we do, as individuals or as nations, deeply affects everyone else" (*T of Y* 472). This was something, she believed, that had been missing from her own sheltered upbringing. Thus, Brittain blamed personal and national isolation as two causes of the war, and used the events of her own life as an illustration to foster a more universal understanding of their ramifications.

Remembering the Dead

I recognized my world for a kingdom of death. (*T of Y* 416)

"I don't require two minutes' silence to think of the dead," Brittain wrote Winifred Holtby on Armistice Day in 1921. "They're with me always; it's like putting two minutes aside in which to breathe" (*Selected Letters* 18). Thus Brittain related the haunting of her life by the dead and her obligation to their remembrance. This took the form of literal haunting, as when she recounted her patients' witness of dead soldier comrades fighting with them (*T of Y* 416), and in Brittain's account of a dream of her resurrected brother when she was writing *Testament of Youth* (*Chronicle of Friendship* 81).

In *Testament of Youth,* Brittain provides extraordinary, if contradictory, insight into death, treating it harshly on the one hand and yet finding moments of beauty on the other. She wrote after Edward had died, "I couldn't see that it mattered to myself or anyone else if I caught and even died from one of my patient's dire diseases, when so many beautiful bodies of young men were rotting in the mud of France and pine forests of Italy" (458). From isolation and loss arose a carelessness about her own life amid the brutality of death. Yet, after a patient's death throes from venereal disease, she depicted the body's removal in far more poetic terms:

There was a brilliant moon that night . . . and it was very solemn and impressive to watch the orderlies carry him across the compound on a stretcher to the mortuary, with the Union Jack over him and the moonlight shining on all—it is a queer moonlight in these places [Malta], very black shadows and startling outlines; everything is transfigured. (*T of Y* 333)

Thus Brittain provides a dignity in death in her description of what society might consider an ignominious end. As moonlight transfigured the body, so Brittain transfigured and transcended death, and remembered the individual soldier with dignity, with an effort to transforming brutality into something more endurable.

As she memorialized the dead, Brittain identified an effort to minister to the living in producing *Testament of Youth:* "I was writing, I thought, to try to console others who like myself had known despair— about the loves they had lost, perhaps, or their work's frustration—and to prove that this universal emotion could be overcome even by individuals whose courage was as small as mine" (*T of E* 80). She, casting herself as a coward,[3] despite all she had endured, indicated a wish to serve and help others, in providing a story of great trial and ultimate survival.

In serving her generation, she wanted in *Testament of Youth* to capture the "peculiar quality of the youth of our generation . . . its native idealism, its gallantry, its dogged, unshaken persistence even when faith was lost and hope was gone" (*Selected Letters* 249). She viewed herself and her dead as the personification of these qualities and wished to have them remembered so that the idealism of future generations would not be exploited as she felt hers and her contemporaries had been.

Brittain's inclusion of Roland's poetry, her touching account of Victor Richardson's sympathetic ear for her troubles and her decision to marry him when he was wounded, Geoffrey Thurlow's shy gift of flowers for her, and her sisterly pride in her brother's Military Cross are small touches that turned the dead into human beings—a reclamation. Brittain's assiduous quest for answers to Roland's death and her equally determined pursuit of Edward's colonel for every scrap of detail about her brother's death illustrate her dogged need to believe that they had not died in vain, despite her expressed disillusion about the war itself. She wrote, "Edward had died in saving this beauty [of Italy] from the fate of Ypres"—her clear attempt to give her brother's death a larger and more noble context (523).

She also attempted to resolve her feelings of guilt and frustration over Roland's premature loss. Brittain well described the rush of courtship to engagement; she and Roland had only known each other a little over two years, with few actual face-to-face meetings, before he was killed. Her comment that she wished not to "astonish the world by some brilliant and glittering achievement, but some day to be the mother of Roland Leighton's child," expresses her sexual desire for Roland (*Chronicle of Youth* 141). A constant refrain is her frustration at the conventions that hampered their being alone together, and when they were, her regret over the quarrels that resulted from the clash of two strong personalities. Brittain's later treatment of this situation in her novel *Honorable Estate* (1936), where her heroine, Ruth Alleyndene, sleeps with her American soldier before he goes to the front, clearly indicated how Brittain wished her relationship had progressed.

"It is through me that the victory is incomplete," Brittain wrote to Winifred Holtby in August 1924, "because I cannot always quite feel that their deaths matter less to me than the fact that they lived, nor reconcile their departure, with all their aspirations unfulfilled, with my own scheme of life" (*Selected Letters* 41). Through *Testament of Youth,* Brittain gave her young men's deaths—and lives—meaning, in memorializing them, and in refusing to forget.

Establishing a Literary Reputation

> There was only one possible course left—to tell my own fairly typi-
> cal story as truthfully as I could against the larger background.
> (*T of Y* 12)

Brittain wrote just a few years before her death that "only ambition held me to life" after the war.[4] As a child inventing stories, she had envisioned a future career as a writer. *Testament of Youth* allowed her to carve out her own niche in the literary world.

She attempted several literary forms for her experiences before settling on autobiography. Poetry was the first. Brittain had published the largely awkward *Verses of a V.A.D.* in 1918, the first literary outlet for her war experiences.[5] She was one of the editors for *Oxford Poetry 1920*, which included her poem "The Lament of the Demobilized," that expressed her bitterness at the harsh readjustment to postwar life. Oxford's Louis Golding said this poem could have been produced "by Godfrey Elton out of Siegfried Sassoon"—comparing Brittain to two male war memoirists (*T of Y* 491). In 1922, Brittain sought to publish her World War I diary,[6] later terming the diary as the more immediate trees, and *Testament of Youth* as the broader, fuller, and more interpretative forest (*Chronicle* 15). When the diary failed to find a publisher, she thought to write the book as a novel, but found the form created "a false atmosphere" in using pseudonyms and "the events about which I was writing were still too near and too real to be made the subjects of an imaginative, detached reconstruction" (*T of Y* 12).[7] Thus Brittain indicated that a bare record or fictional account of her experiences was an unsatisfactory literary form; she needed an outlet in which to explore them most freely, with the maturity of age.

Brittain's subheading of *Testament of Youth* is "An Autobiographical Study of the Years 1900-1925." Only the distance of fourteen years and autobiography could most honestly convey the full impact of her experiences, although Brittain often used novelistic techniques with great effect. Jean Kennard notes Brittain's frequent use of foreshadowing, which effectively contrasts the young, idealistic Brittain with the mature, sadder woman (132).

For example, Brittain relates standing in a fairy ring and wishing to be married to Roland; when her brother presses her for her wish, she replies that she will tell him in five years, "for by then the wish will come true or be about to come true, or it will never come true at all" (103). It is chillingly apparent that the wish never comes true.

Clearly, Brittain wished to make the war and the hard lessons she had learned accessible and understandable to the popular reader, and this goal was reflected in the first-person, narrative style she adopted. Giving a sense of immediacy, Brittain quoted extensively from her diary.

"O Roland," I wrote, in the religious ecstasy of young love sharpened by the War to a poignancy beyond expression, "Brilliant, reserved, extravagant personality—I wonder if I shall have found you only to lose you again, or if Time will spare us till it may come about that the greatest word in the world—of which now I can only think and dare not name—shall be used between us. God knows, and will answer." (*T of Y* 114-15)

In quoting directly from her diary, Brittain provided a passionate window into her youth, the immediate flush of love and the fear of its fragility. The diary captures the turbulence of that emotion as no measured retrospective could, yet also provides a sense that her love for her wartime fiancé would never be recaptured in another man.

She also quoted from the young men's letters, firmly establishing them as real human beings and grounding war in very personal terms. Most poignant is the letter from Edward, dubbed "the immaculate man of the trenches" by his men for his habit of daily shaving, who writes after their three friends are dead:

We started alone, dear child, and here we are alone again; you find me changed, I expect, more than I find you; that is perhaps the way of Life. But we share a memory which is worth all the rest of the world, and the sun of that memory never sets. And you know that I love you, that I would do anything in the world in my power if you should ask it, and that I am your servant as well as your brother. (*T of Y* 361)

By directly quoting Edward, Brittain provided a tender, unfiltered affirmation of the closeness and understanding between brother and sister, and their sense of isolation from others by their shared experience of their friends' deaths.

In a 1963 article, "The Place of Autobiography in Modern Literature," Brittain listed the elements of the modern autobiography and thus her thinking on her Testaments' construction. She emphasized that since autobiography was foremost a quest for self-enlightenment, it did not matter at what age it was written. "A spiritual odyssey does not depend —especially in an age of literary change—upon how long a person has lived," she said, replying to criticism of calling her autobiography a "testament" at the early age of forty, and emphasizing the inner rather than outer journey of the individual. To be accessible, Brittain said, autobiography required a quality of universality with its readership, a smooth transition from event to event and an analysis of the impact of each upon the author, and a conscious effort to shape the product as "a work of art." Most of all, she felt the ordinary person's autobiography to be far more representative than a monarch's, politician's, or military official's—typical authors of traditional autobiographies. Thus, Brittain viewed this revamped genre as a form of self-empowerment, as the author told his or her own story instead of having it imposed by outside sources, and valuable as a vehicle for artistic self-expression and interpretation.

Upon *Testament of Youth*'s publication, 5,000 copies sold in one week, prompting a second edition (*Chronicle of Friendship* 150) and 1,300 letters to Brittain in the four years following its first publication (*On Being an Author* 161). During World War II, a new edition of 15,000 was immediately snatched up by bookstores (*Wartime Chronicle* 223). Brittain's biographers estimate that *Testament of Youth* has sold a total of nearly 750,000 copies in Great Britain alone.[8] *Testament of Youth* also renewed Brittain's ties to Somerville College, which had banned her Oxford-critical novel, *The Dark Tide*, upon its 1923 publication and ten years later, welcomed her return in a debate (*Chronicle of Friendship* 162). Virginia Woolf criticized Brittain's "stringy, metallic mind" but praised *Testament of Youth* as "a very good book of its sort. The new sort, the hard anguished sort, that the young write; that I could never write" (177). Although Woolf was only eleven years older than Brittain when *Testament of Youth* was published, Woolf labeled Brittain's work as a new form of writing tied to youth—a raw, powerful, even uncomfortable, confessional.

Yet at the outset, the idea for *Testament of Youth* was met with scorn and has continued to attract criticism for its treatment of history. Brittain's American publisher, George P. Brett of Macmillan, wondered, after reading the manuscript, if the work in actuality was a "novel masquerading as an autobiography" (*T of E* 89). Brittain's friend Roy Randall told her, "I shouldn't have thought that anything in *your* life was worth recording"—a position, Brittain thought, that resulted from the failure of her experiences to stamp themselves on her demure features (*T of E* 79). When Henry Andrews, a friend of Brittain's husband, agreed with Randall, his wife, author Rebecca West, retorted, "You mean she's not a field marshal? But it's the psychological sort of autobiography that succeeds nowadays—not the old dull kind" (*Chronicle of Friendship* 30). Thus, West acknowledged an emerging form of autobiography that would fully engage readers by its more intimate and quotidian approach.

Brittain thought in 1933 that many people would believe "a personal story should be kept private," no matter how valuable its lessons to a wider audience (*T of Y* 12).[9] By interpreting her own life, Brittain refused to remain silent on her experiences and those of other women.

Expressing Women's Experience in War

[W]hat mattered was not the quality of the work, but the sex of the worker. (*T of Y* 58)

Testament of Youth is Brittain's journey of self-discovery, emphasizing her resentment of societal obstacles and her fight for her own rights as a woman. Her war experiences became a part of her identity, as the means of her escape from provincial isolation and ignorance, and living an active vocation that she felt had been experienced in some form by other women but ignored by the literary world.

In the book, Brittain portrayed both an emotional and an intellectual education of a woman. She described the effects of the acquisition of intimate knowledge as a war nurse:

Throughout my two decades of life I had never looked upon the nude body of an adult male. . . . Short of actually going to bed with [the wounded], there was hardly an intimate service that I did not perform for one or another in the course of four years, and I still have reason to be thankful for the knowledge of masculine functioning which the care of them gave me, and for my early release from the sex-inhibitions that even to-day . . . beset many of my female contemporaries, both married and single. (165-66)

Through her nursing experience, Brittain candidly illustrated her release from Victorian repressions as well as a sense of gratitude towards her patients for giving her knowledge. Clearly, Brittain did not view herself as a ministering angel but as someone with a job to do, a student of her patients, and a opponent of societal taboos against sexual knowledge.

Phyllis Rose states in her introduction to *The Norton Book of Women's Lives* that the one story that dominates in women's autobiography is "the liberation narrative and its dark underside, the captivity narrative" (31). The majority of subjects in *Women's Lives* speak of escapes from physical, intellectual, and emotional prisons. An excerpt of *Testament of Youth* is included in the volume.

Brittain's *Testament of Youth* is a liberation narrative, in her discussion of her rebellion against authority and patriarchy to attend Oxford, and escape from provinciality to embrace war nursing and sorrow in the wider world. Yet she illustrated the persistent demands on women in her account of her father's command to leave nursing in France and return home when her mother fell ill—something she resentfully noted her soldier brother would never be expected to do. "My father's interpretation of my duty was not, I knew only too well, in the least likely to agree with that of the Army," she noted (421). In this episode, Brittain identified a difference in men's and women's war experience, stating, "What exhausts women in wartime is not the strenuous and unfamiliar tasks that fall upon them . . . it is the incessant conflict between personal and national claims which wears out their energy and breaks their spirit" (422). Thus Brittain described women's perpetual tug-of-war over fulfilling their familial versus their civic duty. "Feeling a cowardly deserter" (424), Brittain broke her nursing contract to return home, clearly depicting the pain of divided loyalties. Her chapter 3 and 4 headings, "Oxford versus War" and "Learning versus Life" illustrate her sense of conflict between personal and national duty, and her struggles to break out of her prison of provincial narrowness to confront love and learning.

In other passages, she described a harsher form of education in enduring the horrors of war. A self-described "complete automaton," Brittain conveyed her duties in graphic language:

An incongruous picture came back to me of myself standing alone in a newly created circle of hell . . . and gazing, half hypnotised, at the dishevelled beds, the stretchers on the floor, the scattered boots and piles of muddy khaki, the brown blankets turned back from smashed limbs bound to splints by filthy bloodstained bandages. Beneath each stinking wad of sodden wool and gauze an obscene horror waited for me—and all the equipment that I had for attacking it in this ex-medical ward was one pair of forceps standing in a potted-meat glass half full of methylated spirit. (*T of Y* 410)

In this passage, Brittain does not shrink from nor sanitize war's realities. Although she was a nurse—a traditional supportive role—she challenged the perception of women's passive place on the sidelines in her "I was there" narrative. She confronted her own memories and also forced readers to confront them directly.

Brittain also depicted a form of emotional education, bringing to vivid life the anguish of love in wartime, especially in the description of what followed her farewell to the front-bound Roland:

I crouched beside the morning-room fire for almost an hour, unable to believe that I could ever again suffer such acute and conscious agony of mind. On every side there seemed to be cause for despair and no way out of it. I tried not to think because thought was intolerable, yet every effort to stop my mind from working only led to a fresh outburst of miserable speculation. . . . I felt . . . a weak and cowardly person . . . to shrink from my share in the Universal Sorrow. . . . It was my part to face the possibility of a ruined future with the same courage that he is going to face death. (133-34)

Brittain illustrated the suffering of the "woman left behind" but at the same time indicated her consciousness of sharing this emotion with a community. In her misery, there was an exhortation for courage, a casting of her mental anguish and perception of self-cowardice as a battlefield similar to the physical one faced by Roland.

In describing the palpable experiences of nursing, mental struggles, and often painful acquisition of knowledge, Brittain clearly felt that her experiences were not unique. "I always felt that my story was a universal story, beginning with the Trojan Women and repeated through all ages and all generations," she wrote to Winifred Holtby in April 1933, identifying her book as one with a long history that would strike a chord within everyone (*Selected Letters* 249). Yet she wondered why the woman's perspective was not reflected in the popular war books of the early 1930s. "Why should these young men have the war to themselves?" she asked. "Didn't women have their war as well?" (*T of E* 77). In a review of *Testament of Youth,* novelist Storm Jameson explained women's silence on the war when she noted women lacked the community of comrades that ex-servicemen possessed and experienced a "feeling of inferiority . . . when they set their war experience beside that husbands, brothers or lovers. . . . From the difficulty of the task, and from diffidence, most of them kept silence" (28 Aug. 1933). Thus she noted a reluctance of women to articulate their war experience out of an erroneous sense of its insignificance, their personal inadequacy for the job, or their lack of an organized community where they could share their experiences.

Brittain intended to speak for her generation of "obscure young women" whose views and activities had been ignored (*T of E* 77), and indeed, some of the reviews recognized Brittain's as the definitive women's voice of World War I. Beatrice Kean Seymour in the September 1933 *Women's Journal* called *Testament of Youth* "the authentic feminine voice in contemporary literature—heard, alas, far too seldom!" Cecil Roberts termed the book "the autobiography of a feminist" (334). One reviewer, A. G. Macdonell, called *T of Y* "a clearer, more fearful, more moving picture of what a modern war does to a generation than all the Remarques and Sherriffs, all the Sassoons and Graves, and all the reminicenses of literary privates put together" (Macdonell 486). Thus Macdonell suggested that *Testament of Youth*'s female point of view—with its emphasis on the personal cost that in turn had an impact on the wider world—was more effective as an interpretative work than the lauded male war autobiographies.

Some later criticism, however, has taken a harsher view of Brittain as a voice for her female contemporaries. Marvin Rintala argues that Brittain was not particularly representative of her generation, as a well-off woman of the British upper middle class who had the atypical experience of World War I nursing, and that she "chose to write her own story"—not the one of the men who had died (33). Yet as Brittain's experience of disillusionment and loss reflected so many others, whether they came from her social class or not, and *Testament of Youth* illuminated the story of four young soldiers as well as her own life, Rintala's does not seem to be an appropriate conclusion. As Brittain herself put it, "[W]omen as well as men had endured war experiences, which had led them to certain common conclusions about the state of the world" (*On Being an Author* 165)—clearly a statement that identifies both points of view as worthy of an audience.

Claire M. Tylee attacks Brittain's "novelistic conception of history," and argues that *Testament of Youth* only rates as "emotional protest" and lacks political insight (211). Brittain, says Tylee, simultaneously identifies herself as speaking for women of her generation yet repudiates them in preferring male society to female in her youth.

In *Testament of Youth,* Brittain described female society as found in her village of Buxton and at her school, St. Monica's. Most girls and women of her acquaintance were solely concerned with matrimony and denigrated Brittain's intellectual pursuits. It is logical to assume that Brittain would seek male companionship if she could not find a receptive female audience, and from all indications found acceptance as an equal with her easygoing brother and his friends.

Brittain's account of her struggles for knowledge and independence and ultimate triumph in building a new life out of sorrow would seem to evoke a certain universality among women who also had endured loss. Her approach to history, while atypical, made it accessible and real to the popular reader—one avenue to awareness. Brittain reported in *Testament of Experience* (314) that a copy of *Testament of Youth* was found beside the body of a World War II soldier—one indication of the book's appeal to men, women, and successive generations.

Exploring the Personal Relationship to Public Events

[W]hat I have written constitutes the indictment of a civilization.
(*T of Y* 12)

From the beginning of *Testament of Youth,* Brittain illustrated the tension between public duty and private life. She noted, "When the Great War broke out, it came not as a superlative tragedy but as an interruption of the most exasperating kind to my personal plans" (18). She then related a memory of the Boer War in which an uncle died. Thus, from the book's genesis, Brittain began to demonstrate the impact of international events on individual lives versus the individual absorption in personal affairs, and examined the siren call of patriotism on her own life. As a student on the home front, she feared a "permanent impediment to understanding" (143) between herself and her fiancé at the front, but cited "the persistently beating drum" of patriotism as a strong reason for volunteering as a nurse. She quoted Roland's view of her Oxford in this period as "a secluded life of scholastic vegetation" (140). Brittain therefore signaled a shift in her thinking as a result of the call by her country: from a perception of her long-awaited Oxford study as a vital, constructive occupation to a static, impractical activity in the excitement and obligations of wartime.

In *Testament of Youth,* Brittain did not intend to write a dry political treatise; rather, she sought to examine the impact of often cataclysmic events on everyday life—a more intimate analysis of the relationship between the individual and the state. One example of this is through an episode of nursing in France:

To us, with our blistered feet, our swollen hands, our wakeful, reddened eyes, victory and defeat began—as indeed they were afterwards to prove—to seem very much the same thing. . . . I stumbled up to the Sisters' quarters for lunch with the certainty that I could not go on. (418-19)

Brittain then recounted Lord Haig's "Special Order of the Day" that exhorted, "With our backs to the wall and believing in the justice of our cause each one of us must fight on to the end" (*T of Y* 419). "After I read it," wrote Brittain, "I knew I should go on, whether I could or not" (420). Thus she illustrated the dangerous pull of patriotism, the persuasive power of the state over the individual mind. However, her agenda is not hidden; Brittain admits candidly to her purposes and conclusions about the war—"It is not by accident that what I have written constitutes, in effect, the indictment of a civilization" (*T of Y* 12). With the deaths of her loved ones and her war service, she conveyed a permanent mistrust of government, and a commitment to be ever-vigilant against its excesses to avoid the repetition of war. She indicated a hard-bought education: that individual ignorance and isolation from world events were responsible for the war's occurrence and its continued support; and that it was each individual's responsibility to teach successive generations. "Perhaps, after all," Brittain wrote, "the best that we who were left could do was . . . to teach our successors what we remembered in the hope that they, when their own day came, would have more power to change the state of the world than this bankrupt, shattered generation" (*T of Y* 646). For Brittain, there was to be no ducking of duty nor mindless co-option as a tool of the state; she vowed to be informed and inform others through her Testaments and other writings.[10] Thus her autobiographical writing assumed a political dimension in addition to its personal expression.

In *Testament of Youth,* Vera Brittain wished to "put the life of an ordinary individual into its niche in contemporary history" (*T of Y* 12). The book also was her attempt to find a literary niche for herself, and a demonstration to her contemporaries that a new life could be built after so much death. She wrote, "I lost one world and after a time rose again, as it were, from spiritual death to find another . . . resurrection is possible within our limited span of earthly time" (495-96). In Brittain's account of coming out of her personal darkness into the light, she provided a wrenching memorial to the dead, but ultimately a tale of the long journey and rebirth of a courageous survivor.

Notes

1. Catlin did not share the same opinion, and asked his wife to make substantial changes in the last chapter, believing her portrayal of himself would harm his academic and political prospects (Berry and Bostridge 257). He also believed Brittain was still in love with Leighton which she denied. "For years he went on believing that Roland's passionate young ghost stood between us when he had in fact laid it by his own loving-kindness," wrote Brittain (*Testament of Experience* 92). The idea of Roland's ubiquitous presence, whether in a real or literary form, seemed to have cast a shadow over the marriage. See John Catlin's *Family Quartet* for his perception of his parents' marriage (96-97).

2. Brittain always maintained that *Testament of Youth* got the war "out of her system" but it is clear that she was haunted by it over the course of her life. Brittain's daughter Shirley Williams noted, "It was hard for her to laugh unconstrainedly; at the back of her mind, the row upon row of wooden crosses were

planted too deeply" (*T of Y* preface). Brittain wrote to Phyllis Bentley in 1961, "I shall welcome death when it comes because it will release me from remembering the things I still have to remember."

3. In World War I and II, Brittain tended to place herself in harm's way—not out of foolhardiness, but to prove something to herself. She wrote in 1942, "I get a 'guilt complex' when out of dangers that other have to endure—and therefore tend (as in the Blitz) to go into them deliberately, for no purpose but the maintenance of my self-respect" (*Wartime Chronicle* 181).

4. See Brittain's unpublished "Testament of Faith."

5. Like novel writing, poetry was not Brittain's most proficient metier, although certain of her poems display tremendous power, such as "Sic Transit" from *Verses of a V.A.D.* (1918). Brittain herself called *Verses* "an insignificant and short-lived volume" (*On Being an Author* 150).

6. All of Brittain's diaries ultimately saw publication after her death: *Chronicle of Youth* (1980), *Chronicle of Friendship* (1986), and *Wartime Chronicle* (1989).

7. Brittain's sense was proved true in *England's Hour* (1941), which was supposedly an autobiographical account of the Blitz, but is lent an air of falsehood by its use of pseudonyms for George Catlin, and John and Shirley Brittain-Catlin.

8. Berry, Paul, and Mark Bostridge. *Vera Brittain: A Life* 2.

9. While *Testament of Youth* was well received critically, charges of egotism were leveled against Brittain's later autobiographies. Graham Greene, calling *England's Hour* "excited, sentimental, and egotistic," added scathingly, "Miss Brittain . . . is strenuously in the centre of the picture—the book might have been called more accurately *Brittain's Hour*" (Greene 178).

10. This perspective is especially evident in Brittain's refusal to do propaganda for the Ministry of Information and her initiation of her "Letter to Peace Lovers" at the outbreak of World War II. See *Testament of Experience* 217, 221.

Works Cited

Berry, Paul, and Mark Bostridge. *Vera Brittain: A Life*. London: Chatto & Windus, 1995.

Brittain, Vera. *Chronicle of Friendship: Vera Brittain's Diary of the Thirties 1932-1939*. Ed. Alan Bishop. London: Gollancz, 1986.

———. *Chronicle of Youth: The War Diary 1913-1917*. Ed. Alan Bishop. New York: Morrow, 1982.

———. *On Being an Author*. New York: Macmillan, 1948.

———. "The Place of Autobiography in Modern Literature." Manuscript. Later published in *Cultural Forum*. Sept./Oct. 1963. Vera Brittain Archive,

William Ready Division of Archives and Research Collections, McMaster University (Canada).

——. *Testament of Experience*. London: Gollancz, 1957. London: Virago, 1979.

——. *Testament of Faith*. Unpublished Manuscript. Vera Brittain Archive.

——. *Testament of Youth*. London: Gollancz, 1933. New York: Wideview, 1980.

——. "War Service in Perspective." *Promise of Greatness: The War of 1914-1918*. Ed. George A. Panichas. New York: Day, 1968. 363-76.

——. *Wartime Chronicle: Vera Brittain's Diary 1939-1945*. Ed. Alan Bishop and Y. Aleksandra Bennett. London: Gollancz, 1989.

Brittain, Vera, and Geoffrey Handley-Taylor, eds. *Selected Letters of Winifred Holtby and Vera Brittain 1920-1935*. London: Brown & Sons, 1960.

Catlin, John. *Family Quartet*. London: Hamish Hamilton, 1987.

Greene, Graham. "A Pride of Bombs." *The Spectator* 14 Feb.1941: 178.

Jameson, Storm. "Miss Brittain Speaks for Her Generation: War As a Woman Saw It." *Yorkshire Post* 28 Aug. 1933.

Kennard, Jean. *Vera Brittain and Winifred Holtby: A Working Partnership*. Hanover: UP of New England, 1989.

Macdonell, A. G. "Bystander Bookshelf." *The Bystander* 13 Sept. 1933: 486.

Rintala, Marvin. "Chronicler of a Generation: Vera Brittain's Testament." *Journal of Political and Military Sociology* 12 (Spring 1984): 23-33.

Roberts, Cecil. Rev. *Testament of Youth*, by Vera Brittain. *Sphere* 26 Aug. 1933: 334.

Rose, Phyllis. *The Norton Book of Women's Lives*. New York: Norton, 1995.

Seymour, Beatrice Kean. Rev. *Testament of Youth*, by Vera Brittain. *Women's Journal* Sept. 1933. Vera Brittain Archive.

Tylee, Claire M. *The Great War and Women's Consciousness: Images of Militarism and Womanhood in Women's Writings 1914-64*. Iowa City: U of Iowa P, 1990.

Woolf, Virginia. *The Diary of Virginia Woolf, Volume 4, 1931-1935*. New York: Harcourt, 1977.

Crossing the Boundaries:
Appropriating Other Genres

12

"Write it upon the walles of your houses": Dorothy Leigh's *The Mothers Blessing*

Martha J. Craig

In the early years of the seventeenth century, an ailing widow named Dorothy Leigh wrote a book to guide her three sons after her death. Leigh, who is identified as a "gentle-woman" on the title page, was part of a small tradition of women who wrote books of advice to their children regarding morality and behavior, creating a subset of the larger genre of male courtesy manuals and manners books. The number of surviving women's advice books is but a fraction of the only one hundred or so books published by women between 1500 and 1640 in England. But the fact that women were writing at all, particularly women of the "middling sort" such as Dorothy Leigh, who did not enjoy the social protection of the high aristocracy, is proof of the strength of their resolve to address posterity in the face of overwhelming cultural constrictions on women's public voice.

In the late sixteenth and early seventeenth centuries in England, women were in an ambiguous position domestically and socially. Renaissance society in general accepted a hierarchical view that was a mixture of Aristotelian misogyny and patriarchal Christian "truths" regarding the inferiority of women and the necessity of their submission to men's domination. Law, religion, and custom discriminated against women. And yet they were expected to be productive forces for the moral good, overseeing, despite frequent disparagements from the pulpit, the piety and stability of the newly revalued family. Largely illiterate as a body, they were charged with the moral education of their small children, as well as the fundamentals of learning that would be taken over by tutors and schools as the children grew older. Dominated by a pervasive ideology that devalued women while it played on the individual's craving to attain ultimate salvation, women were prey to notions of fundamental guilt that inspired, and at the same time subverted, efforts to prove redemptive piety by doing exactly what society dictated for "good" women.

Within the skewed moral climate that Dorothy Leigh grew up in, humanist writers extended their didactic energies toward the problem of educating women to be constructive members of a moral society while discouraging them from assuming a public role. To this end, humanist literature promoted women's education as long as it was pursued in the privacy of the home. Even the books and tracts considered the most enthusiastic toward women's education, including those of Vives, More, Mulcaster, and Elyot, did not disagree with the prevailing attitude that the optimum feminine virtues were chastity, silence, and obedience, and that therefore women needed education on a par with males' only in circumstances of extraordinary brilliance, such as Sir Thomas More's daughters,[1] Mary Sidney Herbert, and other advantaged and gifted women, and the rare case of a woman who might rule, like Vives's pupil the Princess Mary. The home was women's prescribed territory. In his influential *Instruction of a Christian Woman* (trans. 1529), Vives endorsed this circumscribed view of women's sphere of influence:

A woman should study . . . if nat for her own sake, at the least wyse for her chyldren, that she maye teache them and make them good . . . For that age childhood can do nothynge it selfe but counter fayte and followe others, and . . . taketh its fyrst conditions and information of mynde [from the] mother. . . . therefore it lyeith more in the mother than men wene, to make the conditions of the chyldren. (13^v)

Protestant emphasis on the individual's duty studiously to develop a personal theology (therefore needing to read, at least the Bible) reinforced the humanist initiative in education. Wealthy individuals, often from the merchant classes, developed a fervor for education as a conduit to salvation—and, incidentally, to a higher social position. They began endowing schools so that their values of thrift and industry would be brought to all citizens society recognized as eligible for public intercourse—that is, to the boys.[2] But preparation for these schools was begun in the home, by the mothers, and this early education was extended to girls as well, as the future nurturers of their own children's education. Thus education, intended to preserve morality and the integrity of the individual within the family, became a dynamic process that involved the whole community, and brought attention to the lynch-pin of the family, the mother. With the recognition of this role, women seemed to find their voices in greater numbers than ever before. Female literacy climbed, especially in urban areas, and women began to write. This was not an easy accomplishment, and although significant, the number of women writers was still small: David Cressy claims that between 1580 and 1640, between ninety and ninety-five percent of Englishwomen appearing in Ecclesiastical Court (a population that might not generally include the better-educated upper classes) could not write their own names. He adds, "[Y]et the number of copies sold of books specifically written for women indicates a substantial literary rate. Teaching women to read the words of men without teaching them to write their own was one effective means of silencing them" (236).

But feminist scholars of literature, history, art, and culture have proven to us in the latter half of this century what only a few writers mentioned earlier:[3] That women in the early modern period were articulating personal, moral, and practical positions in writing, a potentially public medium. They were doing this both in direct discourse, such as letters, tracts, pamphlets, and even wills and other legal documents, and in "fiction,"[4] poetry, drama, meditations, and translations. Few of these texts were printed for sale, but some were circulated beyond the family. Many more women wrote their thoughts in private diaries, instructions, lists, and even annotations in daybooks, cookbooks, and literary works of others, some of which have found their way to posterity.

Although women were enjoined to avoid the public forum in the interests of modesty, the differentiation between their private and public writing was, ironically, blurred. Driven by the problematics of feminine virtue as articulated by all the literary artifacts of their culture, women writers engaged in what Elaine Showalter has called "double-voiced discourse," combining representation of their own voices with their negotiations with patriarchal ideology. It is safe to say that nothing was written without the author's addressing, directly or indirectly, the issue of her *right* to write—based on privilege, proficiency, piety, or the compulsion of circumstances.[5] Thus the author herself was always a subtext, one that maintained a continual *sub rosa* dialogue with an audience on the subject not just of her writing but of her persona. For Leigh and a few others like her to negotiate the dangerously shifting boundaries of social regulation to write for possible publication in the early 1600s, therefore, required education, determination, and moral independence.

Some early modern English women writers, including Mary Sidney Herbert, Aemilia Lanyer, and Elizabeth Cary, secured the right to write partly because of the sanction and educational opportunities class and connection afforded the aristocracy. Others justified religious writing on grounds of piety; and a few, usually under protective pseudonyms, employed anger to enter the print debate about feminine virtue that had been raging since time immemorial.

But the women advice-writers wrote in their own personae, contributing quiet voices to this subgenre that has escaped widespread modern attention. While male authors of courtesy manuals used the vehicle to glorify their own experiences and values as they fine-tuned contemporary definitions of honor, courage, and accomplishment,[6] women's advice-writing, in keeping with the gender differentiations embedded in Renaissance philosophy, was far more moralistic, concerning itself with women's responsibility for children's souls, rather than for their social status and success. Women's advice-writing was also a form of communication among females, often including a direct appeal to other women to respond. They are "life-writings" that articulate personal beliefs and experiences as they reach out to a community of women with similar concerns for approbation and a shared sense, however subliminal, of value and purpose.

The popularity of the English advice tracts by women is noteworthy, attesting to the hunger with which the products of these infrequent incursions into a male-dominated genre were greeted by a seventeenth-century public audience swelled by the ranks of increasingly literate women. Arguably one of the first English women's advice-writings is "The Northren Mothers Blessing: The Way of Thrift," a charming lyrical poem of advice from a middle-class woman to her daughter that purports to have been written "nine yeares before the death of G. Chaucer" and was reproduced in many books of poems and manuscripts printed in sixteenth and early seventeenth centuries.[7] Leigh's tract, which most scholars agree was first published in 1616, enjoyed at least fifteen printings by 1630 and still saw editions coming out in 1707 and 1718 (Bell et al. 125). Joan Larsen Klein claims that it "went through at least twenty editions and an untold number of reprints" (287). In the modern world, however, perhaps because they are women's personal reflections, women's advice tracts have been largely ignored until recently, or are still treated in short excerpts in volumes of early women's writing.[8] But at a time when women's life-writings are needed to illuminate how women thought, felt, and sought affirmation in a period known to us largely by the echoes of men's voices, they deserve closer scrutiny. Early editions, printed in small leather-bound books that were so popular in their day, slumber in manuscript boxes at institutions like the Newberry Library in Chicago and the Huntington Library in San Marino, California, waiting to be reawakened.[9]

Part of a "minor" tradition, at least as far as printed materials are concerned, Dorothy Leigh's tract fits into an even smaller subgroup: advice-writing by women who feared they were dying. Leigh and Elizabeth Grymeston, author of *Miscelanea, Meditations, Memoratives* (1604) wrote of imminent death (Grymeston identifies her disease as consumption), and Elizabeth Joceline wrote *The Mothers Legacie to her*

Unborn Childe in 1624 when she was pregnant and fearful that the perils of contemporary medicine and child-birthing practices would prevent her ever from meeting her child. Joceline died within days of giving birth. The impunity death would bring these writers from the consequences of transgressing culturally determined boundaries might have contributed to their temerity in creating documents that could find their way into the public sphere. Margaret King writes that becoming a nun (interpreted by some orders as "dying" to the world)[10] freed women from the gender constrictions of contemporary life and allowed them the coveted chance to "develop the most esteemed craft or artistic or intellectual skills " (93-94). So, by fact and not by process, did impending death.

Dorothy Leigh's book of advice to her sons was published under the title *The Mothers Blessing: Or, The godly Counsaile of a Gentle-woman, not long since deceased, left behind for her Children: contayning many good exhortations, and godly admonitions, profitable for all Parents, to leave as a legacy to their children.*[11] Like the "Northren Mother," Dorothy Leigh is known to us best through the pages of her book. Time and the apparent lack of interest even in Leigh's period in investing the author of this popular tract with a history have shrouded the woman behind *The Mothers Blessing* from modern recognition almost as effectively as death shrouded her physical body from her primary intended audience, her sons. No facts reside in her biography except the dates of the manuscripts that have been found of this one book, and the fact that her patronym was Kemp.[12] She is referred to in Betty Travitsky's *Paradise of Women* as of the "middling class" (10) and by the subtitle to *The Blessing* itself, as noted above, as "a Gentle-woman." Deconstructing Leigh as an individual, therefore, is impossible—and unnecessary. Like other advice-writers and "feminist" tract writers, Dorothy Leigh's value to scholars of early modern culture lies not in individual status but in her articulation of women's importance and authority in private life, her sense of the common experience of all women, and her vision of the scope of the duty women shared to instruct and save.

Leigh's voice could have been lost to history like the voices of many other early women but for the fact that she wrote her thoughts down, an action that asserted the importance of preserving her words of advice and moral perspective. Her reasons for writing and thus violating what she calls "the usuall order of women" are complex. Initially, Leigh provides herself with the best possible reason given the dangerous ground she is treading: piety. She asserts she is driven by Christian fear that her impending death will prevent her from teaching her children the lessons necessary to leading godly and productive lives. She must commit her words to paper, and thus, significantly, to posterity, because she is "troubled, and vvearied with feare, lest my children should not finde the right way to Heauen" (A²-A²ᵛ). Leigh might well have been skeptical of the potential of zealous reformist sermons or the multiple handbooks on piety effectively and practically to guide her sons. She indeed expands the usual role of women by supplementing and supplanting these institutionalized voices with her own articulate and thorough exposition of individual piety and probity: her text is forty-five chapters and 269 pages, exclusive of dedications.

Another justification Leigh offers for writing is obedience. She notes in her dedication to sons George, John, and William that her deceased husband "charged in his will, by the love and duety which I bare him, to see you well instructed and brought up in knowledge" (A⁵). Had she not been ill, she might have taught them verbally; under the circumstances, she saw one sure way to carry out her husband's (and her) wishes: "Seeing my selfe going out of the world, and you but coming in, I know not how to performe this duety so well, as to leaue you these few lines" (A⁵ᵛ). Next she had to safeguard her manuscript so that "all the vvicked vvinde in the world could not blowe it away" (A⁴), to make sure that it would survive for her sons. "I could not see to what purpose it should tend," she writes, "unlesse it were sent abroad to you: for should it be left with the eldest, it is likely the youngest should haue little part in it" (A⁶).[13]

Like many of the women writers of her period, Leigh chose another woman as the executrix of her instructions to her children. In her first dedication, she describes with Shakespearean cadence her concern for "how this scrole should be kept for my children: for they were too young to receiue it, my selfe too old to keepe it, men too wise to direct it to, the world too wicked to endure it" (A³-A³ᵛ). Convinced that feminine virtue was the best "Protectress of this my booke" and that "the highest bloud had the lowest [humblest] minde" (A³ᵛ), she dedicates her book to Princess Elizabeth, daughter of James I of England. In dedicating her work to a woman she joined an ongoing tradition among women artists. As Bell, Parfitt, and Shepherd point out, "Appeals by women to other women as patrons or protectors are frequent in the published writing of this period: dedications, prefaces and dedicatory sonnets addressed to other women make an explicit request for protection against men and the world in general" (248). Mary Sidney Herbert, for example, dedicated her Psalm translations to Queen Elizabeth, and Aemilia Lanyer sought the protection of the Queen and various of her women.[14]

In the body of the text, Leigh establishes a preemptive apology for female writing that asserts maternal love and responsibility as the passions that combine with piety and obedience to provide the driving force of this work:

Bvt lest you should maruaile, my children, why I doe not according to the usuall custom of women, exhort you by word and admonitions, rather then be writing: a thing so vnusuall among vs . . . knowe therefore that it was the motherly affection that I bare vnto you all, which made me now . . . forget my selfe. (3-4)

Leigh enumerates several "causes" or justifications for writing in the course of the text ("for you may thinke that had I but one cause, I would not haue changed the usuall order of women") in an astute compromise between "self-assertion and self-abnegation," a phrase Barbara Everett uses to illustrate the necessarily close tie between aggression and submissiveness in Renaissance courtly ritual.[15] Leigh's intention is to save, and in order to do that she has to assert herself, "to write them the right way that I had truely obserued out of the written Word of God, lest for want of warning they might fall where I stumbled, and then I should thinke my selfe in the fault, who knew there were such downe-fals . . . and yet had not told the[m] therof" (A²ᵛ).

Knowing the Pauline injunction against women teachers, Leigh argues: "Can any man blame a Mother (who indeed brought forthe her childe with much paine) though shee labour againe till Christ be formed in them? Could Saint Paul wish himselfe seperated from God for his brethrens sake? And will not a Mother venture to offend the world for her childrens sake?" (11-12).

Leigh's book, in fact, resonates with her certainty that showing children the right way is a mother's work, comparable to what "euery man will doe for his friend" (A²ᵛ). Leigh voices distrust of men, enemies of female chastity who "lye in waite every where to deceive us" (33). But her devotion to her male children is evident, and she displays respect for her deceased husband's interest in their welfare. She embraces the task of bringing them up piously, her husband's desire and her aim, implicitly emphasizing the second part of a quotation from Proverbs on the title page: "My sonne, heare the instruction of the father and forsake not the law of thy mother."

Leigh's numerous passages of apology and explanation appear on first reading to set a self-deprecatory tone for the whole piece. But these, and her insistence on her religious and parental mission, enable her to sidestep the double-bind Lisa Jardine claims beset educated Renaissance women. Their articulateness, although encouraged by liberal humanists, exposed them to social backlash such as that suffered by Veronese humanist Isotta Nogarola, whose scholarly activities met with virulent attacks, one critic characterizing her conduct as "obscene." "I have long believed that saying of numerous wise men," he writes, " 'The woman of fluent speech (eloquentem) is never chaste, and this can be supported by the example of the great number of most learned women.'"[16] Skill in rhetoric damned women in the eyes of Protestant reformers. In her *Still Harping on Daughters,* Jardine describes

the actual . . . helplessness of the wife in a liberalized marriage which laid strong emphasis on dialogue between partners, but continued . . . to treat articulateness in women as unseemly and unreliable. Liberal theory encourages the partner-wife to speak her mind; illiberal tradition, on the look out for signs of female disruptiveness, reduces her to a silence which renders her more powerless than ever. (46-47)

Leigh manipulates the tradition of silence first by explaining the reasons why her love of God and of her children compels her to break it, and ultimately by the survival of her manuscript, which proves that women's words could be valued by society, and that the silencing of the body does not mandate the extinction of the mind or its influence. With her book, she transcends what the editors of historian Joan Kelly-Gadol's *Women, History, and Theory* call that "false division within theory between a female sphere of 'private' as opposed to a male sphere of 'public' activity" and another "false division between personal experience and knowledge, the subjective and the objective" (xxiii). Leigh is both intimate and public, self-effacing and self-proclaiming, modest and knowledgeable. These transcendences would make her, by some definitions of feminism, a revolutionary in her time.

Not only did Leigh render her thoughts public and lasting, she made them inclusive. The heading to chapter 1 states, "The occasion of writing this Booke, was the consideration of the care of Parents for their Children." She does not say "a Parent for her Children," but rather reinforces the statement of universality made by the subtitle to the *Blessing* ("contayning many good exhortations, and godly admonitions, profitable *for all Parents, to leave as a legacy to their children*" [italics hers]). This inclusiveness, and her act of entrusting the manuscript to a powerful woman outside her family, confirm Leigh's desire to speak to a wider audience than her own sons. Employing a modest pose typical of the times, Leigh admits that her writing might not be equal in quality to the "many godly bookes in the world" written by men, but she aims criticism at the gender that had, in greater numbers than women, the education to read. She notes that often good books "mould in some mens studies, while their Masters are mard, because they will not meditate vpon them" (4). This image of men too busy to enrich their own souls or to take responsibility for others', and a direct appeal to women that follows, proclaim a belief that once they are shown the way, women might take a leadership role in social morality. Leigh challenges other members of her sex to speak up about what they know best. Women, she claims,

who, I feare, will blush at my boldnesse [should] not be ashamed to shew their infirmities . . . give men the first and chiefe place: yet let vs labor to come in the second; and because wee must needs confesse, that sinne entred by vs into our posterity, let vs shew how carefull wee are to seeke to Christ . . . to follow Christ, who will carry them to the height of heauen. (16-17)

This is an interesting call to action for women. Leigh seems to be suggesting that women owe it to themselves to speak up ("shew," "confesse") on social and moral issues because of the bad name they inherit from Eve. They should commit themselves to prove publicly that they are pious and responsible and to encourage others to be the same, for to do so will insure their salvation. In the forty-five chapters of her text, Leigh "shews" her own godliness and didacticism, addressing such matters as education, personal thrift and industry, social responsibility, religious devotion, marriage, servants, and facing death. She demonstrates that woman can wield the authority to offer spiritual and practical advice to all members of the Renaissance family.

Leigh characterizes at length the nature of the family she is referring to. This was a time when many children were sent out to wet nurses, and later to other households to be raised and trained, practices that influenced writers like Lawrence Stone to maintain that children were still not accorded much attention in Renaissance society. But Leigh describes a fierce parental entanglement with the welfare of children:

My Children, when I did truely weigh, rightly consider, and likewise perfectly see the great care, labour, trauaile, and continuall study, which Parents take to inrich their children, some wearing their bodyes with labour, some breaking their sleepes with care, some sparing from their owne bellies, and many hazarding their soules, some by bribery, some by simony, others by periurie, and a multitude by usury . . . not caring if the whole Common-wealth bee impouerished, so their children be inriched: for themselves they can bee content with meate, drinke, and cloth, so that their children, by their meanes, may bee made rich. (I-12)

Leigh's own determination to guide her children, even beyond the grave, reflects the same deep commitment to their welfare that reverberates in this passage. But she takes it upon herself to correct a portion of this dedication to the Protestant ethic: she reminds parents that the best things they can procure for their children are spiritual. She specifically insists on education for all young children, "bee they Males or Females," advocating beginning children's instruction as early as age four, or "so soone as it can conueniently learne," and firmly exhorting parents to teach their children to read the Bible "in their own mother-tongue" (24-26). Not to do so, she darkly warns, is a sign of parental idleness and sloth. In fact, she suggests that adults refuse to become godparents unless the natural parents agree to teach the children to read at an early age. Reading is terribly important to Leigh, whose writing suggests that she was something of a scholar. Her text asserts that reading is the labor of a chaste woman, a godly man, and an industrious child. It is the biggest key to salvation besides prayer, which she devotes many chapters to, because each individual who reads can study the Bible, the printed sermons, and other worthy books. Leigh mentions reading frequently, and devotes a separate chapter to "How to reade with profit" (chapter 25).

Along with reading goes the responsibility to teach, and hence to write. *"I know (sayth God) that Abraham will teach his Children, and his childrens children,"* Leigh quotes, pointing out that Deuteronomy enjoins humankind "to write it upon the walles of your houses" (25-26). Leigh devotes a chapter to urging parents to teach their children to write, so they can, like her, pass on the word of God. Writing is labor that strengthens the spirit, and just as Leigh takes risks to do so, she hopes her sons will also. She explains her own writing, yet again: "I thought it fit to give you good example, and by writing to entreat you, that when it shall please God to give you both vertue and grace with your learning, he having made you men, that you may write and speake the Word of God" (14-15). Leigh hopes that her sons, when they are grown, will "remember to write a booke vnto your children of the right and true way to happinesse, which may remaine with them and their for euer" (16). Writing should be for them, as it is for her, an act of industry, moral didacticism, and familial responsibility. It is a self-proclamation as well.

Leigh proclaims more than rigorous feminine devotion in her book. She demonstrates her superior intelligence and learning not just in her articulate delivery, which could have been enhanced by an editor, but by her intellectual imagery, which is less likely to have been tampered with. In her first dedication, she visualizes her children on a path that should lead them to heaven but which is obstructed with "downe-fals" that impede progress up "the Hill to Heauen." Her role as guide is to steer them away from the false paths. Her language and imagery are highly derivative of the literary prototypes that existed by the early modern period for this kind of spiritual and/or heroic journey, including the Bible, the devotional language of the myriad piety books and the sermons that circulated in manuscript, and the books on saints' lives that were so often referred to in defenses of women's chastity.[17] In fact, Leigh's pursuit of her children's piety often veers into discussion of feminine chastity, a topic that arises when she considers her own religious responsibility to her children, her choice of a protectress for her book, her sons' selection of wives, their wives' fidelity, and even the choice of children's names. Leigh's combination of self-assertion and eloquence is however not in the least rendered self-conscious by her firm assumption of feminine virtue. It serves to invest her practical advice with quiet authority and not to distract from this goal with flattering intellectual or moral self-congratulation.

Even more than pride, the greatest threat to virtue and piety in Leigh's lexicon is idleness. Leigh prefaces the many different areas of advice in *The Mothers Blessing* with an appeal to industry. In a little section entitled "Counsell to my Children" that precedes even the table of contents, she presents a seven-stanza lyric to the "laborous" bee, the time-honored defender against idleness, that "cardinal sin according to bourgeois economy," according to Louis B. Wright (44). Interestingly reversing the usual gender of the worker bee, she renders it a female symbol not just of hard work but of vision (she foresees how long the winter will last and doesn't stop working too soon), persistence (she visits each flower), and obedience: she doesn't question the task or the nature of it, but labors faithfully to preserve herself and her community from death.

> Shee lookes not who did place the Plant,
> nor how the flowre did grow;
> Whether so stately vp aloft,
> or neere the ground below.
> But where shee finds it, there shee workes,
> and gets the wholsome food,
> and beares it home and layes it vp,
> to doe her Country good. (A⁶ᵛ-A⁷)

Leigh's industrious bee vanquishes the ravishments of death itself, which beset the idle bee, who rests too soon and too soon "looketh out, and seeth death/ready her to devoure" (A7). She represents the bee as a symbol of feminine virtue and of faith and good works. Leigh's prescription for salvation is finely honed with such analogies, which identify the good work that sanctifies the mother who has labored to bring children into this world and to teach them how to secure a place in the next.

One of the words written on the walls of her sons' houses should be fidelity, and Leigh counsels men to choose their future wives carefully so that they can be loyal husbands who treat their wives as equals rather than subjugating them. Likewise, she counsels women to be chaste and totally faithful to their husbands, recalling the heroines of antiquity who "before they would bee defiled, haue beene carelesse of their liues" (38). But Leigh firmly dispells the onus of Eve's sin. Through Mary, God redeemed woman, "for shee hath taken away the reproach which of right belonged vnto vs, and by the seed of the woman we are all saved." Mary, in fact, is God "working in a woman," just as Jesus is God working in a man. And whereas woman played a part in Jesus's creation, "man can claime no part" in Mary (44).

It is the prerogative, Leigh seems to be saying, of the mother, more than any other female, to usurp male ownership of creation, of godliness, of authority. Her profound responsibility lends her eloquence she might not otherwise have. It is no mild disclaimer when she remarks that she may "offend the world." But the compulsion of Leigh's pious motive and the power of her sense of agency outweigh considerations of social conformity and fly in the face of public opinion that could (but interestingly did not) decry her writing and suppress her text. "Therefore let no man blame a Mother, though she something exceede in writing to her children, since every man knows that the love of a Mother to her children, is hardly contained within the bounds of reason" (12). Her disregard for her social reputation counterbalances any complicity her location in a patriarchal culture forces her to demonstrate in her conventional definition of female virtue as piety and obedience, and greatly enhances the authority of her words when she simultaneously defines her virtue in terms of forthrightness, assertiveness, and publication. It is precisely her "forgetting herself" that validates her piety and enables her to speak to the world as well as to her sons.

As far as we know, Dorothy Leigh did not see her words into print personally. But her desire to use her intelligence and education for good, to instruct her sons and to speak to other parents as well, clearly influenced her patroness or someone close to her to do so for her. Public acceptance of this action, to which so many reprintings attest, rent the fabric of silence patriarchal Renaissance society had woven around its women.

Leigh's literary experiment was joined, as suggested above, by other texts of this new genre. Both Elizabeth Joceline's *Mothers Legacie* and Elizabeth Grymeston's book to her son argue an earnest case for the obligations of motherhood that resembles Leigh's own. Joceline had carefully prepared herself for the eventuality of death, buying her own

winding sheet and writing this tract, the presumption of which she justi-
fies by her "motherly zeale," and because "that I wrote to a child, and
though I were but a woman, yet to a child's judgment, what I understood
might serve for a foundation of better learning" (B²ᵛ-Bˢ). And Grymeston
adds an honest admission of another motive also clear in Dorothy
Leigh's text: self-representation. "There is nothing so strong as the force
of love," Grymeston wrote in 1604:

There is no mother can either more affectionately shew hir nature, or more naturally manifest hir affection, than in aduising hir children out of hir owne experience. . . . Out of these resolutions, finding the libertie of this age to be such . . . I
resolued to breake the barren soile of my fruitlesse braine, to dictate something
for thy direction; the rather for that as I am now a dead woman among the
liuing, so . . . thou maiest see the true portrature of thy mothers minde. (A³-A3v)

By fashioning their work as pious reflection, these writers were able to
leave lasting documents that allowed their children, and posterity, famil-
iarity with the personal images and distinctive cadences with which they
conceived their own minds and souls.

It is especially significant that Dorothy Leigh and the other women
advice-writers mentioned above, whose works so successfully crossed
the barrier of privacy society had erected around women, all published
posthumously. It is irresistible to speculate that they were conscious,
however tragically, of manipulating the rule of feminine silence in order
to record their thoughts publicly, and to create mothers for their children
who would never disappear. Further, it seems possible that it was just
this circumstance of their maintaining bodily, deathly, silence while their
words were carried to the public in another medium that facilitated
public acceptance. Their successful circumvention of cultural taboos had
literary precedent. Shakespeare's outspoken and didactic heroines in the
comedies and romances often resorted to disguise to exercise their arts
of persuasion, preserving the illusion of chaste silence on the part of the
women the public believed to be elsewhere while a man with a different
name spoke their words. Even more to the point, Juliet and *Much Ado*'s
Hero used (pretended) death as persuasion—quietly to oppose and win
over the forces ranged against them. And *The Winter's Tale*'s Hermione's sixteen-year death safely transferred her words, ignored by her
husband, Leontes, while she was alive, to the tongue of Paulina, who
kept them viable by continually repeating them, publishing them, as it
were, in successive editions. Paulina redeemed Hermione's honor and
virtue the more effectively by continually referring to her death. Just so,
the words of advice Grymeston, Jocelin, and Leigh offered to the world

beyond the confines of their own sphere were more poignantly effective because they were spoken, in a way, by silent women.

By avoiding the antagonism that the articulations of women often incited, Dorothy Leigh and the other women advice-writers quietly repositioned women in society, characterizing them as civilizing influences on their fellow humans rather than agents of corruption, as male writings so often viewed them. In this sense they formed a new female subject with an agenda, and a discourse, all their own. These writings appropriated the existing audience of male courtesy manuals, and created a new one. Fitting into this new tradition was the diary of Lady Grace Mildmay (1552-1620), which reflects the author's concerns about the education of her grandchildren,[19] *The Countess of Lincoln's Nursery,* a tract designed to convince the author's daughter and other women to breast-feed their own children, and *The Mothers Counsell, or Live Within Compasse. Being the Last Will and Testament to her dearest Daughter, which may serve for a worthy Legacie to all the Women in the world, which desire good report from men in the world, and grace from Christ Jesus in the last day* (1630) by an author identified as "M. R."

An articulate leader in this tradition that was often interrupted by historical circumstance and prejudice, Dorothy Leigh tried to make new sense of the world that was, and would be for a long time to come, organized by a male ideology. The advice she tenders in *The Mothers Blessing* is more, ultimately, than the specifics it enumerates. She advises women to recognize their expertise, to trust their beliefs, to embrace their maternal responsibility, to use their voices, and, ultimately, to take charge of the world's morality, challenging not just the usual order of women but the judgments of society and history. This is an impressive, but apparently not daunting, task, and a task suited best to a mother, whose labor for her children, Leigh insists, is "a pleasant labour, a profitable labour: a labour without the which the soule cannot live" (5). The reward of the text, as Leigh poignantly declares, is that although "nature telleth mee, that I cannot long bee heere to speake vnto you . . . this my minde will continue long after me in writing" (12).

Notes

I presented an earlier version of this essay under the title "'That all men may say thou art true as steele': Female Fashioning in English Advice-Writing" at the Women and Power Symposium at the National Museum of Women in the Arts in Washington, D.C. in March 1993. That paper is bound with the other conference proceedings on the shelves of the National Museum's library. I am indebted to Merry Wiesner-Hanks, whose seminar at the Newberry Library in 1992 on gender and power in the Renaissance first led me to the library's fine collection of early manuscripts, and to both her and Charles Ross for reading the original paper on women advice writers and subsequent versions that focused more specifically on Dorothy Leigh. I am grateful, too, to the participants Workshop 34, "Teaching Women Writers," at the 1994 Attending to Women in Early Modern Europe Symposium and the audiences of my sessions at the 1995 Central Renaissance Association and the Sixteenth Century Studies conferences for their responses to my theories about the similarities between women's manipulation of silence in Shakespeare and in early women's advice-writing.

1. One thinks particularly of daughter Margaret More Roper, whose translation of Eusebius from Greek to Latin many consider brilliant. But More encouraged her not to have it published, and she did not. (See Travitsky 11, 36.)

2. This fact inspired the middle classes while it irritated some above them. Renaissance satirist Thomas Nashe remarked, "Pride the perverter of all Vertue, sitteth appareled in the Marchants spoils, and ruine of yoong Citizens: and scorneth learning, that gave their upstart Fathers, titles of gentry." This quote is reprinted in Wright (47-48), as is a similar but earlier complaint registered in the late fourteenth-century *Peres the Ploughmans Crede:* "Now may every cobbler set his son to school, and every beggar's brat learn from the book. . . . So that the beggar's brat becomes a bishop, to sit esteemed among the peers of the land, and lords' sons bow down to the good-for-nothing" (J. W. Adamson, *A Short History of Education* [Cambridge: University P, 1922] 66, a modernization of the original manuscript, published about 1394. Quoted in Wright 45.)

3. Two scholars who included early female advice-writers long before they came to the attention of other literary historians were Ruth Willard Hughey, whose unpublished doctoral dissertation at Cornell in 1932 was entitled "Cultural Interests of Women in England from 1524-1640: Indicated in the Writings of the Women: A Survey," and Charlotte Kohler, whose unpublished doctoral dissertation for the University of Virginia was "The Elizabethan Woman of Letters: The Extent of Her Literary Activities."

4. Fiction is used here to refer to the genre that combined the epic and the romantic adventure, such as Sidney's *Arcadia.*

5. Travitsky notes that "writing by women was seen as a form of public instruction and as a public speaking out, two types of activity disapproved [of] in women by even the most liberal of their advocates" (xviii).

6. Among the fathers who wrote advice books for their sons are Sir Walter Ralegh, William Cecil, Richard Vaughan, and Francis Osborne.

7. For example, one of the volumes I found the manuscript in contains "Certaine Worthy Manuscript Poems of great Antiquitie Reserved long in the

Studie of a Northfolke Gentleman." It was published in 1597 (London: Robert Robertson).

8. For brief discussions of Dorothy Leigh's *Mothers Blessing,* for instance, see Tavitsky, *Paradise* 55-57; Beilin 275-80; Bell, Parfitt, and Sheperd 125; and Henderson and McManus 54-55. Joan Larsen Klein has a longer essay on Leigh in her *Daughters, Wives, and Widows,* as does Kristen Poole in "The Fittest Closet," an essay in *SEL* that came to my attention while I was making the final revisions on this one. It highlights many of the sections in *The Mothers Blessing* I note and comes to conclusions similar to mine to support her view of Leigh's successful negotiation of the boundary between public and private writing.

9. But they do not, as Leigh suggests many good books do, "mould" (282). I first read the manuscript of the 1627 edition of *The Mothers Blessing* at the Newberry Library in 1992, and later found the 1618 manuscript at the Huntington. Both were in remarkably good condition given their age.

10. An example is Julian of Norwich, a fourteenth-century nun who, scholars believe, underwent a burial service to demonstrate her total break with the world, but became so famous as an anchoress that she was sought out by other pious women such as Margery Kempe, who visited her.

11. Unless otherwise noted, all quotations from *The Mothers Blessing* are taken from the 1618 manuscript (fourth edition).

12. See Leigh's short entry in Bell et al. (125). Travitsky also lists her maiden name as Kemp (55). Klein cites an October 1868 *Notes and Queries* article that suggested that Leigh "might have been the daughter of William Kemp of Finchingfield and the wife of Ralph Leigh, a soldier under the Earl of Essex at Cadiz," but she adds that the *Dictionary of National Biography* mentions that William Kemp had no children. She also suggests that Leigh could have been the daughter of Robert Kemp and wife of Ralph Lee. Poole also attempts to track Leigh's heritage, arguing for a link between the family Dorothy probably married into and the Brooke family of Elizabeth Brooke Joceline. But this detective work is inconclusive; and would it, in any event, really tell us who Leigh was? Klein concludes that "not only to we not know who she was, even late in the nineteenth century attempts to identify her did so by trying to discover her father, husband, and son" (288).

13. Poole discounts this justification for writing as an "unlikely excuse," but I am reminded of Shakespeare's Orlando, whose complaint in the opening scene of *As You Like It* is precisely that his dead father's wish that he be educated was entrusted to his eldest brother, who ignored this legacy for him, the third and youngest son.

14. Bell et al. add Anne Prowse, who dedicated to the Countess of Warwick, and Alice Sutcliffe, who dedicated her *Meditations of man's mortalitie* to the Duchess of Buckingham and the Countess of Denbigh, asking for their pro-

tection against "mocking Ishmaels" and remarking "it being, I know not usuall for a Woman to doe such things" (248).

15. Everett juxtaposes these terms in her July 8, 1994, *Times Literary Supplement* article on Shakespeare's sonnets.

16. Quoted in Lisa Jardine's *Still Harping* 57, re T. W. Baldwin's *William Shakspere's small Latine and lesse Greek*, 2 vols. (Urbana: U of Illinois P, 1944) and Aphthonius, *Progymnasmata*, Latin translation, R. Agricola.

17. Leigh's various paths to the hill to heaven are also reminiscent of the beginning of Canto One of Dante's *Inferno*, but Leigh might have had no access to Dante, or to Chaucer, whose dream sequences seem to echo in her first dedication.

18. For portions of Lady Mildmay's diary, see Rachel Wiegall's "An Elizabethan Gentlewoman" and Betty Travitsky, *Paradise* 83-85.

Works Cited

Beilin, Elaine V. *Redeeming Eve: Women Writers of the English Renaissance.* Princeton: Princeton UP, 1987.

Bell, Maureen, George Parfitt, and Simon Shepherd. *A Biographical Dictionary of English Women Writers, 1580-1720.* Boston: Hall, 1990.

Cressy, David. "Literacy in Pre-industrial England." *Societas: A Review of Social History* 4 (Summer 1974): 229-40.

Everett, Barbara. "Shakespeare's Greening." *Times Literary Supplement* 8 July 1994: 11-13.

Grymeston, Elizabeth. *Miscelanea, meditations, memoratives.* London: Printed by M. Bradwood for F. Norton, 1604.

Henderson, Katherine Usher, and Barbara F. McManus. *Half-Humankind: Contexts and Texts of the Controversy about Women in England, 1540-1640.* Urbana: U of Illinois P, 1985.

Hughey, Ruth Willard. "Cultural Interests of Women in England from 1524-1640: Indicated in the Writings of the Women: A Survey." Diss. Cornell, 1932.

Jardine, Lisa. *Still Harping on Daughters: Women and Drama in the Age of Shakespeare.* New York: Columbia UP, 1983, 1989.

Joceline, Elizabeth. *The Mothers Legacie to Her Unborn Childe.* London: John Haviland, 1624.

Kelly, Joan. *Women, History, and Theory.* Chicago: U of Chicago P, 1984.

King, Margaret. *Women of the Renaissance.* Chicago: U of Chicago P, 1991.

Klein, Joan Larsen. *Daughters, Wives, and Widows: Writings by Men about Women and Marriage in England, 1500-1640.* Urbana: U of Illinois P, 1992.

Kohler, Charlotte. "The Elizabethan Woman of Letters: The Extent of Her Literary Activities." Diss. U of Virginia, 1936.

Leigh, Dorothy. *The Mothers Blessing: Or, the Godly Counsaile of a Gentlewoman, The Fourth Edition*. London: [S. Stafford] F. J. Budge, 1618.

Lincoln, Elizabeth Clinton, Countess of. *The Covntesse of Lincolnes nvrserie*. Oxford: Printed by I. Lichfield and I. Short, 1622.

M.R. *The Mothers Counsell, or, Liue within compasse: being the last will and testament to her dearest daughter*. London: Printed for I. Wright, 163(1?).

"The Northren Mothers Blessing. The Way of Thrift." *Certaine Worthye Manuscript Poems of Great Antiquitie. . . .* London: Robert Robinson for Robert Dexter, 1597.

Poole, Kristin. " 'The fittest closet for all goodness': Authorial Strategies of Jacobean Mothers' Manuals." *SEL* 35 1995: 69-88.

Showalter, Elaine. *A Literature of Their Own: British Women Novelists from Brontë to Lessing*. Princeton: Princton UP, 1977.

Stone, Lawrence. *The Family, Sex, and Marriage in England, 1500-1800*. New York: Harpers, 1977.

Travitsky, Betty. *The Paradise of Women: Writings by Englishwomen of the Renaissance*. New York: Columbia UP, 1989.

Vives, Juan Luis. *A very fruteful and pleasant boke called the instruction of a Christen woman made fyrst in Latin and dedicated unto the quene good grace by the right famous clerke mayster Lewes Vives*. London: 1529.

Wiegall, Rachel. "An Elizabethan Gentlewoman." *Quarterly Review* 215 (1911): 119-35.

Wright, Louis B. *Middle Class Culture in Elizabethan England*. Ithaca: Cornell UP, 1958.

13

"When a Woman So Far Outsteps Her Proper Sphere": Counter-Romantic Tourism

Angela D. Jones

Mary Wollstonecraft is the particular woman who, according to the anonymous reviewer for the *British Critic*,[1] ignored proprietary boundaries in her autobiographical travelogue, *Letters Written during a Short Residence in Sweden, Norway, and Denmark*, published by Joseph Johnson in 1796.[2] Under attack for dismissing "facts" too hastily and for promoting fallacious thinking about women's oppression in her "letters for the press" (Author's Appendix 197; 346), Wollstonecraft is finally likened to Phaeton in this 1796 review. Thus this record of Scandinavian travel, permitting its author to cycle continuously through landscape description, personal revelation, and political commentary, threatened at least one male reader if we take his allusion at face value. This reviewer expresses a minority opinion, however, on the potential destructiveness of Wollstonecraft's travelogue. Most contemporary reviewers, in fact, praised her description of natural scenery, sympathized with the personal trauma related, and chastised to varying degrees the "woman-as-thinker" represented therein.[3] What interests me, however, is this anonymous reviewer's sense of a "proper sphere." It is tempting to conclude that because he charges Wollstonecraft with "derid[ing] facts which she cannot disprove, and avow[ing] opinions which it is dangerous to disseminate," this reviewer is likewise saying that traveling women are dangerous, and that their "proper sphere" is the domestic sphere. Yoking Wollstonecraft to another traveler, the neophyte chariot-driver who nearly destroyed the world, certainly supports this argument. I suggest, however, that it is the travelogue form, licensing Wollstonecraft to roam philosophically as much as she does literally, all the while blurring boundaries between personal and descriptive modes, that upsets this reviewer. I further propose that critics oversimplify the matter of separate spheres and the subversiveness of women's travel in claiming that "women in the late eighteenth and nineteenth centuries were expected

209

for the most part to remain in the domestic sphere. The very act of travel for them was not only a novelty but also a challenge to the standards and norms of society" (Hartley 5). Although I will ultimately demonstrate that Wollstonecraft's travelogue—like so many produced by romantic women travelers—subverts popular aesthetic and tourism discourses, its "challenge to the standards and norms of society" rests more with its complication of landscape perspective than with the woman writer's waywardness.

My understanding of counter-romantic tourism hinges on Rita Felski's concept of a "feminist counter-public sphere" (9), located specifically within the society of late capitalism and continuous with eighteenth and nineteenth century struggle for women's political and social enfranchisement (12). Felski suggests that women's autobiographical writing, specifically, twentieth-century feminist confession, facilitated the production of this "oppositional discursive space" (121). Despite her acknowledgment that the eighteenth century saw the beginning growth of a counter-public sphere, Felski ignores the specific contributions romantic women lifewriters like Wollstonecraft made to it: "the autobiographical writing inspired by the women's movement differs . . . from the traditional autobiography of bourgeois individualism, which presents itself as the record of an unusual but exemplary life. Precisely because of this uniqueness, the eighteenth-century autobiography claims a universal significance" (94).[4] Felski clearly has in mind the androcentric bias apparent in autobiography studies, but she also implies that self-expression in the eighteenth century is much more monolithic than is the case. She suggests that autobiographies produced by "exemplary" men were the predominant, if not exclusive, form of published self-expression in the period, and that twentieth-century feminist confession has little in common with earlier women's life-writing.

Felski thus paves the way for Anne Mellor's discussion of "feminine Romanticism" as an ideology articulating an alternative to the doctrine of separate spheres:

Many women writers of the Romantic era . . . explicitly or implicitly advocated . . . the value of rational love, an ethic of care, and gender equality as a challenge both to a domestic ideology that would confine women within the home and to a capitalist laissez-faire system that would set the rights of the individual, free-will or rational choice, and an ethic of justice above the needs of the community as a whole. (*R&G* 84)

I read Mellor as sorting gendered romantic traditions from one another by specifying Felski's notion of a "feminist counter-public sphere" within a late-eighteenth-century context. She is not ahistorically applying this notion of a "feminist counter-public sphere" to romantic women writers but attempting to identify its particular eighteenth-century history. It is then just a small step from Mellor's characterization of "feminine romanticism" to my contention that Wollstonecraft's travelogue contributes to counter-public discourse on romantic tourism, thus forbidding any simplistic reading of separate spheres. Wollstonecraft did not, to paraphrase Mary Morris, move through the world differently than a man (xvii), but confronted paradigms of travel that privileged normatively masculine ways of perceiving and representing oneself and one's surroundings. Her travelogue did not so much challenge preexistent expectations for private containment, but suggests that the conventions used to represent landscapes placed her in a different social relationship to the act of travel. Insofar as it is read as life-writing, moreover, Wollstonecraft's travelogue helps us account for its own erasure as a form of self-representation within literary romanticism.

Wollstonecraft produced and published *Letters Written during a Short Residence in Sweden, Norway, and Denmark* in spite of, or, perhaps, because of, tremendous personal upheaval at the age of thirty-six. In April 1795, Wollstonecraft returned home from France a single mother with French nursemaid, Marguerite Fournée, in tow. A short-lived affair with American author and captain, Gilbert Imlay, whom she had met in 1793 while living in Paris with Girondist leaders, yielded her daughter, Fanny, and, ultimately, a broken heart as well. Wollstonecraft arrived in London that spring to find Imlay aloof, already in pursuit of other women. Regardless of whether she set out for Scandinavia in the summer of 1795 to secure the necessary £1000 to emigrate to America with him and/or to support herself and her daughter by producing a travelogue, there appears little doubt that Wollstonecraft intended to act as business agent for her lover abroad. Indeed, a Norwegian captain, Peder Ellefsen, had apparently bilked Imlay out of goods being transported for him from France past the English blockade. Wollstonecraft was thus commissioned by Imlay to represent his interests in Risør, Norway, arguably leaving him to pursue other women freely as well. So from June to September Wollstonecraft traveled Scandinavia with her daughter and nursemaid as escorts, recording her impressions of landscapes "little-known to most Britons" at the end of the eighteenth century (Hartley 58). Back in London that autumn and unequivocally rejected by the lover on whose behalf she had acted, Mary Wollstonecraft attempted suicide, throwing herself off Putney Bridge. She survived, of course, to see her experiences abroad published in the form of twenty-five letters, ostensibly addressed to an "assumed audience of one," Imlay (Hartley

79). A separate set of posthumously published letters to Imlay implicitly contests the privacy of those made available to the public in this travelogue.[5]

Nearly all critical responses to Wollstonecraft's travelogue foreground self-disclosure as a dramatic feature of the text, though the form that expression takes is not always of interest. Hartley locates Wollstonecraft's *Letters from Norway* within an eighteenth-century trend toward greater personal expression in travel work, but also identifies it as a precursor for its degree of self-revelation (31). Mitzi Myers, one of the earlier commentators on the travelogue, regards it as "a generic hybrid, a kind of subjective autobiography superimposed on a travelogue" (166). Myers's sense that Wollstonecraft used the travelogue to enhance self-awareness and to sort through her attitudes toward human progress more than to describe Scandinavia is faintly echoed by Eleanor Ty. Citing it as "a virtual failure as a travel guide" and as indicative of the problems of self-representation for an eighteenth-century woman (66), Ty emphasizes the travelogue's hybridity as a consequence of alienation from "the rational linguistic world of the Father" (67). According to Ty, Wollstonecraft's decision to represent herself in the form of a travelogue suggests the author's profound alienation from the symbolic and her resultant "polarized subjectivity" (63). The epistolary travelogue is read, in other words, as a "covert" form, one that would permit Wollstonecraft to write "from the perspective of the daughter" through identification with her infant daughter, Fanny (61). Although Ty attempts to account for the gendering of form in stressing Wollstonecraft's identification as a daughter, she also implies that writing as both a mother and a daughter disables her as an author. Jeanne Moskal's contention that Wollstonecraft accented "the affectionate tie between the traveling mother and daughter" in order to revise cultural biases against women travel writers seems far more compelling (264).[6] I would also add that the traveling mother motif which organizes the travelogue is essential to Wollstonecraft's ability to remove the Burkean sublime from a paradigm of individualism by associating it with social and familial contexts. Her self-representation as a new mother traveling with her infant daughter is, in other words, crucial to characterizations of *Letters from Norway*[7] as both life-writing and travel writing.

No reader could ignore the presence of the strong writing subject in *Letters from Norway*, including the author herself. Indeed, Wollstonecraft opens with an "Advertisement" attesting to the selfhood she reveals in her travelogue: "I found I could not avoid being continually the first person—'the little hero of each tale.' . . . I give [my readers] leave to shut the book, if they do not wish to become better acquainted with me" (5; 241).[8] Wollstonecraft speculates briefly that such egotism may be a "fault," only to dismiss the concern as secondary to the negative consequences of self-censorship: "[I]n proportion as I arranged my thoughts, my letter, I found, became stiff and affected: I, therefore, determined to let my remarks and reflections flow unrestrained . . . relating the effect different objects had produced on my mind and feelings, whilst the impression was still fresh" (5; 241). Leaving in the personal apparently accomplished more than just spontaneity and fluidity, as her future husband, William Godwin, decided, "[I]f ever there was a book calculated to make a man in love with its author, this appears to me to be the book" (St. Clair 161). Similarly, Robert Southey declared to Joseph Cottle that Wollstonecraft's Scandinavian travelogue had "made [him] in love with a cold climate, and frost and snow, with a northern moonlight" (Holmes 17). And Jane Moore has recently argued that Samuel Taylor Coleridge was so threatened by the powerful female subject represented in *Letters from Norway* that he attempted to master it through plagiarism in "Kubla Khan." In spite of what these hyperbolic responses imply about the author's projected self, Wollstonecraft, according to Debra Hartley, felt "a need to justify the fact that she is 'the little hero of each tale'" which her romantic counterpart, William Wordsworth, could ignore, claiming unapologetically "that the theme of *The Prelude* will be 'the story of my life'" (87). Owing to its personal character, however, Wordsworth did refuse to publish his autobiography in his lifetime. Nevertheless the material conditions for his self-production were distinct from Wollstonecraft's and are worth teasing out here. I would add as well that I read Wollstonecraft's apparent apology as a trope of qualification common to much eighteenth-century women's writing, one that arguably draws more attention to her selfhood than it negates.[9]

Wollstonecraft links the writing of her journal with increased self-awareness. Her daily experience as a traveler constitutes her subject matter, but it also facilitates deeper self-reflexivity:

What a long time it requires to know ourselves; and yet almost every one has more of this knowledge than he is willing to own, even to himself. I cannot immediately determine whether I ought to rejoice at having turned over in this solitude a new page in the history of my own heart, though I may venture to assure you that a further acquaintance with mankind only tends to increase my respect for your judgment, and esteem for your character. (IX: 90-91; 289)

This page-turning metaphor unambiguously relates her expanding self-knowledge to the literal pages of her travelogue. Her ambivalence about this enhanced self-awareness may, in fact, have been as much an attempt to inspire guilt in her addressee, Imlay, as an expression of the growing pains associated with consciousness-raising.[10] As the private "letters to Imlay" attest, he had done little to inspire "respect" or "esteem" and, thus, her expanded self-knowledge would also include awareness of rejection. Still, *Letters from Norway* presents a solitary traveling woman struggling to understand herself and her new environment.

Wollstonecraft's strategies for self-representation cannot be disentangled from her role as a mother and as a daughter. In this way, gender is a crucial feature of the writing, but one that gets complicated by the author. Hartley persuasively identifies, for instance, gender as a foundational difference in the attitudes Wollstonecraft and William Wordsworth exhibit toward their self-display. Her argument that "both writers define themselves partly in contrast to the person to whom they address their work" is too narrow, and, thus, far less convincing (88). To make such a claim ignores how Wollstonecraft continuously misaligns herself with the other women she represents, obliquely announcing herself as a different kind of woman. In the first letter, for instance, Wollstonecraft, restless from having been on a ship for eleven days, attempts to go ashore near Gothenburg against the captain's wishes. She finally persuades two sailors to row her, Fanny, and Marguerite to the mainland, but the whole enterprise is disconcerting:

The day was fine; and I enjoyed the water till, approaching the little island, poor Marguerite, whose timidity always acts as a feeler before her adventuring spirit, began to wonder at our not seeing any inhabitants. I did not listen to her. But when, on landing, the same silence prevailed, I caught the alarm, which was not lessened by the sight of two old men, whom we forced out of their wretched hut. . . . I was not sorry to see a female figure, though I had not, like Marguerite, been thinking of robberies, murders, or the other evil which instantly, as the sailors would have said, runs foul of a woman's imagination. (I: 9-11; 244-45)

Here and throughout her travelogue, Wollstonecraft implicitly distinguishes herself from Marguerite, the kind of woman who would allow her femininity to render her vulnerable to attack. In this particular instance, she conjures the sailors' patronizing attitude toward women travelers, disclaiming it by projecting it onto one of her female escorts. She also, of course, tries to distance herself from the very real danger that could befall a woman traveling alone. Much later in the travelogue Wollstonecraft expresses dissatisfaction with Marguerite, whose "train of thoughts had nothing in common" (XXII: 175; 333) with the author's ample insights. Wollstonecraft also distinguishes herself from that other female traveler, Fanny, who "found a few wild strawberries more grateful than [the] flowers or fancies," which preoccupy her mother as "omens or sentiments" (I: 14; 247). Although Wollstonecraft establishes traveling women as endangered in a way that men are not, she simultaneously presents herself as a different kind of traveler. Wollstonecraft appears, for instance, to align herself with the men accompanying her for a short jaunt within her longer solitary travels:

The gentlemen wishing to peep into Norway, proposed going to Fredericshall, the first town, the distance was only three Swedish miles. There, and back again, was but a day's journey, and would not, I thought, interfere with my voyage. I agreed, and invited the eldest and prettiest of the girls to accompany us. I invited her, because I liked to see a beautiful face animated by pleasure, and to have an opportunity of regarding the country, whilst the gentlemen were amusing themselves with her. (V: 46-7; 265)

Wollstonecraft's proclaimed intention to distract her male companions implies that she would be the unwilling object of their attention without another female traveler. In this Wollstonecraft is clearly gendered as this other woman is and as these gentlemen are not. But in saying that she "liked to see a beautiful face animated by pleasure" she expresses a desire not unlike that which she imagines the gentlemen amusing themselves with her would. She distinguishes herself from this woman by aligning herself with the men who gaze and who are not gazed upon. Finally, Wollstonecraft distinguishes herself from even these male travelers in expressing her desire to take in the landscape, uninterrupted by the men who are busying themselves with the other woman. Instead of the normatively male picturesque tourist, a subject I will elaborate later, Wollstonecraft here figures herself as a manifestly female picturesque traveler, her companions as myopically concerned with flirtation. Taken together with her continuous emphasis on the novelty of being a female stranger and a Swedish lieutenant's comment that Wollstonecraft "was a woman of observation, for [she] asked him *men's questions*" (I: 15; 248), these indirect self-presentations clearly suggest that consciousness of gender informs the kind of subject represented in *Letters from Norway*.

Wollstonecraft's decision to produce an epistolary travelogue has been read by Mary Favret as an attempt to "transform the familiar letter into a public critique" (96). It is one of the few romantic women's travelogues organized as letters, suggesting that it has more in common with precursors like Montagu's *Embassy Letters* and Helen Maria Williams's *Letters from France* than with, say, Ann Radcliffe's travelogue, *A Journey Made in the Summer of 1794, through Holland and the western frontier of Germany*, published in Dublin in the same year that Wollstonecraft traveled to Scandinavia. Favret contends that *Letters from Norway* blurs static boundaries between the commercial and the sentimental uses of the letter in the period. These letters, that is, facilitate Imlay's blockade-running enterprise, and, thus, function as correspondence in the legal sense of "commercial communication" (97).[11] And yet they also represent "the conventional voice and posture of the 'feminine' letter-writer" (96). The corollary set of posthumously published letters to Imlay suggest that *Letters from Norway* is primarily to be understood as a public form, produced for both Imlay's and the author's profit. Continuous, seamless blending of private reverie and political critique within each individual letter, however, complicates formalistic boundary designations.

Wollstonecraft frequently turns from seemingly personal observations to political and social critique without signaling this move to her readership. She digresses from descriptions of Swedish food to the oppression of women and servants (III: 26; 253); from the lack of Swedish children seen outdoors to a critique of mothering and overreliance on wetnurses (IV: 33-34; 257-58); from the details of travel to Godwinian meditation on the "future improvement of the world" (XI: 102; 294; XXII: 182; 338); from anxiety for her child's welfare to the "oppressed state of her sex" (VI: 55; 269); and, from the appearance of soldiers at Schleswig to "an old opinion of mine, that it is the preservation of the species, not of individuals, which appear to be the design of the Deity throughout the whole of nature" (XXII: 179; 336). Myers notes this dilution of public and private boundaries, emphasizing the fluidity of the travelogue: "[T]here are no rigid separations in the *Letters*: personal and social themes, rational assessments and emotional epiphanies, flow one into another joined by a use of associationism quite subtle and sophisticated" (181). Watery boundaries are, for Myers, an indication of the author's desire to engineer a different form of self-representation; for Ty, they signal the author's "divided subjectivity" (65). These textual swerves from personal notation to social critique are, however, far less subtle than the few sustained passages yoking national identity to domesticity and the body politic to the literal body of individuals. Wollstonecraft writes, for instance, of her first night in Sweden:

I contemplated all nature at rest; the rocks, even grown darker in their appearance, looked as if they partook of the general repose, and reclined more heavily on their foundation.—What, I exclaimed, is this active principle which keeps me still awake?—Why fly my thoughts abroad when every thing [sic] around me appears at home? My child was sleeping with equal calmness—innocent and sweet as the closing flowers.—Some recollections, attached to the idea of home, mingled with reflections respecting the state of society I had been contemplating that evening, made a tear drop on the rosy cheek I had just kissed; and emotions that trembled on the brink of extacy and agony gave a poignancy to my sensations, which made me feel more alive than usual. (I: 16; 248)

It is unclear initially what is "home" and what is "abroad" here, though these contrasting metaphors secure nationality as part of the equation. That the author's thoughts fly "abroad" hints that she misses England, and, likely, Imlay, such that "abroad" is really "home." But the quick elision of her surroundings with her child—"every thing around me appears at home"—suggests that the presence of her infant makes Sweden home. One is then left to wonder how Wollstonecraft is understanding her national identity at this moment, though the implication is that her role as a mother supersedes identity related to geographical moorings. I am suggesting, in other words, that Wollstonecraft is very deliberately introducing ambiguity about the national status of home here in order to suggest its proximity to domesticity. And as if playfully to underscore this point, a mother's thoughts about home and "the state of society" are linked to the daughter by a tear. Wollstonecraft reinforces the continuity of the domestic affections with politics, commerce, and nationality just a few letters later: "They [Norwegian sea captains] love their country, but have not much public spirit. Their exertions are, generally speaking, only for their families; which I conceive will always be the case, till politics, becoming a subject of discussion, enlarges the heart by opening the understanding" (VII: 63-64; 274). Here Wollstonecraft distinguishes domesticity from the political, the family from the social, but only to undercut these distinctions. That is, political discussion supports the domestic affections—figured here as an enlargement of heart—by challenging narrow-minded preoccupation with commercial pursuits which benefit the individual family while eroding "public spirit." In both examples domesticity galvanizes national identity in its irreducible relationship to it, not separation from it. The implications of yoking the domestic to the political stem beyond characterizations of the text as fluidly negotiating public and private modes to include these negotiations as examples of counter-public discourse.

The personal and political are once again intertwined in Wollstonecraft's observations of the effects of alcohol on the body. She rails against excessive alcohol consumption among Scandinavians throughout this entire text, a feature made all the more revealing by Janet Todd's note that the author's father was an "impecunious drunkard" (Introduction to *Mary* viii).[12] Intoxication, according to Wollstonecraft, "is the pleasure of savages" (XX: 163; 327), derails advancement of the intellect, spoils the teeth, and, in her most sweeping indictment, precludes national improvement in England and the northern states (XX: 163; 327). The effect of alcohol on the body is, in the passage below, literally figured in terms of the classed body politic:

> The enjoyment of the peasantry was drinking brandy and coffee, before the latter was prohibited, and the former was not allowed to be privately distilled. The wars carried on by the late king rendering it necessary to increase the revenue, and retain the specie in the country by every possible means. . . . The prohibition of drinking coffee, under a penalty, and the encouragement given to public distilleries, tend to impoverish the poor, who are not affected by the sumptuary laws; for the regent has lately laid very severe restraints on the article of dress, which the middling class of people found grievous because it obliged them to throw aside finery that might have lasted them for their lives. (III: 27-28; 254-55)

The "late king" is Gustavus III, who, as Carol Poston notes, aggressively encouraged Swedes to drink heartily because spirits were heavily taxed and the monarchy needed to generate revenue to pay for a long and expensive war with Russia. So much so that, as Poston notes, "vats of liquor were located outside of churches" (27). Thus the king's subjects, the body politic, are here literalized as a dressed body, decaying with the monarch's assistance. In figuring the body politic as a natural organism, Wollstonecraft is quite potentially troping on Burke's trope of revolution as "disease" in *Reflections on the Revolution in France*. Wollstonecraft, that is, picks up on Burke's conservative trope of the diseased body politic, but revises it such that it is the monarch, not the revolutionary initiatives of the people, which causes deterioration. Her sympathy here appears to be with the rising bourgeoisie much as they are her intended audience in *Vindication of the Rights of Woman*. Given this oblique attack on Burke's view of the French Revolution, it is not surprising that she concludes, just a few sentences later, that "the death of the king, by saving them [the people] from the consequences his ambition would naturally have entailed on them, may be reckoned a blessing" (III: 29; 255). Thirty years later, Wollstonecraft's as yet unborn daughter Mary Shelley, will develop a similar trope of the decaying body politic to critique Burke in her futuristic narrative of the annihilation of the human race, *The Last Man* (xxi).[13]

   The published text of *Letters from Norway* contested public and private designations by representing the intensely personal concerns of its author while serving "the demands of 'business'" (Favret 97). It departs from standard romantic autobiographies which maintain rigid distinctions between personal and political life. Moreover, *Letters from Norway* complicates Michel Foucault's claim that "a private letter may have a signatory, but it does not have an author" because the private status of the letter is thrown into question by its content (124). One cannot, that is, rely solely on the formal characteristics of the text to determine what is private and/or public about it. And although I want to steer readers away from formal considerations, I also intend to demonstrate that *Letters from Norway* is a travelogue. Without associating itself with late-eighteenth-century English ideologies of tourism, her travelogue could not be understood as participating in those discourses, and, subsequently, as revising assumptions about representations of the traveling subject and gendered biases against forms like letters and journals. In this *Letters from Norway* performs its most impressive function as lifewriting: it authorizes marginalized modes of perception which help account for its rare appearance in romantic studies.

Wollstonecraft was more than conversant with public discussions of tourism and landscape representation, flourishing as her travelogue went to press in 1796. Before she embarked for Scandinavia in 1795, Wollstonecraft had, in fact, reviewed at least twenty-five travelogues and works more generally concerned with the pictorial for the *Analytical Review*.[14] Only one of these travelogues issued from a woman's pen, Hester Lynch Piozzi's *Observations and Reflections, made in the Course of a Journey through France, Italy and Germany* (1789). Although not, strictly speaking, a travelogue, Helen Maria Williams's *Letters written in France, in the Summer, 1790, to a Friend in England* also impressed Wollstonecraft considerably, its "sincerity" perhaps providing a model for the author's subsequent travel record.

Her reviews corroborate many of the opinions she advances in her travelogue, especially as they relate to the purposes and ideology of touring. For Wollstonecraft, traveling is, first and foremost, an organized, premeditated intellectual pursuit. In her review of the Reverend William Hamilton's *Letters Concerning the Northern Coast of the County of Antrim* (1790) she writes: "The art of traveling is only a branch of the art of thinking, or still more precisely to express ourselves, the conduct of a being who acts from principle" (*Works* 7: 277). Wollstonecraft's most pithy rendering of the value of travel combines both thought and action, mind and body. Travel is here predicated on the application of principles, thus, the ability to systematize and prioritize. Wollstonecraft may, in fact, have been emphasizing the systematic, informative, even scientific, nature of her travels in titling her travelogue, *Letters Written during a Short Residence in Sweden, Norway, and Denmark*. Characterizing her journey as a "residence" implies that she is not a mere tourist passing through, but a traveler with refined taste, keen observation, and knowledge. As Barbara Stafford contends, "[W]riters frequently distinguished between being a mere tourist and being a serious traveler: the former gives general impressions, whereas the latter conveys particular information about the region" (59). Indeed, Wollstonecraft's September 1791 review of J. P. Brissot's *Nouveau Voyage Dans Les Etats-Unies de L'Amerique Septentrionale, fait en 1788* makes apparent what her title only suggests about the knowledge and thoughtfulness integral to travel:

The question is not what a man *should* observe who wishes to collect information, and afford instruction by drawing judicious results from obvious comparisons, but what he has *actually* observed. If he has seen with his eyes, heard with his ears, and pondered every thing [*sic*] in his mind, the example would render precepts superfluous, if not impertinent; but should the hapless wight have sauntered along 'unknowing what he sought,' he has only employed a flourishing pen to shew us that he was unfit for the task he undertook. (*Works* 7: 390-91)

Wollstonecraft here urges that the traveler not process his views through popular theories of the pictorial, but balance immediacy ("seen with his eyes") with mindfulness about his journey.[15] Preparing to travel does not mean that one either formulaically reproduces scenery in terms of popular paradigms or that one rambles about arbitrarily, taking in and representing landscape haphazardly. She reiterates this compromise four years later in her own travelogue: "As in traveling, the keeping of a journal excites to many useful enquiries that would not have been thought of, had the traveler only determined to see all he could see, without ever asking himself for what purpose" (III: 30; 256). Here, then, the travelogue form is wrenched to the task of chronicling her journey, helping her to experience her surroundings more deeply by organizing impressions.

When Wollstonecraft aligns travel with principled action, she intends premeditation in the way I have been suggesting, but far more too. Acting from principle, of course, suggests moral action, for instance, taking responsibility for one's behavior. To this end Wollstonecraft identifies herself with serious, conscientious travelers by faulting those tourists who distort information:

Behold us now in Norway; and I could not avoid feeling surprise at observing the difference in the manners of the inhabitants of the two sides of the river; for every thing shews that the Norwegians are more industrious and more opulent. The Swedes, for neighbors are seldom the best friends, accuse the Norwegians of knavery, and they retaliate by bringing a charge of hypocrisy against the Swedes. Local circumstances probably render both unjust, speaking from their feelings, rather than reason: and is this astonishing when we consider that most writers of travels have done the same, whose works have served as materials for the compilers of universal histories. All are eager to give a national character; which is rarely just, because they do not discriminate the natural from the acquired difference. (V: 48; 266)

A lack of reason, that favorite of Wollstonecraftian buzz-words, yields irresponsible reporting on the part of tourists. Travel is not just a measured activity but a reasonable one that requires more than superficial observation. Reason is here synonymous with and necessary for principled activity. Wollstonecraft further implies, just a few sentences later, that travelers must also use their reason in order to censor their own biases: "[T]ravellers who require that every nation should resemble their native country, had better stay at home" (V: 49; 266).[16] Those who travel in order to gratify themselves, imposing their own identities onto others, and, who venture to give general impressions, filtered heavily through their own context, ought not, in other words, travel or write.

Wollstonecraft's caveats against self-indulgent tourism are integral to her general understanding of travel and travel writing as reasonable pursuits. Specifically, she develops paradigms for principled activity, understood in its methodical and moral senses, through running critiques of late eighteenth century travel as dilettantish entertainment. In continuously distinguishing travel which informs from that which amuses, Wollstonecraft casts picturesque touring as an intellectual activity and its written records as historically and aesthetically valuable. Although one can point to at least four other instances of Wollstonecraft correcting idle seekers of self-amusement and self-forgetfulness in travel, her favorable review of William Gilpin's *Three Essays: On Picturesque Beauty; on Picturesque Travel; and on Sketching Landscape* (1792) stands apart. Wollstonecraft quotes at length from Gilpin's essays, sarcastically recommending them to "those favorites of fortune who travel for pleasure" (*Works* 7: 456). She identifies the idle rich as the specific pleasure-seeking audience whose habits are incongruous with a Gilpinian (and, implicitly, Wollstonecraftian) view of picturesque touring as manifestly intellectual. Wollstonecraft cites Gilpin's claim that "the art of sketching is to the picturesque traveler, what the art of writing is to the scholar" in order to correct such self-aggrandizing habits. She writes: "landscape sketching is certainly a most pleasing amusement, and affords the idle, we mean the rich, an employment that by exercising taste, leads to moral improvement" (*Works* 7: 456-57). Wollstonecraft thus corroborates Gilpin's implied intention to improve the status of sketching by likening it to scholarly writing and augments the analogy with a class critique, suggesting that this bourgeois intellectual pursuit might improve the morality of moneyed but mindless tourists. Ties between social class and the pictorial are reiterated in her travelogue too, but here the bourgeoisie bear the burden of the critique: "the lower class of people here amuse and interest me much more than the middling, with their apish good breeding and prejudices. The sympathy and frankness of heart conspicuous in the peasantry produces even a simple gracefulness of deportment, which has frequently struck me as very picturesque" (IV: 35-36; 259).

Wollstonecraft approves of much of Gilpin's writing on the picturesque, which, in his own words, is "that kind of beauty which would look well in a picture."[17] His essays profoundly influenced late-eighteenth-century taste in landscape representation and helped produce the fashion for picturesque touring: the practice of experiencing nature in terms of the artistic principles of representing it. Gilpin's desire to cultivate taste among painters and poets of landscape was, at one level, perfectly commensurate with Wollstonecraft's own tireless efforts to connect aimless tourism with the excess and dilettantism of the rich. They are, that is, allies in their pursuit of paradigms of travel and its representation. But she clearly parts company with Gilpin when it comes to his penchant for tinting sketches. Tinting landscape sketches, or coloring, as she often refers to it, is associated with amusement, artificiality, femininity, and harmful reading practices in her frequent contributions to the *Analytical Review* from 1788 to 1797. These reviews, taken together, suggest the author's strategies for revising the logic conjoining them, especially as it relates to prescriptions for female behavior.

In his *Observations, relative chiefly to Picturesque Beauty, made in the Year 1776* (1789), Gilpin encourages picturesque tourists to "catch" nature by tinting sketches on the spot which can later be painted up in a "second translation." Wollstonecraft dissents, associating this practice with artificiality, the beautiful, sentimentality:

Mr. G.'s advice respecting colouring, obviates, we think, in a very slight degree, the objection he raises against *artificial effect*: nay, we are apt to believe, from experience, that a small landscape, when it is tinted, assumes a more diminutive and artificial appearance than plain, shadowy drawings, because the unnatural, striking glow in them, awakens the imagination, which bold strokes might have cheated, if the veil had not been removed; for unnatural must the charming tints of nature ever appear, when they are not mellowed, by melting into a large expanse of grey air.

However, prettiness, and a high manner of finishing drawings, render many people blind to this defect: the eye is amused by a kind of glaring beauty, or childish neatness, and the absence of these touches which display sentiment, and rouse it, is not felt by common observers, the sense is amused, but the imagination still remains quiet. (*Works* 7: 197)

Wollstonecraft criticizes Gilpin's recommendation to tint nature because it encourages gratification of the "senses," not the imagination. This amusement of the senses is further linked with the beautiful, a specifically gendered designation in the period owing to Edmund Burke's influential treatise, *Philosophical Enquiry into the Origin of Our Ideas of the Sublime and the Beautiful* (1757). I will leave discussion of the gendering of the sublime and the beautiful aside for the moment, noting that "glaring beauty" is here associated with childishness. Four months prior to her review of *Observations, relative chiefly to Picturesque Beauty,* Wollstonecraft penned a nearly identical criticism of Gilpin's *Observations on the River Wye* (1789):

[H]is elegant sketches oftener gave us an idea of the beautiful than the sublime. There is, besides, a want of nerve and boldness in the lines, which might, in some measure, arise from too scrupulous a desire to render them perfectly picturesque. The tints sometimes appear artificial and unnatural, though we are convinced that they are not so. (*Works* 7: 162)

In the first review I cited the beautiful is ideologically yoked with color, neatness, and high finishing in art, and is here unmistakably contrasted with the sublime and associated with the artificial effect of tinting landscape. Her critique of tinting takes on more literal dimensions in her travelogue. Traveling toward Christiania (Oslo), Norway, Wollstonecraft remarks with disgust the red stain left on the rocks where alum has been produced:

The view, immediately on the left, as we drove down the mountain, was almost spoilt by the depredations committed on the rocks to make alum. I do not know the process.—I only saw that the rocks looked red after they had been burnt; and regretted that the operation should leave a quantity of rubbish, to introduce an image of human industry in the shape of destruction. (XIII: 118-19; 303)

This passage has been read by critics as expressing anti-commercial sentiment, but the link between the literal tinting of the landscape and the production of alum has been completely ignored. Aesthetic and industrial discourses collide in this critique of coloring, implying the detrimental impact of both on nature.

Wollstonecraft does not limit her criticism of tinting practices to landscape representation either. In her 1791 review of *A Short Journey in the West Indies* (1790), for instance, she criticizes the sentimentality and artificiality of the writing: "some of the descriptions appear to have been taken on the spot; but they are so fantastically coloured, that the whole wears an air of romance and fiction" (*Works* 7: 355). Again, tinting is singularly aligned with artificiality, falseness. The mention of romance here, moreover, recalls several other instances where Wollstonecraft makes unambiguous the link between artificiality, reading practices, and gender. Her 1790 review of J. Hassell's *Tour of the Isle of Wight* (1790) asserts the author's debt to Gilpin as well as his failure to live up to the precursor's balance of perception and feeling. Wollstonecraft closes this review, lamenting that the "book will probably fall into the hands of females; and we are sorry to find that it is written in an artificial style, calculated to pamper the imagination and leave the understanding to starve" (*Works* 7: 279). That Wollstonecraft imagines a largely female audience for Hassell's "sentimental" travelogue associates feminine reading habits with an overreliance on "extatic feelings" and, concomitantly, amusement, even as it points to the unfortunate, but not inevitable, nexus. Finally, Wollstonecraft unites childishness, femininity, and amusement in her criticism of Hester Lynch Piozzi's *Observations and Reflections made in the course of a Journey through France, Italy, and Germany* (1789): "we find in her journey all the childish feminine terms, which occur in common novels and thoughtless chat, sweet, lovely, dear dear, and many other pretty epithets and exclamations" (*Works* 7: 127).

Although Wollstonecraft's rhetoric of the pictorial infantilizes women and denigrates their reasoning abilities, it also revises such stereotypes. Much as she takes issue with the cultivation of affectation in females in *Thoughts on the Education of Daughters* (1787; *Works* 4: 14-15) and condemns novel reading for women in *Vindication of the Rights of Woman* (1792; *Works* 5: 256), Wollstonecraft uses her reviews of travel—and her travelogue itself—as yet another forum to decry the oppressive construction of women.[18] But it's also not just another avenue for social critique. Associating the logic of the picturesque with the logic of female manners enables an impressive revision of both. She exposes the discursive production of picturesque touring as similar to but also as distinct from the discursive production of women. Thus a critique of artificiality, sentimentality, and mindless pursuits in travel doubles, by association, for a critique of these same qualities in female manners.

That Wollstonecraft understood travelogues as useful to such multi-tiered critiques is evident in her 1790 review of Samuel Ireland's *A picturesque Tour through Holland, Brabant, and Part of France; made in the Autumn of 1789*. Therein she announces that travel journals that serve as actual guides are deficient to their purpose, though she is not overly specific about what ends they should serve: "[M]ore employed to describe things than men, many of their voluminous productions contain such dead matter, that they will only be read as guides in travelling, or to renew the impressions of memory, which variety has rendered faint, when the journey is over" (*Works* 7: 301). Thus Eleanor Ty's offhand remark that "the text is a virtual failure as a travel guide" (66) might be closer to Wollstonecraft's intention than she realizes. What Wollstonecraft meant in juxtaposing "things" to "men," is not entirely clear, but we are left with the unambiguous impression that her travelogue does more than direct tourists to their destinations. Wollstonecraft's rhetoric only begins to hum in critical elaboration of the picturesque, moreover, reaching its ideal pitch in *Letters from Norway*'s revision of the Burkean sublime.

Since *Letters from Norway* advances critiques of sensibility similar to those expressed in Wollstonecraft's far more widely read texts, we are left to puzzle out this particular brand of erasure. Although recuperation of late-eighteenth-century women writers is far from systematic, feminist critiques of New Historical work on literary romanticism help explain why an author who receives more than her share of critical attention also gets ignored.[19] Dismissal of particular texts, in this case, an autobiographical travelogue, is neither arbitrary nor related to deceptive, ostensibly value-neutral claims about the intrinsic merit of the work. It has, in fact, everything to do with ideologies of genre, especially those dramatically reducing the literary productions of the romantic period to poetry. As Kay Cook points out, even critics like Jerome McGann who seek self-consciously to define romantic ideology neglect all genres except those apparently dominant at the time and all writers except men, suggesting "that only certain literary genres are capable of expressing or responding to an ideology or to the political and social forces that have created it" (88). Cook goes on to suggest that the immersed narrative perspective, attention to detail, dailiness as a structuring principle, and parataxis common to many forms of life-writing by romantic women run counter to theories of the beautiful and the sublime that promote the notion of perspective as distance. Let me put this another way: the kind of journalizing that emphasizes particularity as a way of structuring reality is viewed as inferior in the late eighteenth and early nineteenth centuries because it is incommensurate with aesthetic conventions of the sublime and the beautiful emergent in the period. Cook specifically contends that Dorothy Wordsworth's usage of detail in her *Journals* "indicates a refusal to conform to the dictates of the 'sublime,' which sought absence of the feminine and of detail" (94). Similarly, I propose that Wollstonecraft revised popular tropes of the sublime and the beautiful.

Her travelogue put forth counterpublic discourse on touring, ideologically aligned with the narrative structures of private life-writing produced by many romantic women. By this I mean that the distance ostensibly necessary to sum up one's subjectivity, say, William Wordsworth's totalized, epic self-representation in *The Prelude*, is akin to historical trends accenting sublimity in landscape. Wollstonecraft's travelogue honors, moreover, the continuous daily process of self-revision, resisting, consciously or not, the temptation to quantify her whole self for an anticipated readership. Much as her reviews rearrange the picturesque, her travelogue manipulates conventions of landscape description in an effort to revalue the minute particulars of personal experience.[20]

The concept of the sublime sponsored by Edmund Burke and the male romantic poets is, according to Anne Mellor, "associated with an experience of masculine empowerment; its contrasting term, the beautiful, is associated with an experience of feminine nurturance, love, and sensuous relaxation" (*R & G* 85). Massive mountain peaks inspiring awe and fear in onlookers are frequently troped in the language of masculine conquest, virility, and mastery by male climbers. Likewise, verdant pastures that soothe the weary traveler are cast as maternal, as feminine in their comfort. Recall, for instance, William Wordsworth's description, in Book I of *The Prelude*, his boyhood experience pilfering a skiff, rowing out from the shore of Ullswater only to be stunned by a "huge cliff" so terrifying that the author thought it a "living thing" in pursuit of him (I: 11. 409-11). In the highly gendered, sexualized language of this passage, the boat is unmistakably female, "she was an elfin pinnace" (l. 401), "her mooring-place" is the "cavern of the willow tree" (l. 414-15), and the rower, consummately male, "lustily" propels the "swan"-like skiff forward till his fright at the living crag causes him to turn back to shore. The implication is clear: the "silent" moonlit lake plays passive female against the terrifying cliff that the author imagines as chasing him, mastering him as he thinks of himself as mastering the silent female.[21]

Wollstonecraft too contrasts the terrifying grandeur of the sublime with the serenity of the beautiful in her travelogue. Although she takes shelter from the wind in the cliffs of Norway, she also finds them threatening: "[A]fter mounting the most terrific precipice, we had to pass through a tremendous defile, where the closing chasm seemed to threaten us with instant destruction, when turning quickly, verdant meadows and a beautiful lake relieved and charmed my eyes" (V: 47; 265). She elsewhere privileges the mind-expanding character of "grand views" and "sublime prospects" over the comfort afforded by beautiful Norwegian landscapes (XIII: 112; 300; 119; 304). But these gendered oppositions are infrequent. Wollstonecraft spends far more of her time reinventing tropes of the pictorial and epistemological than recuperating Burke. My claim that her travelogue challenges this gendered logic is thus somewhat akin to recent feminist claims that Emily Dickinson, Marianne Moore, and Elizabeth Bishop developed a female sublime in their poetry. Patricia Yaeger maintains, for instance, that these women writers invented a mode of self-empowerment based on communion with, not domination of, others. She calls this "the sublime of nearness," or, the horizontal sublime, which revised the vertical, self-absorbed sublime of William Wordsworth, Walt Whitman, Hart Crane, and others (195). This notion of mutuality is further expanded in Mellor's discussion of an "ethic of care." While cultivation of mutuality and the domestic affections between mother and daughter is certainly a cornerstone of Wollstonecraft's strategy to revise the solitary masculine sublime, it is not the entire foundation.

Wollstonecraft repeatedly places the sublime and the beautiful on a continuum with one another, thus, refashioning this opposition. She writes, "the sublime often gave place imperceptibly to the beautiful, dilating the emotions which were painfully concentrated" (I: 14; 247).[22] Wollstonecraft's association of pain with the sublime implicitly identifies Burke's *Philosophical Enquiry into the Origin of Our Ideas of the Sublime and the Beautiful* as contextual backdrop. Burke claimed in the 1757 treatise that "whatever is fitted in any sort to excite the ideas of pain, and danger, that is to say, whatever is in any sort terrible, or is conversant about terrible objects, or operates in a manner analogous to terror, is a source of the sublime" (39). When Burke refers to "danger" excited by the sublime he intends the thrill of illusory self-annihilation one experiences amidst sublime scenery. Wollstonecraft, however, manipulates this idea of the sublime when she states that fostering "a quick perception of the beautiful and sublime, when it is exercised in observing animated nature, . . . is dangerous . . . in such an imperfect state of existence" (VI: 58; 271). On Wollstonecraft's rendering, the danger is Burke's cultivation of this idle notion of a momentary loss of ego when what is needed is "an unfolding of that love which embraces all that is great and beautiful" (VI: 58; 271). She further metaphorizes this self-annihilation as wind activating an aeolian harp, an image she develops in order both to critique the passivity involved in the Burkean sublime and the association of masculine agency with a refusal of responsibility.

Other examples of Wollstonecraft purposefully confusing Burke's sublime and beautiful fill the pages of *Letters from Norway.* She revises the logic of this opposition by describing the "beauties" of nature as "sublime" (XIV: 126; 307); she associates the pain of the sublime with the self-forgetfulness so frequently railed against in her reviews (XII: 109; 298-99); and, her experience of "beautiful" mountain scenery momentarily suspends ego consciousness, not in avoidance of self or fear of being engulfed, but in expansion towards her "Creator" (VIII: 74; 280). In a more direct assault on Burke, Wollstonecraft unites the "characteristic sublimity" of neo-gothic architecture with unimaginative commercialism. Sublimity with no "elegance," no attention to the minute particulars, "has an emphatical stamp of meanness, of poverty of conception, which only a commercial spirit could give" (XIV: 125; 307). And in perhaps her most direct address to Burke's experience of the sublime as painful, Wollstonecraft depicts despair as quickly transformed to pleasure by the sublimity of a cascade. She does not recede from "the rebounding torrent" before her, but experiences it as "pleasurable" and as capable of quelling her troubled thoughts about existence (XV: 132-33; 311).

Wollstonecraft frequently veers from landscape description to meditation on her intimate relations with loved ones as if there were no conceptual distinction between these modes. These emotion-filled passages tend, quite significantly, to follow closely on the heels of corrections to would-be tourists about their enterprise. Just after her diatribe against travelers who seek sublime scenery as a consciousness altering experience, for example, Wollstonecraft relates her profound grief at the death of her friend, Fanny Blood, and her "melancholy" at a brief separation from her daughter during a particularly dangerous part of the journey:

The grave has closed over a dear friend, the friend of my youth; still she is present with me, and I hear her soft voice warbling as I stray over the heath. Fate has separated me from another, the fire of whose eyes, tempered by infantine tenderness, still warms my breast; even when gazing on these tremendous cliffs, sublime emotions absorb my soul. And smile not, if I add, that the rosy tint of morning reminds me of a suffusion, which will never more charm my senses, unless it reappears on the cheeks of my child. Her sweet blushes I may yet hide in my bosom, and she is still too young to ask why starts the tear, so near akin to pleasure and pain? (VI: 59; 271-72)[23]

Wollstonecraft's sharp segue from a critique of the sublime to the death of her childhood soulmate in this passage suggests yet another distortion of Burke. This time Burke's annihilated subject is refigured as the literal dead, mediated through memory. It is as if Wollstonecraft undercut Burke's experience of the sublime as threatening self-preservation by representing the real pain of losing an intimate friend. More importantly, though, Wollstonecraft's experience of the sublime in the "tremendous cliffs" of Norway is mediated through another Fanny, her child by Imlay.

Wollstonecraft thus removes the sublime from the externalized landscape to the inscape. The sublime is associated both with the majestic scenery Wollstonecraft represents in her travelogue as well as with the domestic affections, the tenderness she feels for her friend and her daughter. Maternal affection, singularly aligned with the beautiful, is thus invested here with the sublime. Much later in her travelogue, Wollstonecraft, still separated from her infant daughter, relates a dream in which Fanny reappears in the landscape: "[M]y little cherub was again hiding her face in my bosom. I heard her sweet cooing beat on my heart from the cliffs, and saw her tiny footsteps on the sands" (X: 98; 293). Only days later Wollstonecraft is reunited with her "Fannikin," whom she fears will no longer remember her mother. These anxieties thus explain Wollstonecraft's landscape projections and support Moskal's conclusion that maternal affection revises conventional renderings of the sublime and the beautiful (264).

Wollstonecraft closes this meditation with one more parting shot at Burke: in suggesting that Fanny is still too young to ask how her mother's grief is associated with pleasure and pain, she associates the Burkean sublime with oppressive modes of socialization. That is, Fanny will have to be indoctrinated into Burke's theories of perception, grounded on psychologies of pleasure and pain. The implication being, of course, that the "imperfect state of existence" earlier mentioned will perhaps be improved, thus offering competing interpretations of perception. This notion of the progress of the intellect is, moreover, continuously taken up by the author throughout the travelogue. The question mark punctuating what seems to be a statement more than a query about the relationship of her grief to pleasure and pain further underscores Wollstonecraft's awareness that while her identity may be overdetermined by the subject-object relations she investigates, Fanny's is not yet.

Wollstonecraft's revision of the sublime as masculine empowerment fits within Anne Mellor's schema of women romantics' general responses to these aesthetic conventions. Women writers, according to Mellor, either equated the sublime with patriarchal tyranny (*R & G* 91) or troped it as a female friend with whom they could commune in mutuality (*R & G* 97). The tradition that associated sublimity with male aggression against women frequently displaced the power of the landscape onto the home. Thieves who rove the landscape, threatening women, are refigured as fathers and priests who commit incest (91). Through this displacement these writers, notably Ann Radcliffe, "expose the dark underside of the doctrine of separate spheres, the sexual division of labor, and the domestic ideology of patriarchal capitalism" (91). Wollstonecraft's domestication of the sublime certainly seems related to this tradition of the female gothic, but also extends it significantly. When Wollstonecraft brings the literal implements of the kitchen to bear on sublime architecture she is blurring the boundary between domesticity and commerce as well as revaluing details and dailiness submerged by theories of the sublime:

When I first saw it [the Chapel of Windsor], the pillars within had acquired, by time, a sombre hue, which accorded with the architecture; and the gloom increased its dimensions to the eye by hiding its parts; but now it all bursts on the view at once; and the sublimity has vanished before the brush and broom; for it has been white-washed and scraped till it is become as bright and neat as the pots and pans in a notable house-wife's kitchen. (VII: 69-70; 277-78)

It is, thus, not the crimes of banditti moved from the landscape to the home, but, rather, the implements of the home which, metonymically, improve the sublime by particularizing it.[24]

Only once in her travelogue reviews does the author explicitly link details and dailiness to travel: the same review in which Wollstonecraft yoked traveling and thinking to one another. She enthusiastically recommends the Reverend William Hamilton's *Letters concerning the Northern Coast of the County of Antrim*, saying that it succeeds because the author knew what he was in search of on his journey:

We have before observed, that travels would be very useful repositories of knowledge, if the traveller always had a particular pursuit in his head; not merely to serve as a clue to the judgment, plunged into a maze of enquiries; but as a solid foundation for the work, only trusting to chance for the ornamental parts of the structure. The imagination would not then be racked to give the air of adventures to common incidents, or to spin sentiments out of the brain that never agitated the heart:—not [*sic*] would the trivial occurrences of each day be noted with puerile exactness, and vacant indiscriminate surprise. But when a man only travels to *while-away* the time, when leisure is, literally speaking, idleness, his eyes are turned on every prominent novelty, and the mind, quite afloat, catches at every straw and bubble that crosses it. (*Works* 7: 276)

It would seem from a glance at this passage that Wollstonecraft finds the details of daily life inherently "trivial" or "puerile," but, in fact, the accent is on mindlessness as triviality, not dailiness. The unthoughtful writer who sallies forth without a sense of himself or his travels is, in Wollstonecraft's thinking, the writer likely to catch at novelty, reproduce arbitrariness in his writing. Moreover, her emphatic distaste for writers who color "common incidents" because they haven't truly experienced their surroundings implies that ordinariness and the ability to render the ordinary significant are vital to Wollstonecraft. Certainly the amount of detail and dailiness in *Letters from Norway* attests to this fact. But there is also an important distinction to be made between Wollstonecraftian detail and the dailiness of, say, Dorothy Wordsworth's *Grasmere Journals*. Wordsworth's *Journals* captures the day's cleaning, cooking, and strolls around the lakes in all their particularity while Wollstonecraft's travelogue intersperses minuteness with a theoretical undercurrent about this attention to detail. Wollstonecraft, that is, displays a distinct amount of self-consciousness about the usage of detail that appears absent in Dorothy Wordsworth's writing.[25] It might even be argued that Wollstonecraft splits the difference between Wordsworth's apparent lack of self-consciousness about her usage of painstaking detail and her brother's obvious perspectival distance from the self he reproduces in *The Prelude*. What I am suggesting Wollstonecraft accomplishes in her travelogue is exactly the kind of perspectival adjustment that blends critical distance from the landscape and self with immersion in both. *Letters from Norway* partakes of the vocabulary of the sublime, the beautiful, and the picturesque, altering this lexicon by closing the distance between the viewer and the landscape.

Notes

1. Janet Todd characterized this 1796 review as "favorable" overall: "Wollstonecraft is judged to have been improved by her experiences of marriage and motherhood. However, the review criticizes her liberal opinions" (*Annotated Bibliography* 11). Imlay's registration of Wollstonecraft as "Mrs. Imlay" with the American consul in Paris in 1793 is the marriage mentioned. This registration protected Wollstonecraft from the imprisonment that English revolutionaries in France (e.g., Helen Maria Williams) experienced. It is, as William St. Clair puts it, a "marriage document of uncertain legal status" (160).

2. William St. Clair incorrectly supplies "late in 1795" as the date of publication. It was, in fact, 1796.

3. Debra Hartley observes that most of the reviews of Wollstonecraft's travelogue were "more consistently positive than those for Wollstonecraft's other books . . . if reviewers tended to sympathize with the 'woman-in-love' in *A Short Residence*, many of them dealt more harshly with the woman-as-thinker represented in the book" (42).

4. I should also add that Felski's chapter on confession is not primarily concerned with the history of women's self-representation. She only briefly

compares contemporary feminist confession with the ostensible claims to universality made by eighteenth century autobiography.

5. In foregounding authorial trauma, it is not my intention to recycle Victorian judgments against the author, enabled initially by William Godwin's posthumous *Memoirs*. Instead, I offer the circumstances prompting Wollstonecraft's travels because they help to contextualize her domestication of the Burkean sublime. See Margaret J. M. Ezell's discussion of the problems of biography for recovering women's writing in *Writing Women's Literary History*.

6. Moskal's basic premise that Wollstonecraft's own inadequate mothering profoundly influences the representation of the relationship with her infant daughter, her self-representation, and landscape description in *Letters from Norway* is well documented. The strength of the argument lies in her ability to link the representation of mothering to specific manipulations of landscape description. In this Moskal betters the tendency to read the text as expressive of general alienation from the linguistic world of the father.

7. No abbreviated version of Wollstonecraft's title has become standardized among critics. I am following Mary Shelley's lead in shortening Wollstonecraft's title to *Letters from Norway*. Shelley refers to her mother's travelogue as such in her own travelogue, *History of a Six Weeks' Tour* (1817), 62.

8. All quotations from *Letters Written during a Short Residence in Norway, Denmark, and Sweden* will hereafter be cited parenthetically in the text. For each citation, I provide, in the following order: the roman numeral of the letter given by Wollstonecraft, the page number from the Poston edition, and the page number of the Todd & Butler edition. Citations from the "Advertisement," "Appendix," or the "Author's Supplementary Notes" are given by page numbers only.

9. See Moira Ferguson's anthology of British Women Writers, 1578-1799, *First Feminists*, for multiple examples of this trope.

10. Hartley devotes the second chapter of her dissertation, "'Sublimating the Imagination': Mary Wollstonecraft in Scandinavia," to the idea that *Letters from Norway* was designed to chasten the man who spurned her, instructing Imlay in how to develop "a strong affectional relationship" (32).

11. Focusing on the letter form itself, Favret's treatment of *Letters from Norway* differs dramatically from approaches highlighting the text as a travelogue. Favret writes: "Wollstonecraft's use of the letter invokes not simply the sentimental memoir and the philosophical essay, but also the 'open letter' of political controversy, the travel letter and the letter of advertisement. Intimacy and publicity, as much as feeling and thought, form the coordinates for our reading of these letters" (97).

12. Todd suggests that Wollstonecraft's bleak depiction of intimate relations between the sexes in *Mary* stems from the author's own early experiences of "despotic parenting" (viii).

13. My discussion of Wollstonecraft's trope of the body politic as a literal body subject to disease owes a debt to Mellor's contention that Mary Shelley developed her fiction of the annihilation of the human race to critique conservative ideologies of revolution flourishing thirty-five years earlier.

14. All citations from Wollstonecraft's contributions to the *Analytical Review,* 1788-1797, are reprinted in volume 7 of *The Works of Mary Wollstonecraft* and will hereafter be cited parenthetically in the text.

15. Two years prior to this review, Wollstonecraft, in her review of William Gilpin's, *Observations on the River Wye, and several Parts of South Wales,* more explicitly advocates reproducing nature in accordance with "the principles of picturesque beauty" (*Works* 7: 161).

16. Wollstonecraft's implication that travel requires one to be thoughtful about the relationship of self to other is extended in Esther Schor's observation that the author elsewhere breaks from the eighteenth-century tradition of producing an archeology of civilization by documenting "barbaric" cultures (247). Schor claims that in *Vindication of the Rights of Woman,* "Wollstonecraft examines the position—and the positioning—of women in her society, a group of which she herself is a member. In choosing as her subject the other who is already the self, Wollstonecraft introduces a radical self-criticism into the agenda of Enlightenment anthropology" (248).

17. This oft-cited Gilpinism has come to serve as shorthand for the late eighteenth century fashion of picturesque touring: searching nature for subjects suitable to reproduce.

18. Wollstonecraft offers critiques of sensibility and affectation in female manners later echoed in *Letters from Norway.* From *Thoughts on the Education of Daughters:* "As humility gives the most pleasing cast to the countenance, so from sincerity arises that artlessness of manners which is so engaging. She who suffers herself to be seen as she really is, can never be thought affected. . . . Feeling is ridiculous when affected; and even when felt, ought not to be displayed. . . . Let the manners arise from the mind, and let there be no disguise for the emotions of the heart" (*Works* 4: 14). And from *Vindication of the Rights of Woman*: "These are women who are amused by the reveries of the stupid novelists, who, knowing little of human nature, work up stale tales, and describe meretricious scenes, all retailed in a sentimental jargon, which equally tend to corrupt the taste, and draw the heart aside from its daily duties (*Works* 5: 256).

19. Although *Letters from Norway* is unknown to many students of romanticism, critical interest in it has increased significantly over the past five years, and it is certainly the most widely read of romantic women writer's travelogues. In fact, the total number of articles addressing the travelogues of Ann Radcliffe, Mary Shelley, and Dorothy Wordsworth is less than half the number devoted to *Letters from Norway.* Still Wollstonecraft's political writings have attracted many more readers than her travelogue.

20. My reading of *Letters from Norway* accords with Moskal's contention that "the affectionate tie between the traveling mother and daughter forms the conceptual center of Wollstonecraft's revision of the gendered aesthetic conventions of the picturesque and its concomitant terms, the beautiful and the sublime" (264). Whereas Moskal centers her investigation on the relationship between Wollstonecraft's personal history and landscape conventions, I am suggesting that Wollstonecraft revised the logic of the pictorial in order to revise the conventions of gendered self-representation.

21. Patricia Yaeger proposes that experiences of the sublime like this one by William Wordsworth are involved with patriarchal sovereignty and oedipal struggle with male precursors. See Hartley (21-26) and Diehl for further elaboration of the masculine sublime and its reproduction in romantic studies.

22. Later in the travelogue, Wollstonecraft reproduces this continuum, substituting, however, "elegance" for "beauty": "Little art appeared, yet sublimity every where [*sic*] gave place to elegance" (XIII: 115; 301).

23. Moskal identifies Imlay as the source of Wollstonecraft's grief (271), but the one from whom the author has been separated could be either Imlay or Fanny (or both). Given the amount of separation anxiety Wollstonecraft expresses in temporarily parting with her daughter and the logic of segueing from one Fanny to another in this passage, there appears little evidence for reading Fanny as a placeholder for Imlay. Reasoning "that the role of mother grew in importance to her [Wollstonecraft] as she faced the loss of the man she considered her husband" (265), Moskal makes plain her assumption regarding the role of the child in the mother's identity.

24. Wollstonecraft domesticates the picturesque in her travelogue too. In an elaborate note on the practice of English picturesque gardening, Wollstonecraft metaphorizes the nation as a garden that will wither if too much shade is introduced. This metaphor thus extends Wollstonecraft's efforts to link domesticity to national sovereignty, suggesting that the two not be understood as distinct (III: 31; 256). A discussion of gardening practices also offers a platform to critique government as well. She yokes domestic and national happiness with health: a garden should be useful to those who wish to exercise their minds and bodies and the government should likewise protect its people by emphasizing utility, not vanity. In deflecting attention away from the visual appeal of gardening, Wollstonecraft is implicitly critiquing the practice of landscape gardening in England made popular by writers like Sir John Vanbrugh and painters like William Kent. See J. R. Watson's *Picturesque Landscape and English Romantic Poetry* for more on picturesque gardening in eighteenth century England.

25. In emphasizing self-consciousness in life-writing I in no way intend to support dismissal of Dorothy Wordsworth's subjectivity "as either repressed or inadequate" (Mellor, *R & G* 144). I distinguish Wordsworth's and Woll-

stonecraft's modes of self-representation to contextualize better the range of romantic subjectivity worth considering. See Kay K. Cook for more on Dorothy Wordsworth's life-writing.

Works Cited

Armstrong, Nancy. *Desire and Domestic Fiction: A Political History of the Novel.* New York: Oxford UP, 1987.

Brissot, J. P. *Nouveau Voyage Dans Les Etats-Unies de L'Amerique Septentrionale, fait en 1788.* 3 vols. Paris, 1791.

Burke, Edmund. *A Philosophical Inquiry into the Origin of Our Ideas of the Sublime and the Beautiful.* 5th ed. London: J. Dodsley, 1767.

——. *Reflections on the Revolution in France, and on the Proceedings in Certain Societies in London, relative to that event* (Nov. 1790). Ed. Thomas H. D. Mahoney. New York: Liberal Arts P, 1955.

Cook, Kay. "Self-Neglect in the Canon: Why Don't We Talk about Romantic Autobiography?" *A/B: Auto/Biography Studies* 5.2 (1990): 88-98.

Diehl, Joanne Feit. *Women Poets and the American Sublime.* Bloomington: Indiana UP, 1990.

Ezell, Margaret J. M. *Writing Women's Literary History.* Baltimore: Johns Hopkins UP, 1993.

Favret, Mary A. *Romantic Correspondence: Women, Politics, and the Fiction of Letters.* Cambridge: Cambridge UP, 1993.

Felski, Rita. *Beyond Feminist Aesthetics: Feminist Literature and Social Change.* Cambridge: Harvard UP, 1989.

Ferguson, Moira, ed. *First Feminists: British Women Writers, 1578-1799.* Bloomington: Indiana UP, 1985.

Foucault, Michel. "What Is an Author?" *Language, Counter-Memory, Practice: Selected Essays and Interviews.* Ed. Donald F. Bouchard. Ithaca: Cornell UP, 1977. 113-38.

Gilpin, William. *Observations on the River Wye, and Several Parts of South Wales, etc., Relative Chiefly to Picturesque Beauty.* London, 1782.

——. *Observations, Relative Chiefly to Picturesque Beauty, made in the Year 1776, on Several Parts of Great Britain, particularly the Highlands of Scotland.* 2 vols. London, 1789.

——. *Three Essays: on Picturesque Beauty; on Picturesque Travel; and on Sketching Landscape.* London, 1792.

Godwin, William. *Memoirs of Mary Wollstonecraft* (1798). London: Constable, 1928.

Hamilton, Rev. William. *Letters Concerning the Northern Coast of the County of Antrim.* 2 vols. London: Robinsons, 1790.

Hartley, Debra Ann. "The Embrace of Nature: Representations of Self and Others by Women Travel Writers of the Romantic Period." Diss: U of Iowa, 1992.

Hassell, J. *Tour of the Isle of Wight.* 2 vols. London: Hookam, 1790.

Ireland, Samuel. *A picturesque Tour through Holland, Brabant, and Part of France; made in the Autumn of 1789.* 2 vols. London: Egertons, 1790.

McGann, Jerome J. *The Romantic Ideology: A Critical Investigation.* Chicago: U of Chicago P, 1983.

Mellor, Anne K., ed. *Romanticism & Feminism.* Bloomington: Indiana UP, 1988.

——. *Romanticism & Gender.* New York: Routledge, 1993.

Moore, Jane. "Plagiarism with a Difference: Subjectivity in 'Kubla Khan' and *Letters Written during a Short Residence in Sweden, Norway, and Denmark.*" *Beyond Romanticism: New Approaches to Texts and Contexts, 1780-1832.* Ed. Stephen Copley and John Whale. New York: Routledge, 1992. 140-59.

Morris, Mary, ed. *Maiden Voyages: Writings of Women Travelers.* New York: Vintage, 1993.

Moskal, Jeanne. "The Picturesque and the Affectionate in Wollstonecraft's *Letters from Norway.*" *Modern Language Quarterly* 52.3 (1991): 263-94.

Myers, Mitzi. "Mary Wollstonecraft's *Letters Written . . . in Sweden*: Toward Romantic Autobiography." *Studies in Eighteenth-Century Culture.* Vol. 8. Ed. Roseann Runte. Madison: U of Wisconsin P, 1979. 165-85.

Piozzi, Hester Lynch Thrale. *Observations and Reflections, made in the Course of a Journey through France, Italy, and Germany.* 2 vols. London: Cadell, 1789.

Radcliffe, Ann. *A Journey Made in the Summer of 1794, through Holland and the Western Frontiers of Germany, with a return down the Rhine, to which are added Observations during a tour to the Lakes of Lancashire, Westmoreland, and Cumberland.* London: G. G. & J. Robinson, 1795.

Rev. of *Letters Written during a Short Residence in Sweden, Norway, and Denmark,* by Mary Wollstonecraft. *British Critic, A New Review* 7 (1796): 602-10.

St. Clair, William. *The Godwins and The Shelleys: A Biography of a Family.* Baltimore: Johns Hopkins UP, 1989.

Schor, Esther H. "Mary Shelley in Transit." *The Other Mary Shelley: Beyond Frankenstein.* Ed. Audrey A. Fisch, Anne K. Mellor, and Esther H. Schor. New York: Oxford UP, 1993.

Shelley, Mary Wollstonecraft Godwin. *History of a Six Weeks' Tour through a Part of France, Switzerland, Germany, and Holland: With Letters Descriptive of a Sail round the Lake of Geneva, and of the Glaciers of Chamouni* [With Percy Bysshe Shelley]. London: T. Hookam, Jun.; and C. and J. Ollier, 1817.

——. *The Last Man*. Intro. Anne K. Mellor. Lincoln: U of Nebraska P, 1993.

Stafford, Barbara Maria. "Toward Romantic Landscape Perception: Illustrated Travels and the Rise of 'Singularity' as an Aesthetic Category." *Studies in Eighteenth Century Culture* 10 [publ. for the ASECS]. Madison: U of Wisconsin P, 1981. 17-75.

Todd, Janet M. *Mary Wollstonecraft: An Annotated Bibliography*. New York: Garland, 1976.

Ty, Eleanor. "Writing as a Daughter: Autobiography in Wollstonecraft's Travelogue." *Essays on Life Writing: From Genre to Critical Practice*. Ed. Marlene Kadar. Toronto: U of Toronto P, 1992. 61-77.

Williams, Helen Maria. *A Tour in Switzerland; or, a View of the Present State of the Governments and Manners of those Cantons, with Comparative Sketches of the Present State of Paris*. London: G. G. & J. Robinson, 1798.

Wollstonecraft, Mary. *Letters from Norway* and Godwin's *Memoirs*. Intro. Richard Holmes. New York: Penguin, 1987.

——. *Letters Written during a Short Residence in Sweden, Norway, and Denmark*. Ed. Carol H. Poston. Lincoln: U of Nebraska P, 1976.

——. *The Works of Mary Wollstonecraft*. 7 vols. Ed. Janet Todd and Marilyn Butler. New York: New York UP, 1989.

Wollstonecraft, Mary, and Mary Shelley. *Mary/Maria/Matilda*. Ed. Janet Todd. London: Penguin, 1991.

Wordsworth, Dorothy. *The Grasmere Journals*. Ed. Pamela Woof. Oxford: Oxford UP, 1993.

Wordsworth, William. *The Prelude, 1799, 1805, 1850*. Ed. Jonathan Wordsworth, M. H. Abrams, and Stephen Gill. New York: Norton, 1979.

Yaeger, Patricia. "Toward a Female Sublime." *Gender and Theory*. Ed. Linda Kauffman. New York: Blackwell, 1989. 191-212.

14

Sugar Ladles and Strainers: Political Self-Fashioning in the Epistolary Journalism of Lydia Maria Child

Anne Righton Malone

In February of 1843, shortly before leaving her post as editor of the *National Anti-slavery Standard*, Lydia Maria Child explained to her readers in one of her final "Letters from New York,"

When I began to write these letters, it was simply as a safety valve for an expanding spirit, pent-up like steam in a boiler. I told you they would be of every fashion, according to my changing mood; now a mere panorama of passing scenes, then childlike prattle about birds or mosses; now a serious exposition of facts, for the reformer's use, and then the poet's path, on winged Pegasus, far up into the blue. (*NASS* 9 Feb. 1843)[1]

And of every fashion they were. For two years, these weekly columns, written in epistolary format and addressed "Dear Friend," provided Child the opportunity to free herself from the bondage of "being chained to the oar" as editor of the *Standard*, as she explained in a letter to Boston abolitionist Ellis Gray Loring (*Lydia Maria Child: Selected Letters* 28 Sept. 1841). On the surface the letters are free-spirited, impartial explorations of New York City. On closer observation, however, they are carefully constructed political epistles, locating the female epistolary genre within the public arena and thus complicating Elizabeth Goldsmith's observation that "female epistolary voices tend to describe confinement more than liberation, isolation more than interaction" (xii).[2] Furthermore, Child's emergence into the crowded streets of New York City marks the entrance of the female spectator into the public arena.

Although Dana Brand argues that the speculative pedestrian essay was an exclusively male genre throughout the nineteenth century, Child's "Letters from New York" clearly establish her as urban spectator and as such allow her to interiorize the city for herself and for her readers. By stepping into the role of public spectator, Child creates a "safety valve" for her "expanding spirit" while nurturing a personal reader-editor relationship. But, most importantly, these letters become a bridge to the *Standard* for those readers who would not otherwise have chosen to read an antislavery newspaper. As Child confesses in her farewell editorial,

The New York Letters were inserted upon something of the same principle that the famous Timothy Dexter sent a stock of Bibles to the West Indies, with warming pans, to be used for sugar ladles and strainers. No purchaser was allowed to have a pan, unless he would buy a Bible also. Thus have I brought some to look candidly at antislavery principles, by drawing them with the garland of imagination and taste. It was an honest and open trick, and I think I may be easily pardoned. (*NASS* 4 May 1843)

In these candid daguerreotypes of the city, Child addresses politically charged issues in an informal rhetorical voice that she had been unable to develop eight years earlier in her highly controversial antislavery treatise, *An Appeal in Favor of That Class of Americans Called Africans*. Although *An Appeal* and its "call for immediate emancipation of the nation's two million slaves" had been highly acclaimed by antislavery supporters, the only review of the book outside of the abolitionist press was a caustic lament in the October 1833 *American Monthly Review* "that a lady who by her writing has done so much credit to herself and her sex, so much for the improvement of her countrywomen should venture with her bark on such a troubled sea" ("Review" 298). Despite Child's acknowledgment in the preface of *An Appeal* that she was fully aware the book's strong abolitionist stance would be the subject of "ridicule and censure," she was stunned that the overwhelmingly negative response came from even her most dedicated audience. As Carolyn Karcher notes, within two months after publication of *An Appeal*,

Child's fashionable acquaintances cut her dead in the streets; a rising star in Boston's political sphere flung her book out of the window with a pair of tongs; the Boston Athenaeum hastily revoked the library privileges she had been only the second woman in its history to receive; outraged parents canceled their subscriptions to her children's magazine [*The Juvenile Miscellany*], bringing about its collapse; and the sales of her other books plummeted. (284)

Thus, by assuming the role as editor of the *Standard*, the official organ of the American Anti-slavery Society, Child again found herself treading water on this troubled sea of abolitionist reform. Although the *Standard* was only one year old when she took the helm, it was already in financial difficulty and the number of subscribers had decreased drastically under the editorship of Nathanial Rogers. At the urging of Maria Weston Chapman and Abby Kelly, Child had agreed to assume the role of editor and had accepted the Society's request that her husband David serve as assistant editor for the sake of those who would not read a newspaper edited solely by a woman. Although a number of women edited newspapers and magazines, by accepting the editorship of the *Standard*, Child became the first woman in the United States to be named editor of a newspaper devoted to issues of public policy.

In many ways her decision to assume the editorship of the *Standard* was more a matter of economics than of politics. She was still suffering from the financial repercussions brought on by *An Appeal* and, as she explained in a letter to her close friend Francis Shaw, the major debts David had incurred in his attempts at sugar beet farming had left her with no choice but "to take the responsible and irksome situation" (*SL* 27 May 1841). Explaining that she had been compelled to assume the editorship of the *Standard* more by her love for David and "the hopes of earning a home, as Jacob did Rachel" than by her zeal for the abolitionist cause, she wrote,

You do me injustice by praising my "moral courage" and "devotion to the cause" in coming here. I would I deserved the praise; but I must disclaim it, because it does not belong to me. It was the driving, not the leading of Providence, which brought me to this position. (*SL* 27 May 1841)

No welcoming committee met Maria when she arrived in New York City on the afternoon of May 11, 1841. After attending the closing ceremonies of the American Anti-slavery Association and securing her belongings in her rented room at the home of Quaker abolitionists Isaac and Hannah Hopper, she set to work on her first issue of the *Standard*. Eight days later, "L. Maria Child, Editor" appeared in the masthead of the *Standard*, and in her first editorial Child explained her willingness to take on this responsibility. In this editorial she vowed to "work according to my conscience and ability; promising nothing but diligence and fidelity, refusing the shadow of a fetter on my free expression of opinion, from any man, or body of men," and at the same time promising to be "equally careful to respect the freedom of others, whether as individuals or societies" (*NASS* 20 May 1841).

Despite the Society's initial agreement with Child's demand for complete editorial control of the *Standard*, her first months as editor were difficult as she fought to achieve editorial autonomy. As she wrote to her friends Ellis and Louisa Loring, the work was often "perfectly intolerable, unless sustained by the conviction that I am doing some good to the anti-slavery cause" (*SC* 17 June 1841). Although she delighted in the intellectual companionship of Hannah and Isaac Hopper and the devoted attention of their 23-year-old son John, Maria's thoughts remained with David on their Northampton farm and with her abolitionist friends in Boston. For this reason letters from friends at home were most welcome gifts. As she explained in a letter to Shaw written shortly after her arrival in New York City, letters from home gave her the strength to maintain her commitment to the *Standard*. Thanking Shaw for his letter, she wrote: "A letter is never so refreshing as during the *first* days after we have left home, when the heart is desolate with remembrance of the past, and unaccustomed to its new relations" (*SL* 27 May 1841). Living in "this disagreeable city," she lamented, makes "[me] feel anxious, responsible, and *alone*," and, thus, compelled to correspond with friends at home because "a very large proportion of my thoughts can find no echo here."

In spite of the support she received from this correspondence, by June she was ready to give up the editorial position and return to Northampton. However, as she would explain several years later in a letter to Louisa Loring, her dislike of New York City was tempered by the stark memories of the previous year and her conviction that the "terrible year of toil and discord at Northampton made any life seem pleasant by comparison" (*SL* 22 June 1845). As she explained to Louisa, she clearly understood that another year of tilling the rocky New England soil and mending David's tattered clothes would in no way advance either her goals for social reform or her career as a writer:

As for my finding "N.York so very delightful in June," I do not find it delightful at *any* season. But . . . I am convinced that N.York is the best place for me to fulfil my appointed mission. I live henceforth for one undivided object; viz: to build up my literary reputation, and make it the vehicle of as much good to the world as I know how. For this purpose, N.York affords advantages that no other place does. (*SL* 22 June 1845)

In her private correspondence during these first months Child continued to write to her Boston friends, each time expressing her doubts and concerns about New York City life, about her marriage, and about her role as editor of the *Standard*. In June 1841 she wrote to Ellis Loring lamenting, "I almost break down sometimes, under the disagreeableness of the employment, and the utter want of interest manifested in the paper. I have not received a line of encouragement from any mortal but yourself" (*SL* 17 June 1841). This letter contains the first seeds for her "Letters from New York" in Child's acknowledgment that these "lines of encouragement" will require that she write the first letter. The power of the epistolary genre, she explains in this letter, is in the fact that letters are gifts exchanged between friends providing an open forum for presenting ideas with "no need of mincing the matter" (*SL* 17 June 1841).

At the end of June 1841, Maria visited David in Northampton, returning to New York City on July 4th. Shortly after her return, she penned her first "Letter from New York" for the *Standard*, positioning it next to the editorial column and presenting it as the first of a series of weekly letters. "Dear Friend," she wrote, as if addressing a distant friend, "You ask what is now my opinion of this great Babylon. . . . Well, Babylon remains the same as then. The din of crowded life, and the eager chase for gain, still run through its streets, like the perpetual murmur of a hive" (*NASS* 19 Aug. 1841). This weekly column, she explained to her readers, would afford her the opportunity to "turn wearily aside from the dusty road of reforming duty," to seek beauty in this city where "the din for crowded life" and "the eager chase for gain" fight for control and where "wealth dozes on French couches" while "poverty camps on the dirty pavement" across the street (*NASS* 19 Aug. 1841). Promising in subsequent letters to "gather flowers in sheltered nooks" and "play with gems in hidden grottos," she signs the letter, "Yours, Affectionately, L.M.C." Despite this promise to seek out tranquil beauty, she ends the second Letter with a description of New York dog-killers "with their bloody clubs and spattered garments," prefaced by an apology and a renewed promise: "The disagreeables of New York, I deliberately mean to keep out of sight, when I write to you. By contemplating beauty, the character becomes beautiful; and in this wearisome world I deem it a duty to speak genial words and wear cheerful looks" (*NASS* 26 Aug. 1841).

Child's weekly "Letters from New York" were an immediate success and for the next two years she included them as a regular feature in the *Standard*. In addition several other newspapers, including the *Boston Courier*, also began publishing her columns. The range of topics Child writes about in these letters varies from the purely observational descriptions of New York City moving day and Ole Bul's concerts to her social and political commentaries on the Washingtonian temperance parades and women's prison reform. Even within each letter, she wanders from one subject to another, creating a mosaic of thoughts and ideas as she seeks ways, not only to understand New York City, but also to deal with her loneliness, her frustration, and her curiosity.

Although Patricia Holland observes, after reading the "Letters from New York," that Child "enjoyed living in New York" in spite of her difficulties with the editorial policy of the *Standard* (48), during the first months, Child's public letters and more specifically her private correspondence indicate that she found city life most difficult. Daily she was confronted with poverty unlike any she had known before. She missed "the green fields and the pure air" of her Massachusetts farm (*SL* "To Francis Shaw" 27 May 1841). Everywhere she turned, she was overwhelmed by poverty and the need for social reform. And as editor of an abolitionist newspaper, she had become convinced that the conflicts between the Garrisonians and the New Organizationists were detrimental to the abolitionist cause as well as limiting to her editorial freedom. Thus, the letters became her safety valve, and at the same time they became the vehicle through which she was able to construct a friendly rather than agonistic editor-reader relationship.

With the "Letters from New York" Child moves immediately and forcefully away from the abolitionist stance of her *Standard* editorials. In her early letters Child describes her walks through the Battery and her meandering strolls through private gardens. Modeled on the popular genre of travel writing, these essays give her license to explore the city with the "I" of authority. During the early nineteenth century, legions of women and men began publishing accounts of their travels. The popularity had increased so dramatically that one nineteenth-century reviewer had observed that almost everybody who "happens once is his life to wander from the precincts of his own native village, thinks it his duty to enlighten the publick with a narrative of his adventures" (Sparks 390).

In his study of the spectator in the city, Dana Brand notes, "In the period . . . up to the middle of the nineteenth century, I have not been able to find any examples of works written by women" as "speculative pedestrian" (199). Suggesting that women tended to confine their narratives to their journeys from home to a distant place and back again, Brand contends that the exploration of city streets and of public space was a uniquely male genre. Women could not assume this role of city spectator, according to Brand, because "there is something inappropriate about women enjoying the degree of access to the consciousness and character of others that the flaneur traditionally claims for himself"(200). In addition Brand notes that "the persona of the flâneur is invariably male" because of "the specific social meaning . . . [that is attributed to] a solitary woman walking the streets without any apparent purpose, looking into the faces of passers-by" (200).

Yet, walking the city streets is exactly what Child does. By assuming the role of urban spectator and writing these weekly excursionary "Letters from New York," Child deliberately steps across even more solidly established gender boundaries than she had when she agreed to edit the *Standard*. In doing so, she grants herself the heretofore exclusive male privilege of the flâneur with his invisibility and inaccessibility within a crowd. With this move, Child, like her male counterpart, gains the freedom to explore, stare, and observe and, therefore, to transform the city "into a legible, accessible and non-threatening version of itself" (Brand 7). Constructing each New York letter as a meandering journey, Child attributes the digressions along the way to the nature of the epistolary genre. Clearly aware of the license this genre allows her, she ends her first letter with a reminder to her readers, lest they have forgotten, of the open-ended nature of letters. In doing so she asks her reader to pardon her seemingly unconnected literary wandering: "I am cutting the lines deep when I meant only to give you airy sketches. . . . Therefore, blame me not, if I sometimes turn wearily aside from the dusty road of reforming duty, to gather flowers in sheltered nooks, or play with gems hidden in grottoes" (*NASS* 14 Aug. 1841).

In these early letters, Child continually seeks to position herself in New York City by locating the familiar in the unfamiliar. This desire for the familiar provides Child with the opportunity to cross and recross genre boundaries. As Diane Freedman has observed, "cross-genre writing often grounds itself in the familiar, a familiar body or body of works, familiar landscapes and seascapes, familiar and friendly tones" (149). Although the private letters Child writes during these early months continue to be filled with laments of loneliness, in her public letters Child clearly acknowledges the presence of spiritual balance. As urban geographer, she describes her walks through the city, questioning what she sees along the way and meditating on the implications. By working within the epistolary genre she is able to shed the fetters that continue to restrict her editorial voice. In writing weekly letters to a friend she is bound to follow no rhetorical structure other than the one she creates for herself.

Stylistically, the "Letters from New York" are stark contrasts to her editorials written in the classical argumentative style and penned with an urgency that matched the rhetorical stance she had assumed in *An Appeal*. In an editorial decrying the "cold-hearted indifference" of abolitionists she lashes out at her readers:

Every week, thousands of innocent babes are born into perpetual slavery; every week, thousands upon thousands groan and shriek under the torturing lash; every week, thousands upon thousands are the forced victims of brutal licentiousness; every week, thousands of mothers are torn from their little ones, stu-pefied or frantic, with agony of heart. . . . And while all this is going on, we are dancing in our saloons, or reclining on spring-sofas, by our comfortable fires, worse than thoughtless concerning this vast amount of misery and crime. . . . Strong language, you call this? But assuredly it is not as strong as any of us would use, if our own children were the victim. (Editorial *NASS* 21 Oct. 1841)

In contrast, the "Letter from New York" she writes for the same issue describes the "infinite varieties" who populate the city and tells the story of a Scotsman's death that "would have melted the heart of his mother" (*NASS* 21 Oct. 1841). In contrast to the carefully constructed editorials, the letters are, by outward appearances, formless narratives, framed only by her excursions about New York and written on whatever topics please her at the moment. On many occasions, she openly acknowledges her inability to clip the wings of her meandering spirit, making observations such as, "To-day I know not what I shall write; but I *think* I shall be off to the sky; for my spirit is in that mood when smil-ing faces peep through chinks in the clouds, and angel-fingers beckon and point upward" (*NASS* 2 Feb. 1843).

As she assumes the flâneur's cape and wanders about the city, first with a guide and later on her own, she weaves for her readers the threads of an intellectual excursion. In each letter she points directly to the nature of the epistolary genre, reminding her readers that letters are not premeditated, structured essays. She requests, "You will, at least, my dear friend, give these letters the credit of being utterly unpremeditated; for Flibbertigibbet himself never moved with more unexpected and inco-herent variety" (*NASS* 21 Oct. 1841). Almost weekly, she reminds her readers that they cannot hold her accountable for the direction these let-ters take, since, "As the boy said of his whistling, 'it did itself'" (*NASS* 14 Oct. 1841). Having studied classical rhetoric with her brother, she was clearly aware that this argument of "writing writing itself" worked well with the epistolary form. This knowledge gave her the freedom to write on whatever subjects she chose, in whatever way she chose, as long as she apologized by reminding her reader in one form or another, "It did itself."

Like Thoreau's romantic excursionary essays, these "Letters from New York" assume overtones of the spiritual quest as Child sets forth on her weekly excursions. In the letter she writes from Northampton, she comments on the spiritual journey she has taken by noting her surprise:

I know not how I wandered here, from the leafless trees on the wintry hill-sides; but in good truth, I never can pen a letter without making myself liable to the

Vagrant Act. . . . My pen . . . paces or whirls, bounds or waltzes, steps in the slow minuet, or capers, in the fantastic fandango, according to the music within. (*NASS* 11 Nov. 1841)

Writing within this transcendental excursionary form, Child is able, as Lawrence Buell notes in his analysis of Thoreau's excursionary transcendentalism, to include in her essays what seems to be "the most perplexing mixture of subject matters and levels of style" (203). And as urban spectator she gains license to take her readers on "panoramic tours" of the city presented in installments, each installment devoted to what she has randomly encountered during the previous week. Rhetorically, these letters become Child's most experimental work, not only allowing her direct access to her readers but more importantly allowing her readers direct access to this woman editor, L. Maria Child. Whereas L. M. Child, editor of the *Standard*, wrote formally structured articles bound by the principles of the American Anti-slavery Association, L. Maria Child, the woman, spoke in a voice bound to no one. At times she told her readers of her difficulties adjusting to New York City life, at other times she invited them on meandering excursions through the city, and always she asked her readers to join her in questioning what they saw and heard.

By casting the "Letters from New York" as excursionary narratives, she provides herself with a forum for open-ended speculation on any subject that comes her way, and in the tradition of the epistolary genre, she discovers a way to describe the specific and make it personal. In the early letters, the beauty she discovers is external, found in her walks along the Battery and her journeys outside the city gates. Although her seaside walks provide tranquillity, this contentment, she continually reminds her reader, is momentary, for she is bound by responsibility to return to the city and to her editorial desk.

On a sultry hot August day three months after her arrival in New York, Child makes her first visit to the slums of New York City. This experience marks her first move from the traditionally detached urban spectator. Beginning her next letter with a wandering narrative on "the God *within* us" and "two beautiful young trees," she asks her readers' patience, acknowledging, "Perchance, you will even call me 'transcendental,'" and offering a brief, hasty explanation:

You too would worship two little trees and a sunflower, if you had gone with me to the Five Points, the other day. Morally and physically, the breathing air was like an open tomb. How souls and bodies could live there, I could not imagine. If you want to see something worse than Hogarth's Gin Lane, go there in a warm afternoon. . . . I regretted the errand of kindness that drew me there; for it stunned my senses with the amount of evil, and fell upon the strong hopefulness of my character like a stroke of palsy. (*NASS* 2 Sept. 1841)

With this letter, there is an immediate shift in her perspective. For the next few months her letters avoid even the slightest glance into these faces that had haunted her on this walk through Five Points. Her first response is to move outside the gates of the city, taking her readers on steamboat excursions to Staten Island and walks along the banks on the Hudson River at Weehawken; however, she observes in a moment of reflection, the "remembrances of the city haunted me like evil spirits" (*NASS* 9 Sept. 1841). Her only New York excursion is within the safety of a Jewish synagogue. However, even here she finds no comfort. Because she and her companion have not joined the other women in the upper part of the synagogue they are chastised by "one of the masters of Israel [who] came, and somewhat gruffly ordered me, and the young lady who accompanied me, to retire from the front seats of the synagogue. It was uncourteous; for we were very respectful and still, and not in the least disposed to intrude upon the daughters of Jacob" (*NASS* 23 Sept. 1841).

Moving further from "the terror and gloom" of the city she travels to Greenwood Cemetery where "fish abound undisturbed" and the air is "redolent with woodland melody" (*NASS* 30 Sept. 1841) and to Grant Thorburn's gardens in Ravenswood, leaving the city "by Hellgate, a name not altogether inappropriate for an entrance to New York" (*NASS* 14 Oct. 1841). Yet as the ferry left the city, her thoughts returned to "the squalid little wretches I had seen at Five Points" and "the crowd of sickly infants in Boston alms-house. . . . And my heart ached, that it could see no end to all this misery" (*NASS* 14 Oct. 1841). This heartache was compounded by her own anxieties and her own loneliness. In September she had written to Ellis Loring,

How I do long to get out of this infernal treadmill. How I do long to be re-united with my dear husband, and have some quiet domestic days again! It makes me groan to think that only four months of the stipulated year have passed. Nothing *but* Mr. Child's pecuniary distress would keep me here another month. I hate it, with an inconceivable and growing hatred. . . . Out of it I will get by hook or by crook. (*SC* 21 Sept. 1841)

Her conflicts increased when several of the more vocal members of the National Anti-slavery Society once again attempted to dictate how she should edit the newspaper, pointing to material, including the

"Letters from New York," that they deemed inappropriate for an abolitionist newspaper. As she wrote to Loring, she was most angered at these
attempts to restrict what she could and could not include in the paper "as
if antislavery were the *only* idea in the universe!" (*SL* 21 Sept. 1841).
Questioning "the morality of letting one's soul be thus ground up for a
cursed reform" and contending that these attempts at control cut into her
editorial freedom, she restated her demand that as long as she was
required to maintain complete responsibility for the production of the
paper she must also be given complete editorial control.

In contrast to these few dissenting Society members, a majority of
the readers of the *Standard* were intrigued with the weekly "Letters from
New York." By mid-September, Child had begun receiving dozens of
letters from her readers responding to her queries, continuing conversations she had begun in her letters, asking her opinion on other subjects of
public policy, telling their stories of slavery and poverty, and at times
correcting her errors and oversights. For Child, this reader-editor correspondence began to provide the personal connection she had been seeking with her readers. As the correspondence increased so did the popularity of the column. Many times subscribers would write to tell her that
the weekly "Letter from New York" was the first column they would
read when the newspaper arrived. And like treasured family letters, they
explained, her letters were read aloud at the dinner table and shared with
friends who came to call. Yet, when Child left her post in early October
1841 for a four-week visit to Northampton, she was still uncertain that
she had the strength to honor her two-year commitment to the *Standard*.
As she explained in a letter to Shaw written just before she left New
York City,

It seems so odd to *visit* [David]. I do hope that circumstances will be so ordered
as to bring about a re-union soon, I am the worst of all temperaments to live
without being beloved. . . . What has fame or wealth to offer compared to a
friend whose welcoming smile and kiss is always ready, and who verily *thinks*
you the wisest, best, handsomest, and above all, the dearest person in the world?
(*SL* 12 Oct. 1841)

During her first weeks at Northampton, Child put aside all editorial
responsibilities, including writing the weekly "Letter from New York."
By the end of the second week, letters poured in to the *Standard*,
expressing concern that Child had given up her editorial post or worse
yet that she had been asked to step down. Readers who thought that
Child's "Letters from New York" column had been dropped wrote passionate letters requesting that it be continued. Surprised and over-

whelmed to hear of this outpouring of letters from devoted readers, Child responded from Northampton with a letter of her own. In this letter she acknowledged their concerns with motherly compassion and assured them that she did indeed plan to return to her position as editor of the *Standard*:

I have not forgotten to write you through the columns of the *Standard*; and I find that the paper itself has become to me as a favorite child, from which I am not well content to be absent, though I know it has passed the three perils of infancy and is left in the best of care. Excess of occupation has alone prevented me from writing sooner. Like Desdemona of old, "still the house-affairs call me hence." The New Organizationists may comfort themselves that I am *sometimes* in my "appropriate sphere"; and you and the subscriber of the *Standard* may rejoice as much as you choose. (*NASS* 11 Nov. 1841)

When she returned to New York City at the end of November 1842, the National Anti-slavery Society was embroiled in a new controversy. The *Pennsylvania Freeman*, the newspaper of the Eastern Pennsylvania Anti-slavery Society, had folded and its subscription list had been added to that of the *Standard*. Among her correspondence was a letter from James Miller McKim, Eastern Pennsylvania Anti-slavery Society president, voicing their concern that a woman serve as the editor of the *Standard* and demanding that this woman editor define her position on the issues of slavery and abolition. Rather than beginning her response with equal anger, she apologized for her delay in responding to the query, reminding McKim that as a woman she also had other obligations. "If you find it difficult to realize this," she explained, "have the goodness to remember that in addition to what men editors have to perform, I am obliged to do my own washing and ironing, mending and making, besides manifold stitches for my husband's comfort" (*SL* 24 Nov. 1841). Her explanation of "her position" portrayed a newfound strength of editorial autonomy:

When you call upon me to "define my position," I do not clearly understand whether you mean me, L. M. Child, or me, the editor of the *Standard*. If you mean individual me, I answer in all respect and courtesy, that I am amenable to no man, or association of men for my opinions. If you mean the editor of the *Standard*, I will say that I respect the freedom of the American Society full as much as I wish it to respect my freedom. The views of a large majority are by no means coincident with my own, on many subjects; but there is sufficient identity for me to manage their organ without interfering with their conscientious freedom, or in any degree violating my own. I have neither the right, nor the wish, to make the paper a vehicle of my own opinions, as distinct from theirs; therefore I am silent about many things which I should probably advocate in a paper of my own. (*SL* 24 Nov. 1841)

As she explained to McKim, the "New York Letters" had provided her with the opportunity to write, not as editor of the *Standard*, but as L. M. Child, urban geographer and observer of humanity. With her return, her relationship with the *Standard* began to change, and she became more keenly aware of the influence her prose could have upon her readers. Although her first letters had portrayed her dislike of living in New York City, by late November she had begun to reconcile these feelings. She no longer sat as an outsider watching the parades of the Washingtonian Temperance Society, she no longer stood as an observer in the rear of a Jewish synagogue, and she no longer retreated from Five Points to pastoral cemeteries and stately gardens.

She began to write "with her sleeves rolled up," clearly acknowledging that she meant these letters to become active agents of social change. As she explained in the first letter written after her visit with David, she returned to the "editorial treadmill" with a strong belief that women were "obviously coming into a wider and wider field of action" (*NASS* 25 Nov. 1841). She spoke out strongly for equality, sometimes adding comments or questions in the midst of descriptive passages. When describing the Jewish synagogue service in an earlier letter, she had mused, "I remembered the contumely with which they had been treated throughout Christendom, and I imagined how they must feel, on entering a place of Christian worship to hear us sing, 'With hearts as hard as stubborn Jews, that unbelieving race'" (*NASS* 23 Sept. 1841).

Her questions now became more direct. In a letter responding to a request that she explain her opinions on women's rights, she "cuts the lines deep," noting that "the present position of women in society is the result of physical force" (*NASS* 16 Feb. 1843). For those who would doubt her statement, she suggests, "let her reflect why she is afraid to go out in the evening without the protection of a man." Further questioning the roles women have been forced to assume in society, she emphatically explains,

This taking away *rights*, and *condescending* to grant *privileges*, is an old trick of the physical force principle; and with the immense majority, who only look on the surface of things, this mask effectually disguises an ugliness, which would otherwise be abhorred. The most inveterate slave-holders are probably those who take most pride in dressing their household servants handsomely and who would be most ashamed to have the name of being *unnecessarily* cruel. And profligates, who form the lowest and most sensual estimate of women, are the very ones who treat them with an excess of outward deference. . . . Just imagine for a moment, what impression it would make on men, if women authors should write about *their* "rosy lips," and "melting eyes," and "voluptuous forms," as they do write about us! (*NASS* 16 Feb. 1843)

   Although Child takes the opportunity on several other occasions to explain her political stance, for the most part the letters now become excursions into the dark corners of the city. She tells stories of penniless women and children huddled together in doorways for winter warmth; she paints word pictures of the street musicians who earn money for food and shelter with their music; she catalogues the effects of a corrupt justice system. She talks with ex-slaves, recounting their stories to her readers as they have told them to her. She questions what she sees at the institutions of reform. Although she still, on occasion, returns to search for tranquillity, as she explained in one of the first letters written after her return to New York City, the sublime landscape belongs, not to her, but "to *him* who has spiritually retired apart into high places to pray" (*NASS* 20 Jan. 1842).

   Begun simply as a way to position herself in New York City, the letters soon become her strongest platform for reform of social wrongs, her vision of the city through a woman's eyes. Whereas the self-reflexive focus of the early "Letters from New York" afforded her the opportunity to calm her doubts about living in "this great Babylon," she now uses the epistolary genre as a vehicle to directly question public policy and to openly encourage her readers to join her in this questioning. Although occasional threads of her earlier loneliness remain, they are now shadows cast in the light of political reform. In a letter written in early February 1843, she confesses,

My spirit is weary for rural rambles. It is sad walking in the city. The streets shut out the sky, even as commerce comes between the soul and heaven. The busy throng, passing and repassing, fetter freedom, while they offer no sympathy. The loneliness of the soul is deeper and far more restless, than in the solitude of the mighty forest. . . . For eight weary months, I have met in the crowded streets but two faces I had ever seen before. Of some, I would I could say I should never see them again; but they haunt me in my sleep, and come between me and the morning. Beseeching looks, begging the comfort and hope I have no power to give. Hungry eyes, that look as if they had pleaded long for sympathy and at last gone mute in still despair. (*NASS* 17 Feb. 1842)

   Writing with deliberate poignancy, Child crafts these letters as invitations for her readers to question what she has seen and to consider more carefully those things they have witnessed with their own eyes. On many occasions she directs her letters to women readers, openly acknowledging the needs for reforms that she claims only women can understand. When she visits Long Island Farms, a state-supported orphanage, she commends the neat outward appearance, but expresses shock at what she sees inside. She invites her readers to share this concern:

In one place, I saw a stack of small wooden guns, and was informed that the boys were daily drilled to military exercises, as a useful means of forming habits of order, as well as fitting them for the future service of the state. . . . Alas poor childhood doth church and state provide for thee! The state arms thee with wooden guns, to play the future murderer, and the church teaches thee to pray in the platoons. (*NASS* 6 Oct. 1842)

On a visit to the penitentiary on Blackwell Island she describes her amazement at the fact that over half the prisoners are women, and that most of these women have been charged with crimes of prostitution. Turning to her readers, she asks them to question the injustice that allows the "men who have made [these women] such" to live in "the 'ceilinged houses' of Broadway, and sit in council in the City Hall, and pass 'regulations' to clear the streets they have filled with sin" (*NASS* 6 Oct. 1842).

In another letter she vehemently expresses her disapproval of capital punishment by describing a public execution that had been averted by the prisoner's suicide only moments before the scheduled public event. Decrying the printed circulars that had been handed out to announce the execution, she observes, "I trust some of them are preserved for museums. Specimens should be kept as relics of a barbarous age, for succeeding generations to wonder at" (*NASS* 19 Nov. 1842). Her greatest concern in this letter is that women were also consumed with the "diabolic passion" to violently terminate this man's life. As she stands with the crowd after the announcement that the prisoner, John C. Colt, has died in his cell, she is stunned by a comment from a woman standing nearby. Turning to the woman Child asks, "Would you feel so, if he were your *son*?" said I. Her countenance changed instantly. She had not before realized that every criminal was *somebody's son* (*NASS* 19 Nov. 1842).

By the time Child's two-year editorship drew to a close, the "Letters from New York" had done what Child had hoped, significantly increased the readership of the *Standard*. In spite of this, several Society members continued to contend that Child's editorial policy had been controlled not by the abolitionist cause but by her "love of popularity" and her "over-anxious desire to please [her] public" (*SL* "To Ellis Loring" 6 Mar. 1843). Thus, she found herself taking an apologetic stance. In a letter written shortly before leaving the *Standard*, she describes sitting at her desk watching "two little ragged girls" walk past her window "their scanty garments fluttering in the wind," and sharply reminds her reader, "Nay, my friend, I do *not* make up such stories" (*NASS* 16 Mar. 1843). Echoing her earlier response to Maria Chapman in which she had stressed her adamant belief that this "line of policy [would] carry abolition more generally among the people" (*SL* 24 Jan. 1843), Child explained, in a letter to Loring, that her goal as editor had been "nothing but a desire to gain the ear of intellectual and judicious people on behalf of slavery" (*SL* 6 Mar. 1843).

As she prepared to leave her editorial post in May 1843, she turned again to explain these editorial decisions. In response to Chapman's argument that the *Standard* had become, under her editorship, no longer an abolitionist paper, Child reminded her readers:

I have repeatedly said that I did not *intend* to edit the paper for *abolitionists*. It seemed to me that the *Liberator*, the *Herald of Freedom*, and various "liberty party" papers, were sufficient to meet their wants; and that the cause needed a medium of communication with people. My aim, therefore, was to make a good family newspaper. (*NASS* 4 May 1843)

Pointing to her first editorial declaration to "work according to my conscience and ability" (*NASS* 16 Aug. 1841), she observes, "I have kept my word" and can thus leave with "a peaceful consciousness of undeviating rectitude of intention" (*NASS* 4 May 1843). Had "personal popularity . . . been my object," she writes in a manner echoing her earlier response to Chapman, "I should not have edited an anti-slavery paper at all. I did it that many might be induced to subscribe to the *Standard*, who would not take an exclusively anti-slavery periodical" (*NASS* 4 May 1843).

Echoing the concerns of Maria Chapman, twentieth-century critics have often accused Child of selling out, of writing these "Letters from New York" to please her readers, and of carefully constructing her prose in an attempt to avoid the repercussions caused by *An Appeal*. However, Child's use of the epistolary format in the *National Anti-slavery Standard* was a carefully chosen rhetorical stance that allowed her to step outside of the narrow confinement of female rhetorical possibilities into the world of the urban spectator and in doing so to cut deep the lines of political reform.

Notes

1. Because Child's two-volume collection, *Letters from New York*, contains selected "Letters from New York" Child wrote during this two-year period and because she made various editorial changes to these Letters when preparing them for publication in this collection, I have used the "Letters from New York" in their original form as they appeared in the *National Anti-slavery Standard* during the period August 16, 1841, through May 4, 1843. The numbering of the letters as they appeared in the *Standard* differs from the numbering in the two-volume collection.

2. In making this statement, Goldsmith is describing women's private letter writing practices during the nineteenth century. However, because Child models her "Letters from New York" on the genre of private letter writing, her deliberate move to explore the intersections of private and public space cuts against the female epistolary tradition grounded in confinement and isolation.

Works Cited

Brand, Dana. *The Spectator and the City in Nineteenth Century American Literature*. Cambridge: Cambridge UP, 1991.

Buell, Lawrence. *Literary Transcendentalism: Style and Vision in the American Renaissance*. Ithaca: Cornell UP, 1973.

Child, Lydia Maria. *An Appeal in Favor of That Class of Americans Called Africans*. Boston: Allen and Ticknor, 1833.

——. "Editorial." *National Anti-slavery Standard* 20 May 1841: 21.

——. "Farewell." Editorial. *National Anti-slavery Standard* 4 May 1843: 191.

——. "From the Editor." Letter. *National Anti-slavery Standard*. 11 Nov. 1841: 91.

——. "Indifference to Slavery." Editorial. *National Anti-slavery Standard* 21 Oct. 1841: 79.

——. "Letters from New York" 1-58. *National Anti-slavery Standard*. Vol. 2.11-3.58 (19 Aug. 1841 - 4 May 1843).

——. *Lydia Maria Child: Selected Letters, 1817-1880*. Ed. Milton Melzer and Patricia Holland. Amherst: U of Massachusetts P, 1982.

Freedman, Diane F. *An Alchemy of Genres: Cross-Genre Writing by American Feminist Poet-Critics*. Charlottesville: UP of Virginia, 1992.

Goldsmith, Elizabeth C. "Introduction." *Writing the Female Voice: Essays on Epistolary Literature*. Ed. Elizabeth C. Goldsmith. Boston: Northeastern UP, 1989.

Holland. Patricia. "Lydia Maria Child." *Legacy* 5 (1988): 45-52.

Karcher, Carolyn L. "Censorship, American Style: The Case of Lydia Maria Child." *Studies in American Renaissance* (1986): 283-303.

Rev. of "An Appeal." *American Monthly Review* 4 (Oct. 1833): 298.

Sparks, Jared. "Riley's Narrative." *North American Review* 5 (1817): 390.

15

Public and Private Tyrannies:
Virginia Woolf, Life-Writing,
and the Feminist Revision of History

Merry M. Pawlowski

[T]he public and the private worlds are inseparably connected; . . .
the tyrannies and servilities of the one are the tyrannies and servilities of the other.

—Virginia Woolf, *Three Guineas* 142

Two works that intertwine in Virginia Woolf's oeuvre near the end
of her life underscore Woolf's insistence upon history as "herstory," a
narrative form that challenges the traditional dichotomies between public
and private worlds and the denial of access to public space and voice for
women. *Three Guineas* and "A Sketch of the Past," separated by less
than a year between the publication of the first and the conception of the
second, choose public and private forms to displace the boundaries
between the public and private arenas as gendered masculine and feminine. In an ironic reversal of masculine narrative strategies that displace
real women into an iconic Woman, Woolf displaces masculine history by
relativizing its importance, placing it between parentheses or in foot-
notes, and contrasting a monumental and essentializing image of Man as
Tyrant with the real stories of women's lives, including her own.[1] Woolf
leads us to recognize, through her deliberate permeation of those realms
that patriarchal society would keep separate, how feminine narrative can
displace the public arena as a masculine forum "unspeakable" in its lust
for war and oppression while materializing the enforced silence and
enclosure of women within the private arena. This narrative strategy of
displacement will lead, ultimately, to a theme of displacement in "A
Sketch of the Past" and *Three Guineas*; for Woolf offers displacement as
a choice for women to remove themselves as outsiders from male society, history, and war—a choice Woolf makes personally and recommends publicly. My remarks include discussion of "A Sketch of the
Past," a manuscript and typescript memoir left unpublished at the time of

Woolf's death, and *Three Guineas*, a political, feminist essay Woolf published in 1938 as an attack on fascism and patriarchy. Each work has the power to interanimate and build a context for the other while demonstrating Woolf's increasing personal commitment to social change. Further, I want to supplement the interlocking historical and emotional context of both works with more intentionally private and autobiographical documents—Woolf's diaries.[2]

On Friday, May 20, 1938, Woolf waited nervously for the response of her readership to *Three Guineas*, scheduled to be out on June 2. "What I'm afraid of," she penned in her diary, "is the taunt Charm and emptiness. The book I wrote with such violent feelings to relieve that immense pressure will not dimple the surface. That is my fear. Also I'm uneasy at taking this role in the public eye—afraid of *autobiography in public*" (*V* 141, emphasis added). Woolf had good reason to be concerned about public exposure; she had written the most radical, controversial book of her career, a book that insisted at its core that English patriarchy in its oppression of women was as fascist as Hitler's Germany or Mussolini's Italy. Few Englishmen were prepared to "like" the mirror Woolf held up before them. Readers of Woolf's novels will recognize that in writing a political tract, Woolf probably felt that she was dropping the veil of fiction to reveal her most passionate beliefs, thereby exposing her "real" face, indeed, a form of autobiography. In fact, Woolf continued in her diary that she had begun to live her beliefs—writing *Three Guineas* had changed her life, and now: "I am an outsider. I can take my way: experiment with my own imagination in my own way. The pack may howl, but it shall never catch me. And even if the pack—reviewers, friends, enemies—pays me no attention or sneers, still I'm free" (*V* 141). Woolf would soon make intensely private by remembering her Victorian past what *Three Guineas* publicly attacks—the building momentum of systematic oppression and exclusion of women from social power and change.

Tantamount among the recognitions forced upon Woolf during her massive research to write *Three Guineas* was her observation of an ideology, gathering momentum in Europe, that insisted upon the return of women to the private home. Woolf knew immediately that such an ideology would remove from women the small gains they had made toward social power, especially their hard-won entrance to the professions in 1919 as a passageway out of the private house. "The door of the private house was thrown open," Woolf writes, ". . . in the year 1919, by an act which unbarred the professions" (*TG* 16). In fact, in this context, 1919 becomes a watershed date in *Three Guineas*, echoing in Woolf's repeated references to women and the professions as a reminder of how recently women had attained access to the professions and how easily any patriarchal society could remove that access.

Furthermore, to indict a public arena inhabited only by men, Woolf refers repeatedly in *Three Guineas* to photographs that she has received from the Spanish Republican government, photographs of ruined houses and dead bodies presenting the graphic horror of war for the public record. We can count at least ten separate references to these photos, locating a refrain that echoes throughout the work and tolls the deadly impact of a public world upon private lives. But the photos themselves are absent from the text; only one viewer—Woolf—can see them. Interestingly, Woolf does include photos in her work, but photos that reinforce her desire to portray the public pageantry of patriarchy—a procession of richly garbed scholars, a row of heralds, a general, and an archbishop. By eliminating the photos of the dead bodies and ruined houses, however, Woolf has displaced the effects of war in the public arena as un*see*able. Such a choice implies a resistance to masculine history and to the public forum, which pervades the nature of Woolf's responses to fascism and to war in the latter years of her life. Her choice also suggests the position from which she writes, penned up within the private house and protected from the ugly images of what men have done to other men, women, and children. Speaking from within the private house, Woolf writes: "Let us then by way of a very elementary beginning lay before you a photograph—a rudely coloured photograph—of your world as it appears to us who see it from the threshold of the private house" (*TG* 18).

Woolf's view of such seclusion for women extends to a radical conclusion:

For, to repeat, if those daughters are not going to be educated they are not going to earn their livings; if they are not going to earn their livings, they are going once more to be restricted to the education of the private house; and if they are going to be restricted to the education of the private house, they are going, once more, to exert all their influence both consciously and unconsciously in favour of war. Of that there can be little doubt. (*TG* 37)

Supporting war was the only way open to women, in Woolf's view, to escape the confinement of the private house. "So profound," Woolf reminds us, "was her unconscious loathing for the education of the private house with its cruelty, its poverty, its hypocrisy, its immorality, its inanity that she would undertake any task however menial, exercise any fascination however fatal that enabled her to escape" (*TG* 39). How sad that women, in an act of desperate resistance, should be drawn into complicity with war, Woolf continues: "Thus consciously she desired 'our splendid Empire'; unconsciously she desired our splendid war" (39). On July 20, 1937, this war became intensely personal for Woolf with the death in Spain of her nephew, Julian Bell. By August 6, when she wrote in her diary for the first time since his death, Julian's loss and her passion to finish *Three Guineas* were inextricably linked. With increased fury Woolf returned to the task of excoriating governments rotten with fascism and patriarchy in *Three Guineas*.

With equal fury two years later, Woolf limned the outlines of her own abusive confinement in the private house. On the 18th of April, 1939, Woolf struggled, as she began her memoir "A Sketch of the Past," for words to describe the "real" Virginia. Woolf had been challenged by her older sister Vanessa to record her memories before it was too late. Only four pages into her memoirs, however, Woolf found she had unleashed a powerful field of reminiscences that indict the patriarchal private house for its containment of the sexual abuse of women as she was drawn to describe a mirror in the house at St. Ives. It was in that very hall that Woolf was sexually abused, possibly for the first time, by her half-brother Gerald Duckworth. In accusing Gerald, Woolf writes:

Once when I was very small Gerald Duckworth lifted me onto this [slab in the hall], and as I sat there he began to explore my body. I can remember the feel of his hand going under my clothes; going firmly and steadily lower and lower. I remember how I hoped that he would stop; how I stiffened and wiggled as his hand approached my private parts. But it did not stop. His hand explored my private parts too. I remember resenting, disliking it—what is the word for so dumb and mixed a feeling? (*S* 69)

Woolf breaks a silence with which she has masked the memory of this early sexual abuse to cry out in rage against a violation of women that is centuries old: "It proves that Virginia Stephen was not born on the 25th January 1882, but was born many thousands of years ago" (69).

In the private house where she should have been safe, secure, protected, Woolf was, instead, physically assaulted by her own half-brother. In Woolf's society (both 1939 and c1888), women were silenced, prohibited from speaking of their abuse.[3] Is it any wonder that the portrait of the brother Woolf constructs in *Three Guineas* would amount to the portrait of a monster? Once again, Woolf refuses the distinctions between public and private as she sketches the "private" brother molded by his "public" society:

Inevitably we look at societies as conspiracies that sink the private brother, whom many of us have reason to respect, and inflate in his stead a monstrous male, loud of voice, hard of fist, childishly intent upon scoring the floor of the earth with chalk marks, within whose mystic boundaries human beings are penned, rigidly, separately, artificially; where, daubed red and gold, decorated like a savage with feathers he goes through mystic rites and enjoys the dubious pleasures of power and dominion while we, "his" women, are locked in the private house without share in the many societies of which his society is composed. (*TG* 105)

I would suggest that the significance of this quote deepens with the knowledge of the private, sexual abuse that Woolf suffered as a young child at the hands of a brother who was a young adult, quite old enough to know what he was doing.

The terror of violation, of loss of self, that Woolf endured in childhood as a result of abuse and tyranny painted powerful images in her dreams and her imagination, while leaving her at that moment outwardly speechless and powerless. However, Woolf coded the images of her text with the record of the abuse on her psyche, indicting her parents and family in the process. One such image in Woolf's memoir returns us to the hall mirror near the spot where Gerald fondled her. Woolf remembers a nightmare around the same time as her sexual abuse which may point to the submerged memory of the abuser: "I dreamt that I was looking in a glass when a horrible face—the face of an animal—suddenly showed over my shoulder. I cannot be sure if this was a dream, or if it happened . . . But I have always remembered the other face in the glass, whether it was a dream or a fact, and that it frightened me" (*S* 69).

As she continues to reflect on childhood memories, Woolf records two especially vivid "moments of being," which comment further upon the fragility of the developing ego. If we draw these two additional images into association with the mirror, we see that clusters of images that began in sexual violation trace the problematic formation of female identity. Such associations include reflections that negate rather than reinforce self-images of wholeness as well as reflective surfaces which threaten to swallow or submerge the self. Woolf's memories paint a tender ego which cringes in fear at the edge of a puddle and huddles in terror in a bath: "There was the moment of the puddle in the path; when for no reason I could discover, everything suddenly became unreal; I was suspended; I could not step across the puddle; I tried to touch something . . . ; the whole world became unreal" (*S* 78). The cumulative impact of her childhood was taking its toll on the young Virginia Stephen; and the puddle, like the horrible face in the mirror of Woolf's nightmare, threatens her with loss of identity. Later that night, the shock of unreality and loss of agency return to Woolf with even greater force: "For that night in the bath the dumb horror came over me. Again I had that hopeless sadness; that collapse I have described before; as if I were passive under some sledge-hammer blow; exposed to a whole avalanche of meaning that had heaped itself up and discharged itself upon me, unprotected, with nothing to ward it off, so that I huddled up at my end of the bath, motionless. I could not explain it" (S 78).

The female body, imaged as violable, weak, powerless, silent, and unsafe *especially* in the private home, inhibits the formation of identity as chronicled in this complex matrix of associations. By the end of her childhood, much damage had been done, and Woolf could only achieve feeling by splitting herself from the body that had caused her shame: "This did not prevent me from feeling ecstasies and raptures spontaneously and intensely and without any shame or the least sense of guilt, so long as they were disconnected with my own body" (S 68). Woolf reminds us that now reality for her resides in words, "I make it real by putting it into words" (S 72). Years of psychic pain and disconnection from her body, however, leave much untold that was just as real. For example, Woolf displaces the historical moment of the inception of her memoir by not making fully explicit when these memories came flooding back. On Tuesday, April 18, 1939, when Woolf began to write "A Sketch of the Past," England was poised on the brink of war as the world waited for Hitler to attack Poland. By allowing deeply suppressed memories of violation to resurface at this moment, Woolf silently underscored the parallels between a very personal oppression and the public violation and suffocation about to be suffered by womankind and mankind alike.

Most painful of all, though, perhaps more painful than the indictment of her brothers, is Woolf's veiled indictment of her father; for Woolf had to be drawn to the recognition of Hitler in the father of her childhood as she wrote "A Sketch of the Past." Her memoirs of her father recall an overt oppression in which he forced her to witness his violent outbursts where her only possible response was silent rage. "Yet he too obsessed me for years. Until I wrote it out, I would find my lips moving; I would be arguing with him; raging against him; saying to myself all that I never said to him. How deep they drove themselves into me, the things it was impossible to say aloud. They are still some of them sayable" (S 108). Could Woolf be suggesting that many things still *remain* to be said, to be written down? Indeed, as Woolf perceives, some of the cause of her rage is sayable through the very act of her writing, but much more is not. Furthermore, the realization that she can only now speak the words that indict her father is made even more acute by the history in whose web she was caught. Only a year after beginning "A Sketch of the Past," and as she began to write in detail of her father, she was witnessing the fall of France to fascism. "The present. June 19th 1940. The French have stopped fighting. Today the dictators dictate their terms to France. I sit in my room at 37 M[ecklenburgh] S[quare] and turn to my father" (*S* 107). Woolf's most precise memories of her father recall those abusive years from the death of her mother to the death of her father, 1895-1904, a period when her father became increasingly tyrannical and she could not fight back.

Juggling the present and the past as she began to formulate her memories of her father, Woolf acknowledged that she had just begun to read Freud seriously for the first time. Indeed, it seems very odd that Woolf resisted reading Freud until 1939 when the Woolfs' Hogarth Press had been publishing his works in English translation for some years.[4] In December 1939 and into the early months of 1940, Woolf read *Group Psychology and the Analysis of the Ego,* probing, through her reading of Freud, the rise of fascism and its threat to civilization. In her notes, Woolf focused on the co-presence of two world wars in her experience and mused on Hitler as the epitome of masculinist attributes: "[T]he present war is very different for now the male has also [anchored?] his attributes in Hitler, & is fighting against them."[5] The irony for Woolf was that the men in her country were blind to their own domestic fascism. As she sought to find the position of woman somewhere in Freud's text or even in society, she concluded that it would be the part of woman to emancipate man.[6]

Part of that emancipation might be effected, Woolf hoped, by forcing Englishmen to see themselves as participants in tyranny. To this end, Woolf indicted her countrymen in *Three Guineas,* offering Hitler and Mussolini as the mirror images of English patriarchy:

And are we not all agreed that the dictator when we meet him abroad is a very dangerous as well as a very ugly animal? And he is here among us, raising his ugly head, spitting his poison, small still, curled up like a caterpillar on a leaf, but in the heart of England. Is it not from this egg . . . that "the practical obliteration of [our] freedom by Fascists or Nazis" will spring? And is not the woman who has to breathe that poison and to fight that insect, secretly and without arms, in her office, fighting the Fascist or the Nazi as surely as those who fight him with arms in the limelight of publicity? (*TG* 53)

Notice that Woolf emphasizes the professional woman fighting fascism in her office as a core element of resistance to an ideology that would return all women to the home. On the very same page as the quote above, Woolf strikes at the heart of fascist ideology, exposing its ugly face beneath the thin veneer of solicitation for women:

Let us quote again: "Homes are the real places of women who are now compelling men to be idle. It is time the Government insisted upon employers giving work to more men, thus enabling them to marry the women they cannot now approach." Place beside it another quotation: "There are two worlds in the life of the nation, the world of men and the world of women. Nature has done well to entrust the man with the care of his family and the nation. The woman's world is her family, her husband, her children, her home." One is written in English, the other in German. But where is the difference? (*TG* 53)

Woolf's refusal of the separation of public and private as separate enclaves restricted to one gender or the other should be amply clear here. Her quotation from the German echoes numerous speeches by Hitler, Goebbels, and Mussolini, all of whom had a hand in the conscious crafting of fascist ideology regarding the subjugation of women.

It is the "daughters of educated men," Woolf reminds her readers of *Three Guineas* repeatedly, who have to fight this fascist worm threatening to spit its ugly poison in the very heart of England. Indeed, Woolf herself is the daughter of an educated man, a member of that class she sees as most underprivileged of all. Her view, of course, is the reverse of received opinion concerning women in the upper middle class to which Woolf's family belonged; but Woolf, autobiographically, paints a far different picture of what it was like to be the daughter of an educated man. By June of 1940, as she memorialized the fall of France in her diary, Woolf was beginning to see that her own father, like Hitler, had been a tyrant, too. For too long, the women of Leslie Stephen's family had excused his violent temper as an expression of genius. Woolf reflected in "A Sketch of the Past," "I think he said unconsciously as he worked himself up into one of those violent outbursts: 'This is a sign of my genius,' and he called in Carlyle to confirm him, and let himself fly" (*S* 109-10). Woolf refuses her father both genius and the right to violent outbursts, naming him now what she knew him to have been then: "It was the *tyrant* father—the exacting, the violent, the histrionic, the demonstrative, the self-centred, the self pitying, the deaf, the appealing, the alternately loved and hated father—that dominated me then. It was like being shut up in the same cage with a wild beast" (*S* 116, emphasis added).[7]

Although for many years Woolf had ridiculed psychoanalysis, reading Freud had finally helped her put her father and her emotions into perspective. She could sketch her father as the tyrant she knew him to be in her personal life while facing the ambivalent emotions he caused her to feel. Yet the implications of what Woolf could say extend far beyond into the unsaid and the unsayable: the memory of her father's irrational rages reflects the growling discourse of Hitler's ranting speeches. Woolf had written in her diary on Tuesday, September 13, 1938: "Hitler boasted & boomed but shot no solid bolt. Mere violent rant, & then broke off. We listened in to the end. A savage howl like a person excruciated; then howls from the audience; then a more spaced & measured sentence. Then another bark. Cheering ruled by a stick. Frightening to think of the faces & the voice was frightening" (*V* 169).

Woolf's descriptions of her father's weekly rages and her own sense of raging, silent frustration vividly parallel the impressions she recorded after listening to Hitler. Woolf remembers with great vividness the "Greek slave" (*S* 106) years when she and Vanessa were teenagers and had to account weekly for the household books. "Then down came his fist on the account book. His veins filled; his face flushed. Then there was an inarticulate roar. Then he shouted . . . 'I am ruined.' Then he beat his breast. Then he went through an extraordinary dramatisation of self-pity, horror, anger . . . I was speechless. Never have I felt such rage and such frustration. For not a word of what I felt—that unbounded contempt for him and of pity for Nessa—could be expressed" (*S* 144). Before she wrote these words, on the 15th of November 1940, Woolf had noted in her diary several severe bombings of London and another of Hitler's speeches, making increasingly evident the interanimation of the personal and the political, the private and the public, in her mind (*V* 338-39).

Such rages as her father's were reserved, Woolf contends, for the women in his family; and the numbing damage to a young girl forced to endure such brutality is revealed through Woolf's anger at the memory: "If someone had said to him simply and straightforwardly: 'You are a brute to treat a girl like that . . .' what would he have said?" (*S* 146). For Leslie Stephen, woman existed only to serve his needs in angelic slavery; and Woolf, reflecting upon her father's verbal abuse of her sister, Vanessa, wrote: "He had an illicit need for sympathy, released by the woman, stimulated; and her refusal to accept her role, part slave, part angel, exacerbated him" (*S* 145-46).

Woolf's vengeance on her father comes in the form of another denial, and she indicates what a daughter who feels robbed of power and language can do to repay such a father. While acknowledging her father's analytical abilities, Woolf would write of his lack of "creativity": "Give him a character to explain, and he is (to me) so crude, so elementary, so conventional that a child with a box of chalks could make a more subtle portrait" (*S* 146). Woolf had effectively weighed her own use of language against her father's and she had silenced him.

Leslie Stephen is to blame for far more in his daughter's eyes than simple ineptitude in the creative use of language, though. What would such a father have said, in fact, if he had been told that his daughters had been sexually abused by his stepsons? We have to wonder if the current of his rage could have been reversed and if Gerald and George Duckworth could have become the targets of his wrath. The evidence from Woolf suggests that Victorian, fascist ideology would have protected the men in Woolf's family from unpleasant recognitions, for it was unnecessary for them to view their behavior from a woman's point of view. In the constructs of the Victorian family, women's servile positions left them helpless and unprotected against onslaughts such as these. What was sayable for Woolf in her autobiographical texts stands as an accusation against her father as well as her half-brothers for a much larger, unsayable, experience of abuse that threatened her tenuous grasp of female identity. Once again collapsing the barrier between public and private, Woolf wrote near the end of *Three Guineas*: "Society it seems was a father, and inflicted with the infantile fixation too" (*TG* 135).

I would add, though, that Woolf's texts not only indict the father and brother basking in the public world of patriarchy; they indict the mother in the private house as well. It is in this indictment of a mother's complicity with the public sphere from within the private domain that Woolf creates a peculiar nexus of things unsayable, unspeakable, and unseeable which become caught in a web of silencing, distancing, and erasure—in short, displacement. First, we should ask, since her mother is the first family member Woolf acknowledges in "A Sketch of the Past," why she holds her mother at a distance during the opening pages. I find in that observation openings for speculation far beyond what Woolf tells us. Woolf cannot bring herself to say that she doesn't believe her mother loved her, or that, in fact, her mother abandoned her child to her devotion to duty as an exemplary Victorian matron. Instead, the text reveals that Woolf's earliest memories of pleasure and ecstasy are not associated with her mother's face, voice, or body; but with other spaces—a garden, the sea—where she feels safe and enclosed in a protective cocoon, a surrogate womb. She remembers the sound of the sea at St. Ives from the safe "uterine" space of the nursery and the colors and sounds of the garden there as though she were "lying in a grape and seeing through a film of semi-transparent yellow" (*S* 65).

Actually, Woolf's only memory of connection to her mother's body, and her earliest memory at the beginning of the memoir, is of sitting on her mother's lap in a train, traveling, perhaps, to St. Ives. Woolf is not sure about this memory, but "it is more convenient artistically to suppose that we were going to St. Ives" (64); and her mother is the mere means of conveyance to Woolf's most pleasurable "safe" space. We could reasonably expect that Woolf, being so close to her mother on this first page of her narrative, would describe her; but instead what Woolf remembers are the colors and shapes of the flowers on her dress. Woolf does not describe seeing her face or hearing her voice; indeed, she will allow her mother only a peripheral entry into the text, holding her at bay for the next fifteen pages.[8]

Woolf suggests by such a rhetorical strategy that, even though now a woman of fifty-eight, she must take her revenge for the child who was ignored by her mother. That revenge encompasses a rhetoric of distancing, of partial erasure, and of silencing during the early course of Woolf's confrontation with her mother in the text. Even as Woolf slowly begins to describe her mother as a presence in her childhood, that presence, as I will demonstrate shortly, is imaged as absence. Woolf's mother, Julia Stephen, managed a huge Victorian household comprised of eight children, numerous servants, and an irascible husband; and she persisted in fulfilling a lifelong dedication to and vocation for nursing, which fit acceptably within the image of the Victorian matron's charitable duties toward the poor. The toll on her, if her photographs are any indication, display her as a woman grim-faced and exhausted at the age of forty-seven. Direct evidence is provided by Woolf: "I see now that she was living on such an extended surface that she had not time, nor strength, to concentrate, except for a moment if one were ill or in some child's crisis, upon me, or upon anyone" (S 83). And although Woolf describes her as central, she is imaged as an "absent" center to be worshipped, "in the very centre of that great Cathedral space which was childhood" (S 81), in a childhood that was itself imaged as "vast empty spaces" (S 78) and a "great hall" (S 79).

Ironically, Julia Stephen does not become a real, approachable body in her daughter's text until she is dead. Woolf's vivid memories of her mother's death scene do not ignore her mother's last words to her: "'Hold yourself straight, my little Goat'" (S 84), words that must have caused Woolf to wince at the mixture of love and reprimand. Woolf denies herself the ability to feel, especially now, at this most painful juncture, as is evident in the memory of her mother's dead body: "A desire to laugh came over me, and I said to myself as I have often done at moments of crisis since, 'I feel nothing whatever.' Then I stooped and kissed my mother's face. It was still warm. She [had] only died a moment before" (S 92). The next morning, Woolf remembers that kissing her mother's body was like kissing cold iron. These death scenes are the few times Woolf remembers being close enough to her mother to touch her, and the touch identifies the mother's dead body as radically depersonalized.

Shortly after her mother's death, Woolf suffered her first serious episode of what has been identified by her family as madness, a violent irrationality that would culminate in a suicide attempt.[9] References to this episode do not surface in the manuscripts published posthumously as "A Sketch of the Past," but references to her insanity do surface obliquely in Woolf's fiction. Her mad character Septimus Smith in *Mrs. Dalloway,* for example, has often been cited as an alter-ego for Woolf;[10] but Woolf rarely admitted her lifelong battle with this illness in any of her autobiographical prose. I suspect that the reasons Woolf chose to silence references to this first episode of mental illness are most complex. In an earlier, rejected, draft of her manuscript memoir, Woolf had written about the period following the death of her mother and before that of her older half-sister, Stella: "This brought on, naturally, my first 'breakdown.'"[11] Even this, a reluctant admission that insists upon enclosing the word breakdown within quotes, problematizes the breakdown and makes suspect its validity as a diagnosing term. Furthermore, since the reference ends after this sentence, it shuts off any attempt at explanation. Woolf chose in later versions to erase the allusion altogether. Had Woolf decided in successive manuscript versions of the memoir to mute her own personal pain to reflect on the larger social picture of 1939? Were Woolf's "breakdowns" caused by more than her mourning a loss? Were they attributable instead to rage at the tyranny of her family, of society, and of its effects on women, including her mother?[12] As we continue to examine the record of Woolf's reconstruction of the past, we find a personal account of abuse that continues to support what I have argued is a condemnation of women's oppression at large, a condemnation of the public and private spheres and the forced separation between them.

An assumption that Woolf's "madness" was a response to rage is certainly bolstered by the knowledge that shortly after her mother's death, Woolf was subjected to caresses from her elder half-brother George that were sexually abusive. In her "Sketch," as we have already seen, Woolf reserves her sharpest accusations for Gerald, the younger Duckworth brother, muting her claims of abuse against George.[13] But Woolf's nephew and biographer, Quentin Bell, fills in some of the space left blank. On the authority of Woolf's husband, Leonard, and one of her doctors, Bell accuses George of making improper sexual advances to Virginia soon after her mother's death (when Woolf was only thirteen) and continuing at least to her father's death; and Woolf herself described the abuse in personal letters and conversations as well as other memoirs.[14]

Increasingly, Woolf implies in the text that Victorian England had deprived her of a mother who had time to attend to her needs, ultimately killing her mother with overwork within her own home and leaving her daughters defenseless against masculine violation. Woolf had already sensed that when she wrote of her mother and father: "Too much obsessed with his health, with his pleasures, she was too willing, as I think now, to sacrifice us to him . . . and so . . . she wore herself out and died at forty-nine; while he lived on, and found it very difficult, so healthy was he, to die of cancer at the age of seventy-two" (*S* 133).

As Woolf thought about her mother, once again, the present moment of the public world impinged upon her consciousness, and she wrote: "Yesterday (18th August 1940) five German raiders passed so close over Monks House that they brushed the tree at the gate" (*S* 124). Perhaps as she wrote of her past, Woolf was making a connection, even in the act of displacing it, for the first time in this memoir—that a power very like fascism had been the governing force in her own family. While her rage at European fascism was real, though, the overt links between father/mother and tyranny were still very tenuous; for Woolf was understandably reluctant to indict her own parents for engaging in and complying with domestic fascism.

Reading Woolf's text as a unconscious indictment, however, deepens our understanding of an additional factor in Woolf's intensely complex relationships to both parents. Not only was Woolf distancing herself from her mother because of her sense of childhood neglect, she was blaming her as well for her complicity in the social status quo. Such blame can be more fully appreciated through continuing our reading of the memoir's contexts, especially the important context of her research notes for *Three Guineas*. Sometime after September 22, 1940, Woolf wrote the words cited above, implicating her society and her father for having literally worked her mother to death. By now, she had been reading and gathering information for years on fascism, male domination, and tyranny, writing copiously in her reading notebooks. Between 1937 and 1938, Woolf copied a quote from Benito Mussolini that suggests a strong parallel to the social requirements for the Victorian matron: "'Woman is reserved to the family and must be a good housewife, a good wife and a good mother.'"[15] Woolf found this citation in an account of Germany and Italy under the sway of fascism, *Women Must Choose: The Position of Women in Europe Today* by Hilary Newitt, and she copied a second quote taken from Newitt's transcription of Nazi propaganda. Here Woolf's quote clearly echoes her memories of her parents' relationship, especially her father's dependence on her mother for approval and support: "The life of man is based on struggle . . . womans [*sic*] task must be to heal his wounds."[16]

Underlining the importance of this quote is the fact that it comes from propaganda written by a woman, Princess Fanny Starhemberg, a high official in Nazi Austria's anti-feminist government. Furthermore, Woolf, in reading Newitt's book, was exposed to the full force of its message. The status of women in Germany and Italy in 1937, Newitt insisted, had seriously deteriorated. Women were being denied their rights, they were being ousted from jobs and professions, and they were being denied an education in an insidious reversal of the minimal gains for social freedom and suffrage that had been made.

Woolf had read about the stark reality of women oppressed by fascist rule; and, within a year or two, she would write remembering how her mother had been mastered by a strikingly similar phenomenon. Yet, unable to forgive her mother's complicity with Victorian ideology, Woolf also silenced her mother, denying her any voice or agency and insisting in an obvious inaccuracy that her mother had never written or published. As she tried to lay hold of her mother's character, she had written in her memoir in May, 1939, the following: "[F]or what reality can remain real of a person who died forty-four years ago at the age of forty-nine, without leaving a book, or a picture, or any piece of work—apart from the three children who now survive and the memory of her that remains in their minds? There is the memory; but there is nothing to check that memory by; nothing to bring it to ground with" (*S* 85). Why did Woolf intentionally silence her mother here by claiming that she wrote no book? Julia Stephen did, indeed, write and publish a pamphlet on nursing in 1883 and composed several unpublished articles on the management of servants and women agnostics.[17] She also signed an antisuffrage manifesto, "holding that women had enough to do in their own homes without a vote" (*S* 120), clearly, in Woolf's eyes, a politically unfavorable position.

Julia Stephen's publishing record reveals her as devoted to nursing as a profession, yet constrained by the social impossibility of pursuing her vocation beyond the acceptable boundaries of charitable bounty. For Woolf, however, her mother was an accomplice with the forces of oppression. Few readers of Woolf could forget her testimony that she had to "kill" the "angel in the house" (her own mother) as the embodiment of feminine self-abnegation in her fiction.[18] The angel in the house, Woolf would contend, meant death to the woman writer (one could not be both a "good" woman and a good writer), so for Woolf her mother *did not* write. Virginia Woolf would emphatically choose *not* to reproduce her mother's choices, her mother's life, her mother's definition of womanhood.

Has Woolf virtually silenced and erased mothers in *Three Guineas* as well? I think the answer has to be yes when we remember that the focus on women in *Three Guineas* is on daughters, but daughters of educated men, not women. Needless to say, this is an important phrase for Woolf to employ for a number of reasons, among them, the potential it offers her for ironic portrayal of the fathers and for the ability to link women of the private house directly with the public world of the father. However, mothers are still largely absent. There is at least one instance, though, when Woolf allows mothers into the text as witnesses of their daughters' burning of the private house:

"Set fire to the old hypocrisies. Let the light of the burning building scare the nightingales and incarnadine the willows. And let the daughters of educated men dance round the fire and heap armful upon armful of dead leaves upon the flames. And let their mothers lean from the upper windows and cry, 'Let it blaze! For we have done with this "education"!' " (*TG* 36)

Once again, later in *Three Guineas*, Woolf exhorts the daughters of *uneducated women* to make the windows of a new house, of a poor house, blaze, and open to the public world of omnibuses and street hawkers. By now, though, quite tellingly with respect to Woolf's own personal history, the mothers of these imaginary liberated women are dead:

And let the daughters of uneducated women dance round the new house, the poor house, the house that stands in a narrow street where omnibuses pass and the street hawkers cry their wares, and let them sing, 'We have done with war! We have done with tyranny!' And their mothers will laugh from their graves, 'It was for this that we suffered obloquy and contempt! Light up the windows of the new house, daughters! Let them blaze!' (*TG* 83)

Ironically, this visionary moment in Woolf's text is just that—a vision, but a vision in which Woolf attempts to restore to mothers the dignity of their own quiet struggle; the reality, however, was a dead mother "ringed with ordeals she was mastered by."[19]

Certainly Woolf had recognized and refused her father's and brothers' tyranny, and she had refused and rejected her mother's complicity as a mode of feminine accommodation to the patriarchal status quo; both efforts provide telling commentary on the wrongful separation of public and private spheres with the attendant relegation of women to secondary "private" status. Woolf had not, however, done with her reconfiguration of "masculine" history. As a part of her resistance to war as public record and, thus, the history of human deeds, Woolf privileges private, feminine history, ultimately recommending a position for women altogether outside of and out of the reach of male-dominated territory. From a motive similar to her refusal to bring literally before our eyes the Spanish photographs of dead bodies and ruined houses in *Three Guineas*, Woolf names the date of her writing specific sections of "A Sketch of the Past" twelve times but displaces history by recording only the most fleeting references to world events of the moment. Clearly, she is writing about the past, so this is no great surprise; but Woolf continually speaks of the link between the present and past, making a compelling observation in the process. On July 19, 1939, Woolf writes:

The past only comes back when the present runs so smoothly that it is like the sliding surface of a deep river. Then one sees through the surface to the depths. In those moments I find one of my greatest satisfactions, not that I am thinking of the past; but that it is then that I am living most fully in the present. For the present when backed by the past is a thousand times deeper than the present when it presses so close that you can feel nothing else, when the film on the camera reaches only the eye. But to feel the present sliding over the past, peace is necessary. (*S* 98)

Woolf, it would seem, has been making a monumental effort, all through her fragmented writing of this memoir, to force the peacefulness of the present. It is necessary for her to create peace in her private sphere as there is none in the public world of her present. More importantly, as a woman she feels compelled to resist rhetorically a public world that will otherwise drown her. On April 15, for example, just three months before the passage just quoted and just three days before she would begin writing her memoir, Woolf acknowledged in her diary "the severance that war brings: everything becomes meaningless: cant plan: then there comes too the community feeling: all England thinking the same thing—this horror of war—at the same moment" (*V* 215). We know that Woolf worked on the "Sketch" over a period of two years, recording the date each time she picked up the thread of her narrative once again. Six times in 1939, Woolf dated her material, once in April, three times in May, once in June, and the last reference in July. On May 2, Woolf claims that she has found a form for these memoirs, one that will use the present as a platform on which to stand to view the past. Yet, throughout 1939, Woolf's references to the present date of her writing never mention the growing war in Europe, the major events in history, and the maelstrom into which her world was being drawn—a maelstrom that she herself was well aware of as clearly indicated in the candid references found in her diary. Woolf carefully resisted the real turgidity of the river of present history, fashioning instead a fictional smooth surface for her memories to penetrate.

By 1940, though, it was increasingly difficult for Woolf to refuse the reality of the present in "A Sketch of the Past." The completion of *Three Guineas* in the spring of 1938 served as a watershed moment in Woolf's participation in, and thinking about, women in the public and private spheres. Six more times Woolf dated her "Sketch," the first picking up the thread of the narrative almost a year after it was dropped in July 1939. On June 8, 1940, having found her notes for "Sketch" in the wastebasket, Woolf took them up again, writing: "Shall I ever finish these notes—let alone make a book of them? The battle is at its crisis; every night the Germans fly over England; it comes closer to this house daily" (*S* 100). Suicide, she concludes, is the only viable alternative; but she continues to write, pushing away the dark curtain of war. "But I wish to go on, not to settle down in that dismal muddle." Now, each reference to a date, with the exception of the last, is keyed, even if ever so briefly, to the fighting. On June 19, Woolf remarks that the French have stopped fighting. On August 19, Woolf mentions that five German raiders have passed over her home at Monks House, flying low. On September 22, she is thinking of invasions and raids; and on October 11, she writes in parentheses: "(London battered last night)" (*S* 136).

Perhaps because the narrative form in her diary is so much more immediate and unlikely to be revised to mute and qualify its emotions, Woolf writes there even more openly of the war during this period. On June 9, Woolf reflects with sadness on the fall of the French government, offering a compelling insight into the crushing private impact on her: "It struck me that one curious feeling is, that the writing "I" has vanished. No audience. No echo. That's part of one's death" (*V* 293).

Earlier, in *Three Guineas*, Woolf had resurrected a feminine icon capable of gathering together so many of these reflections on past and present, public and private, masculine and feminine, resistance and refusal; it is the figure of Antigone. Antigone, carved in Woolf's own autobiographical image, is the figure of feminist resistance by a daughter of an educated man to masculine tyranny. Woolf, having evoked her, can argue through her for the removal of women to a space outside of patriarchal society where mental chastity and resistance to domination become possible. In a powerful passage that collapses over 2000 years of history, Woolf makes Antigone come to life, resisting the law of the tyrant Creon who was to have become her father through her marriage to his son:

And he shut her not in Holloway or in a concentration camp, but in a tomb. And Creon we read brought ruin on his house, and scattered the land with the bodies of the dead. It seems, Sir, as we listen to the voices of the past, as if we were looking at the photograph again, at the picture of dead bodies and ruined houses that the Spanish Government sends us almost weekly. Things repeat themselves it seems. Pictures and voices are the same today as they were 2,000 years ago. (*TG* 141)

Both the public and the private repeat themselves: public abuse is the same today as 2000 years ago, private abuse of a woman named Virginia Stephen Woolf recapitulates centuries of abuse of women. If women are to survive, from Woolf's standpoint, they must proclaim with her (and with Antigone): "'For,' the outsider will say, 'in fact, as a woman, I have no country. As a woman I want no country. As a woman my country is the whole world'" (*TG* 109).

Yet Woolf holds out a faint hope that with the coming together of the public and private worlds, peace may indeed be achieved. As the pages of her text *Three Guineas* draw to a close, Woolf paints a compelling picture of the tyrant behind whom lie the dead bodies and ruined houses. He is "Man himself," and women and men must draw together to recognize that "we cannot dissociate ourselves from that figure but are ourselves that figure" (*TG* 142). Woolf insists:

A common interest unites us; it is one world, one life. How essential it is that we should realise that unity the dead bodies, the ruined houses prove. For such will be our ruin if you [men] in the immensity of your public abstractions forget the private figure, or if we [women] in the intensity of our private emotions forget the public world. Both houses will be ruined, the public and the private. (*TG* 142-43)

On November 15, 1940, armed with the conclusions she had drawn from writing *Three Guineas*, Woolf wrote in her diary that she had plunged into the past and written of her father (in "A Sketch of the Past"). She was poised to write the powerful and compelling indictment we have already witnessed, making private the public tyranny of Hitler and Mussolini. Just three days later, after having made her last recorded dated entry in her "Sketch," Woolf had reached an illuminating moment in her quest for feminine equality. As she writes the results of her private introspection and reflection, she is Antigone looking for the unwritten law, she is the outsider seeking to resist war, she is the daughter of the educated man refusing his domination, and she is everywoman entombed in the private house longing to participate in and change for the better the affairs of the public world: "I am carrying on, while I read, the idea of women discovering, like the 19th century rationalists, agnostics, that man is no longer God. . . . It is essential to remain outside, & realise my own beliefs" (*V* 340). Antigone would be found hanging in the cave where Creon had her entombed, enacting her refusal of tyranny; Woolf's body would be found in the River Ouse three days after she walked into it in her own ultimate act of defiance and displacement.

Notes

An earlier version of a part of this essay was published as "From the Country of the Colonized: Virginia Woolf on Growing Up Female in Victorian England," in *Violence, Silence, and Anger: Women's Writing as Transgression*, ed. Deirdre Lashgari (Charlottesville and London: U of Virginia P, 1995), 95-110. I would also like to acknowledge the Berg Collection of the New York Public Library for their cooperation and kind permission to cite from the Woolf papers in their possession.

1. In "Displacement and the Discourse of Woman," Gayatri Spivak leads us to recognize narrative strategies employed by male writers which displaced real women into "Woman," creating an icon which could then be controlled and deployed by the masculine text.

2. The three texts by Woolf cited in this essay will be indicated by parenthetical citation employing the following abbreviations: *V* and page number for *The Diary of Virginia Woolf, Vol. V: 1936-1941*; *S* for "A Sketch of the Past" in *Moments of Being: Unpublished Autobiographical Writings*; and *TG* for *Three Guineas*.

3. See Louise DeSalvo on Woolf as incest survivor, *Virginia Woolf: The Impact of Childhood Sexual Abuse on Her Life and Work*.

4. Elizabeth Abel notes the following about Woolf's resistance to the psychoanalytic discourse of the 1920s and 1930s: "Woolf's reticence about psychoanalysis is both characteristic and complex; interpreting it requires that we heed her own insistence on authorial silences, on what is left unsaid," 13.

5. See this quote in Brenda Silver's index to Woolf's reading notes, *Virginia Woolf's Reading Notebooks*, 16. I have added my own reading for a word Silver leaves blank: anchored.

6. See for the full quote *The Holograph Reading Notes*, 5.

7. I am indebted to Elizabeth Abel's *Virginia Woolf and the Fictions of Psychoanalysis*, 109, for having pointed me to this passage in Schulkind's 2nd edition of *Moments of Being*. Abel uses the quote to explore Woolf's reading of Freud during her composition of *Between the Acts*.

8. This is a fact that critics like Shari Benstock have noted as well. Benstock writes: "The point is not that Woolf's mother became an 'invisible presence' after her death, but that she was always an invisible presence—too central, too close to be observed," 27. I would add that, for Woolf, having her mother too close to be observed did not ensure against the emotional distancing she experienced as a child.

9. Quentin Bell provides what sketchy information exists on his aunt's first nervous breakdown in his authorized biography of her, *Virginia Woolf: A Biography*, 46.

10. See as an example Roger Poole, *The Unknown Virginia Woolf*, chapter 9.

11. Martine Stemerick, in "Virginia Woolf and Julia Stephen: The Distaff Side of History," points out that the only account of Woolf's first breakdown in these manuscripts is in a preliminary draft for "A Sketch of the Past," *Monk's House Papers* (*MH*/A.5c); but even this account is largely muted by Woolf. What is of most interest to me is the quoted acknowledgment of a breakdown and its later suppression. See Stemerick's essay in *Virginia Woolf: Centennial Essays*, 57.

12. These are very like questions raised by Roger Poole in *The Unknown Virginia Woolf*, his cogent analysis of Woolf's life and work in the context of discourses about her madness, especially those discourses of her nephew-biographer, Quentin Bell, and her husband, Leonard Woolf. Poole's work is very important for initiating a more problematic view of Woolf's insanity.

13. Woolf does, however, accuse George quite directly of indecent advances in "22 Hyde Park Gate," a memoir written twenty years before "A Sketch of the Past": "Sleep had almost come to me. The room was dark. The house silent. Then, creaking stealthily, the door opened; treading gingerly, someone entered. 'Who?' I cried. 'Don't be frightened,' George whispered. 'And don't turn on the light, oh beloved. Beloved—' and he flung himself on my bed, and took me in his arms" (*Moments of Being* 155). Both Roger Poole, *The Unknown Virginia Woolf* 28-32, and Louise DeSalvo, *The Impact of Childhood Sexual Abuse*, argue compellingly that Woolf was subjected to more than cuddling by George.

14. *Virginia Woolf: A Biography* 46. For Woolf's reports of her abuse, see Louise DeSalvo, *The Impact of Childhood Sexual Abuse*, 122.

15. Mussolini, "La Donna, Una Ripresa del feminismo?" *Il Nuovo Stato*, April 1935, quoted in Hilary Newitt, *Women Must Choose: The Position of Women in Europe Today*, 117. Woolf cites this quote in vol. 26: 9 of her *Holograph Reading Notes*.

16. Quoted by Newitt, *Women Must Choose*, 130, from propaganda issued by the office of Princess Fanny Starhemberg, the Nazi Women's Leader of Austria and cited by Woolf in vol. 26: 9, of the *Holograph Reading Notes*.

17. The writings of Julia Stephen have been collected into a volume entitled *Stories for Children; Essays for Adults*, ed. Diane F. Gillespie and Elizabeth Steele (Syracuse: Syracuse UP, 1987).

18. An important reference for this textual "murder" is in *A Room of One's Own* (San Diego: Harcourt, 1929), and another is found in "Professions for Women," *The Death of the Moth and Other Essays* (San Diego: Harcourt, 1970), 236-37.

19. Adrienne Rich's portrait of Aunt Jennifer has always struck an echo of Julia Stephen and the Victorian matron for me, for the complicity coupled with passive resistance suggest the complexity of the Victorian matron's response to patriarchy. "Aunt Jennifer's Tigers," *The Norton Anthology of Poetry*, 796.

Works Cited

Abel, Elizabeth. *Virginia Woolf and the Fictions of Psychoanalysis*. Chicago: U of Chicago P, 1989.

Bell, Quentin. *Virginia Woolf: A Biography*. New York: Harcourt, 1972.

Benstock, Shari, ed. *The Private Self: Theory and Practice of Women's Autobiographical Writings*. Chapel Hill: U of North Carolina P, 1988.

De Salvo, Louise. *Virginia Woolf: The Impact of Childhood Sexual Abuse on Her Life and Work*. Boston: Beacon, 1989.

Newitt, Hilary. *Women Must Choose: The Position of Women in Europe Today*. London: Gollancz, 1937.

Poole, Roger. *The Unknown Virginia Woolf*. 3rd ed. New Jersey: Humanities, 1990.

Rich, Adrienne. "Aunt Jennifer's Tigers." *The Norton Anthology of Poetry*. 3rd ed. Shorter. New York: Norton, 1983. 796.

Silver, Brenda. *Virginia Woolf's Reading Notebooks*. Princeton: Princeton UP, 1983.

Spivak, Gayatri Chakravorty. "Displacement and the Discourse of Woman." *Displacement: Derrida and After*. Ed. Mark Krupnick. Bloomington: Indiana UP, 1983. 169-95.

Stemerick, Martine. "Virginia Woolf and Julia Stephen: The Distaff Side of History." *Virginia Woolf: Centennial Essays*. Ed. Elaine K. Ginsberg and Laura Moss Gottlieb. Troy: Whitston, 1983. 51-80.

Stephen, Julia. *Stories for Children; Essays for Adults*. Ed. Diane F. Gillespie and Elizabeth Steele. Syracuse: Syracuse UP, 1987.

Woolf, Virginia. *The Diary of Virginia Woolf, Vol. V: 1936-1941*. San Diego: Harcourt, 1984.

——. *The Holograph Reading Notes*. Henry W. and Albert A. Berg Collection of the New York Public Library. Vols. 21, 26.

——. "A Sketch of the Past." *Moments of Being: Unpublished Autobiographical Writings*. Ed. Jeanne Schulkind. 2nd ed. London: Hogarth, 1985. 64-159.
——. *Three Guineas*. 1938. San Diego: Harcourt, 1966.

Contributors

Parley Ann Boswell teaches English at Eastern Illinois University in Charleston, Illinois. She studies and writes about American popular culture, from the popular literature of seventeenth-century colonial New England to Hollywood films of the twentieth century.

Jennifer S. Brantley received her Ph.D. from the University of Nebraska-Lincoln and is now teaching at the University of Wisconsin-River Falls. She has published articles in *The Chronology of Women World-Wide* and *Feminist Writers* and has also written on Carson McCullers and Gloria Naylor. She has published in *Literary Magazine Review*. Her poetry has been published in *Women and Language*, *Icon*, and *Gypsy Cab*, *13th Moon*, and *Hurricane Alice*.

Sylvia Bryant teaches as an adjunct professor of English and Women's Studies at Alfred University, in Alfred, New York, where she also directs the Writing Center. Currently she is working on a study of spirituality and community in American women's writing.

Linda S. Coleman is professor of English and Women's Studies at Eastern Illinois University, where she teaches composition, eighteenth-century studies, and women's literature. Her research interests include advanced composition instruction, new historical approaches to the teaching of the eighteenth century, life-writing, and women novelists.

Martha J. Craig has just completed her doctoral dissertation on "Feminine Virtue in Shakespeare's England" for Purdue University. She is a literature instructor at the Indiana Academy for Science, Mathematics, and Humanities at Ball State University, where she teaches Renaissance literature, Shakespeare, and gender studies, as well as American and world literature and creative writing. Her article "The Protocol of Submission: Ralegh as Timias" is forthcoming in *Genre*.

Lynn Domina is completing a Ph.D. in American literature at State University of New York at Stony Brook, where she is writing her dissertation on American women's autobiography and the construction of national identity. She has published articles on the work of N. Scott Momaday, Mary McCarthy, Zora Neale Hurston, and other American writers.

Elizabeth Foxwell is editor and director of publications at the American Association of Colleges for Teacher Education in Washington, D.C. Her M.A. thesis on women pacifists in World War II received distinction from Georgetown University and focused largely on Vera Brittain. She was a presenter at the 1993 Vera Brittain Centenary Conference at McMaster University (Canada).

Jennifer Frangos is a doctoral candidate in English literature at the State University of New York at Stony Brook. She is working on a dissertation on Restoration and eighteenth-century constructions of female sexuality.

Angela D. Jones recently finished her Ph.D. in English literature at the University of Rochester. She has published essays on romantic women travelers, the reception of Mary Shelley's *Frankenstein*, feminist film theory, and feminist pedagogy.

Avra Kouffman is a Ph.D. candidate at the University of Arizona. She is currently in London researching her dissertation, "The Cultural Work of Stuart Women's Diaries." She taught literature and writing courses at the University of Arizona for five years. Interests include autobiographical theory and the long eighteenth century.

Linda Lang-Peralta earned a Ph.D. in comparative literature at the University of California, Irvine, where she wrote a dissertation on Germaine de Staël and Frances Burney. Currently she is editing a collection of essays on the novels of the 1790s. At the University of Nevada, Las Vegas, she teaches writing and literature.

Anne Righton Malone is a veteran teacher of writing and a student of the art of rhetoric who is currently completing her Ph.D. in English at the University of New Hampshire. Her dissertation, "'I take my pen in hand': Letter Writing as a Social Act of Invention," examines the genre of letter writing and its role historically in the college writing curriculum. Malone is also co-author of a pedagogical essay and is currently completing an article for a collection on nineteenth-century composition textbooks as instruments of letter-writing instruction.

Merry M. Pawlowski is associate professor of modern British literature and literary theory at California State University, Bakersfield. She is editor of a forthcoming collection of essays, *Resisting Fascist Seduction: Virginia Woolf, Feminist Theory, and the Ideology of Oppression*, and the author of several articles on Woolf, fascism, and modernism.

Judith Scheffler is associate professor of English at West Chester University of Pennsylvania. Her publications include an anthology and studies of the life-writing of women prisoners. She is currently researching the life and writings of nineteenth-century Quaker industrialist Rebecca Lukens.

Leah White is a Ph.D. candidate in the Department of Communication at Arizona State University, emphasizing performance studies and rhetorical criticism. She is currently working on her dissertation, which is an analysis of shifting subjectivities in Charlotte Solomon's autobiography *Life? or Theater?*